ROME & PARTHIA

POWER, POLITICS AND PROFIT

BY DARYN GRAHAM M.A

2013
PRINTED BY CREATESPACE

ISBN: 1484045661
ISBN-13: 9781484045664
Library of Congress Control Number: 2013906890
CreateSpace Independent Publishing Platform
North Charleston, South Carolina

PREFACE

U PON PICKING UP THIS BOOK, one might wonder what an historian from Sydney could possibly know about ancient Rome and Parthia. That would be natural given the twin-tyranny of distance and time from today's Australia to the classical world. But the reader can feel at ease, because Sydney is in fact in a perfect position for someone like myself to learn about, and then pass on, quite a lot about both Rome and Parthia.

One of the world's most cosmopolitan Western cities, Sydney boasts several world-class universities that have excellent ancient history teaching faculties. As well as that, Sydney's Western heritage means that knowledge about Parthia is easily accessible there, since most modern treatments on its history have been set out in Western European languages, and especially English, which are profuse throughout the bustling capital of New South Wales. Archaeological reports too, are often still written in Western European languages. All of this means is that for an historian like myself, Rome and Parthia can be easily researched and studied, and such was the luxury I discovered while producing this book.

It is my hope that my efforts will help more people – from both East and West – to understand the classical world in a way that is different to what is usually set out in history books. I particularly hope that all readers will appreciate through reading this one that, Rome's and Parthia's histories were so intertwined that, dare I say, it is simply impossible to understand one without some knowledge of the history of the other. Still, today there exist few books that deal with these two civilizations on the same pages, and so it has been my aim to bridge this gap in our general knowledge and inspire more consideration regarding them.

My own journey through Parthian history began as an undergraduate student at Macquarie University, where I learned about, amongst other things, Carrhae, Corbulo, and Trajan. That served to whet my appetite, and so in 2006 I contacted David Coltheart, then editor of Archaeological Diggings Magazine, and asked him if he had done anything in print on Parthia that I could read. The answer he gave me came somewhat as a shock: No. But then he asked me if I would write an article on Parthia for the magazine myself, and I said: Yes. Then the article became a series and that series became a lifestyle. Seven years later I am still happily writing for the publication on numerous ancient topics to do with Rome, Greece, Pompeii, and of course, Parthia. As a result I must thank David Coltheart for setting the ball rolling, so to speak.

Others also deserve thanks, such as David's successor as editor, Michael Browning, who allowed me to write a further series on Parthia; and the present editors, Gary Webster and Shay Mason, who also welcome my offerings on its amazing history. I also thank Dr Kathryn Welch from the University of Sydney for showing me the depth of importance that Parthia had in Augustan Rome, the implications of which I have taken to heart. I also appreciate the time and consideration shown by Dr Paul Roche, who is also from the University of Sydney, towards myself while I wrote my Masters thesis on Roman-Parthian relations and trade from Vespasian to Caracalla while under his supervision.

Thanks is also extended to Gholamreza Farhad Assar, from Oxford, England, who has kindly brought his considerably knowledge and understanding of Parthia's coinage to my attention, and shares my love for Parthian history. Coinage is essential to our understanding of Parthian history so such a gesture is warmly appreciated. A similar appreciation is also extended to John Hill, from Cooktown, Queensland, who has offered me his insights into his field of expertise, that of Parthian and Chinese relations throughout ancient times.

Thank you also goes to Pastor Bob Thurlow from Hawkesbury District Presbyterian Church for his kind support throughout this whole writing process, as well as to the church members themselves for their support. A very special thank you must also go out to Sara Ann Zola and the staff at CreateSpace Publishers for taking the risk to publish my work in this book. I hope the risk will be well worth it. Finally, above all others, I would especially like to thank all of my family and those closest to me who have understood that this book has been a very special and important endeavour for me.

Without the above mentioned people I simply could not have produced this book in its existing form, so they have my sincerest appreciation. For now, though, I pass on all of my knowledge and understanding of Rome's and Parthia's joined history onto you, the reader, and I hope that one day you too might write your own book that gives you the opportunity to express your thanks to those who have also deepened your knowledge of this most wonderful of topics.

Daryn Graham, Sydney, 28th February, 2013.

TABLE OF CONTENTS

INTRODUCTION

F EW RIVALRIES IN THE ANCIENT WORLD match that which existed between Rome and Parthia. For over three whole centuries these two classical superpowers vied with one another for control over the Ancient Near East. In fact that rivalry was to last over twice as long as Rome's other great rivalry – that with Carthage. But Rome was able to prevail over the Carthaginian Empire in the space of one hundred and thirty years since the start of their first Punic War. With Parthia however, even after two hundred and fifty years since the Battle of Carrhae, Rome was never able to prevail over it. In fact, Parthia eventually fell to the armies not of Rome, but of its one-time subjects, the Persians.

It is very disappointing to discover then that only a few books have been written on Rome's relations with Parthia in their complete entirety. With that in mind, I feel, therefore, that a thoughtful book such as this is long overdue, at the very least for the purpose of inspiring further research. Such research would certainly be welcomed by ancient history enthusiasts, particularly those with a passion for all things Parthian. At its peak the Parthian Empire was so large and powerful that even many Romans recognized that it was comparable to their own empire. Of course, there were other neighbours of the Roman Empire that assumed some degree of power or military effectiveness, but none rivaled Rome as Parthia did.

Parthians to the Euphrates

The Parthian Empire began when the nomadic Parni tribe, a people originating in Central Asia, who, like other Central Asian nomads honoured horse riding skills above almost all else, invaded and took control of the kingdom of Parthia. Parthia at that time was a small nation that was situated in Iran's north, and upon the Parni's arrival there still ranked as a Macedonian Seleucid territory. Since Alexander the Great conquered the region it had remained under the control of the Seleucid dynasty, the Macedonian rulers that took over much of the Middle East after Alexander's premature death in 323 BC.

As Seleucid power waned the Parni, under the rule of their own dynasty, the Arsacidae, (so-named after the dynasty's founder Arsaces) grew in power. So much so in fact, that by the second century BC the Parthians, as the Parni now called themselves, had become a clear and very present danger to the Seleucid Empire itself. Moreover, they had become such a threat in the east that they were able to repulse attack after attack launched by their Seleucid rivals. With escalating wars to the east, the Seleucid armies were increasingly absent from the west, and it was there that the Hasmonean Jews were able to throw off the Seleucid yoke and carve for themselves a Jewish nation with a Hasmonean dynasty, all of their own.

By the first century BC Parthia had finally established itself as the dominant power in the Ancient Near East. To the east its empire stretched as far as India, while to the west its armies had penetrated as far as the Euphrates River. But it was there that the Parthians would discover not only the relics of the region's old Macedonian heritage, but another power that like them was also on the rise.

Romans to the Euphrates

Meanwhile, west of the Euphrates, Rome was gaining ground. Rome was founded in 753 BC and possessed an army traditionally made up mainly of foot-soldiers; armies that prided themselves on winning battles with close hand-to-hand hard fighting. By the mid-second century BC Rome had emerged as the dominant power within the Mediterranean basin. But change was in the air by the first century BC. Since 510 BC Rome had been governed by a Senate strongly hostile to monarchy. Kings had actually ruled Rome since its foundation, but after the last king's overthrow there in 510 the idea of a king ruling Rome seemed obscene to many Romans.

But not to all of them. By the first century BC military power was being used as a weapon against the state by gifted Roman generals to further their own semi-monarchical political careers, even at the cost of the life of other Romans. Commanders like Marius, the uncle of Julius Caesar, and Sulla, the patron and master of Pompey, would even go on to wage civil wars in order to wrestle control of the empire from the Senate and from each other.

The ultimate goal for any Roman general, however, was everlasting fame and the wealth that naturally went along with it. That could not be achieved through civil war, but rather through victory over foreign foes. So, when Sulla was commissioned by the Senate to march an army east for the purpose of settling affairs on a diplomatic footing in Cappadocia to the Senate's liking, the general was thrilled and marched off hoping to win some kind of victory in the process. Cappadocia, like Parthia, had once been a part of the Seleucid Empire, and like the Hasmoneans had thrown off its yoke. But as Roman influence in the region increased its rulers saw wisdom in becoming one of Rome's vassal kingdoms. That meant that Cappadocia would support Roman military endeavours in their region, and in return retain some measure of independence at Rome's discretion. It was while Sulla was in Cappadocia that he took stock of the situation in order to plan what he would do next, and it was while there that he came face to face with a Parthian delegation from the Arsacid king himself.

With that began a relationship that would embroil two of the ancient world's greatest superpowers with each other for over three whole centuries. It would pit army against army in times of war, force their politicians to exert themselves diplomatically to their fullest during times of mounting aggression, and see unprecedented commercial prosperity on a global scale in times of peace. It is with great pride therefore, that I present to the reader in this book these three aspects of Romano-Parthian relations: Power, Politics and Profit. Because they were so integral to the relationship that existed between Rome and

Parthia one simply cannot understand their shared histories without understanding those three things. Put together, they make for a very heady brew, but above all, it all makes for a wonderful story to tell.

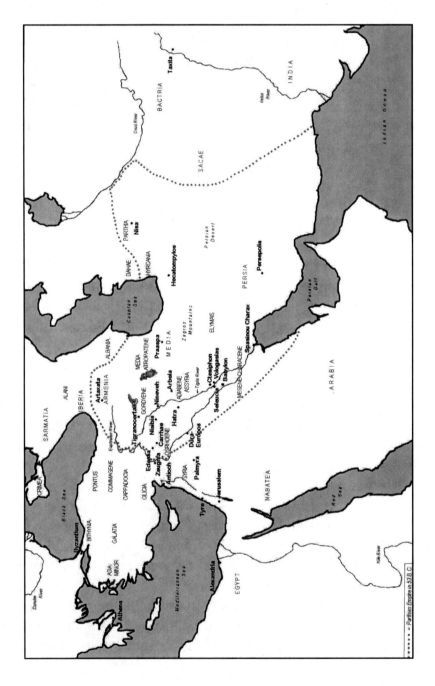

CHAPTER ONE

SULLA TO SINATRUCES

First Contact Made

THE FIRST CONTACT between Romans and Parthians in an official capacity had immense ramifications on the political and military spheres of both peoples. It brought into direct relationship two of the ancient world's greatest and most powerful superpowers; a relationship often more closely akin to sibling rivalry than family warmth, but one that was to last for three centuries regardless. As with all relationships, it would be the initial contacts that would define each side's view of the other. More than anything else, those contacts set in motion a series of events and changes that would have an enormous impact over generations of the people who once lived in what is now called the Middle East under either Roman or Parthian rule. Those changes included the many shifts: from peace to war and back to peace again, cultural hostility to commercial cooperation, and the maintenance of national identity to the transplantation of facets of one society to another, just to name but only a few.

According to Plutarch, the first contact ever between Romans and Parthians, in an official capacity that is, happened when the Roman general L. Cornelius Sulla and the Parthian envoy Orobazus[1] met while Sulla was propraetor in Cappadocia. Sulla, a gifted general and politician who would years later go on to be dictator of Rome, had been dispatched there by the Roman Senate for two ostensibly prime reasons: firstly, to establish the Roman nominee Ariobarzanes on the Cappadocian throne, and secondly, to monitor the actions of Mithridates VI of Pontus. Mithridates was an infamous and a notoriously outspoken enemy of all things Roman, and like the Romans was at that time also expanding his military power base in that region.

While exercising his commission, Sulla stationed himself for quite a considerably long period by the western side of the northern extremities of Euphrates River which ran between Cappadocia and Pontus, and it was there that he met with Orobazus. Orobazus had been specifically dispatched there too on the order of the Parthian king, who Plutarch simply called 'Arsaces'. The main purpose of his commission was to establish ties of friendship and an alliance between Parthia and the Roman state. According to Plutarch, during their meeting Sulla decided to set upon himself to resolve the affairs in Cappadocia with the help of the major power in the region, Parthia. With that in mind he had set up three chairs, one for Ariobarzanes, another for Orobazus, and one for himself in their middle. It was a calculated arrangement that promoted and endorsed Rome's overriding power while in the process of diplomatic meetings with other nations.[2] Unfortunately, Plutarch had little else to about this epoch-making event, but, Plutarch's peer and historian Florus,[3] and later Orosius,[4] did pass on that Orobazus was successful in his mission and that an alliance was agreed upon by the three parties. Ariobarzanes' kingship was also confirmed by those present at the meeting, and it must have appeared on the surface that order was firmly and happily established in the region, and that there was real cause for celebration. But of course, history shows that things turned out not to be so simple. Yet for the moment, the three parties from Rome, Parthia and Cappadocia, who had met together, must have been pleased with what they had achieved. However, in the future many wars would be fought between Rome and Parthia, and they would involve Cappadocia as well. But for the time being such a future must have seemed very distant to Sulla and Orobazus.

Lucius Cornelius Sulla Felix, at the Glyptothek, Munich.
Wikipedia.org

The Response in Rome

It is true that the murky details that have survived to this day are a sad reflection on how seemingly insignificant Sulla's meeting with Orobazus seemed to the vast majority of Romans and Parthians at the time that it took place. But that said, through some investigative work we can determine some things that ran through the minds of Sulla's contemporaries in Rome and Parthia when they learned about it. But in order to do so we must first pinpoint exactly when that meeting took place and follow the social and political ramifications that spilled out accordingly.

By concluding the treaty, Sulla was sticking out his own neck, proverbially speaking, to establish a peace with a power that he perceived needed to be made. But he lacked the Roman Senate's and people's endorsement to do so.[5] Understandably, therefore, there were many people in powerful positions in Rome who were outraged upon Sulla's return the following year, and saw his infringement of law and precedent as something not for the good of the Roman state but a direct result of sheer arrogance and vulgarity.[6] But such frustration was aimed at much more than just Sulla alone. In fact outrage had been developing for some time at the growing trend among Roman commanders to decide official business in the field on their own initiative independent of any consultation with Rome's political establishments. Such distaste had deep roots, stretching back to the common disgust felt in Rome towards one Gnaeus Manlius, who in the 180s BC conquered Galatia in central Turkey for Rome without any Senatorial consent to do so. But, distaste towards such ventures was not total. In fact, besides certain ambitious Roman generals, there were in fact many Romans who supported such conquests. It is a telling fact that although Manlius was severely censured upon his return to Rome for his decisions, he was still awarded a triumph regardless, and ultimately welcomed back not as a criminal, but as a true conqueror and celebrity.[7]

But the actions of Manlius and other like him did divide those in Rome who on the one hand despised unjustified violence with those who, on the other, deemed it a necessary evil to ensure Rome's very own survival. Since the time Hannibal of Carthage had forged a notorious alliance with Antiochus III, the king of the Seleucid Empire that stretched from Asia Minor and Syria to Iran and beyond, it was feared among many in Rome that Hannibal himself, or just as bad, a Hannibal-like eastern king would again stir up war and march on Italy as Hannibal himself once did. In fact, according to Livy, the idea of yet another Punic War, this time involving Antiochus and widespread rebellion among Rome's subjects, frightened many Romans so much that a large number of them saw preemptive strikes against the Asian Seleucid regime as an effective antidote to another war in their own backyard in Italy.[8] As a knock-on effect to all this was that the fear that Hannibal had inserted into the minds of many Romans was projected onto Antiochus and indeed onto all eastern kings. That is why there is a lingering echo of the cultural diversity in Hannibal's armies in Antiochus' own throughout Livy's descriptions of them both.[9] Of course, by Livy's own lifetime under Augustus the Roman Empire itself was far from being culturally homogenous; but the fear of eastern despots leading hordes upon hordes of warriors from countless distant lands against Rome, that had been forged during Hannibal's wars with Rome, remained even to Livy's time almost two centuries later.[10] Thus there were two divergent positions held by most Romans at the first contact between Romans and Parthians: those who deplored war without reserve, and those who saw the possibility of war as justification in itself for a war.

During Sulla's time, however, Rome was also undergoing revolutionary change with traditional power-structures giving way to powerful individuals. That is why the conservative base of authority, the Senate, in time succumbed to the ambitious warlords like Sulla, Pompey and Julius Caesar, that would go on to lay the foundation of the Roman Empire under the rule of the first Roman princeps and indeed emperor, Augustus. Not surprisingly, then, those who wanted change in Rome praised Sulla to the skies for his actions and for humbling so great a potential future eastern threat as Parthia. Indeed, in the end, it was this party that ultimately carried the day and the alliance with Parthia was allowed to stand. But, as support for ambitious generals over traditional institutions continued to increase in Rome, so it happened that it would not be Sulla, but those Roman military leaders that followed him in the East, who would go on to deal with Parthia as they themselves saw fit, just as Sulla had done, irrespective of any opposition there may be back in Rome and in Sulla's circle.

The partial jubilation in Rome for the actions of Sulla in respect to Parthia certainly invites us to wonder what Romans actually knew about Parthia itself. It is unclear exactly how long Romans and Parthians knew about each other. However, that there was some rejoicing in Rome upon Sulla's return over his diplomatic coup means that Romans probably had considerable knowledge of Parthia's growing power.[11] The same could be said for the other side of the Euphrates River: that Sulla was searched out by Parthia is in itself a clear indication of just how important Rome's presence in the East had become in the minds of Parthia's elite. That Sulla spent a considerable time by the Euphrates and that that is precisely where Orobazus met him is certain proof that the two must have expected each other to be there from a much earlier stage.

Besides being the border between Cappadocia and Pontus, where Mithridates of Pontus was operating, the Euphrates River was a busy highway of human traffic and movement, trade and the exchanging of countless ideas along its many docks - facts that would have a bearing on Roman and Parthian trade-relations for centuries to follow. True, Sulla had ostensibly waited by the River to monitor events in Pontus and Armenia, not a bad tactic to keep informed about those places. But, just as importantly, he had sought to meet with Orobazus who had traveled to Sulla along that same bustling river. Although Plutarch was quick to say that this initial meeting was somewhat spontaneous and put it down to Sulla's notorious good luck,[12] the realities of Roman diplomacy were never so simple. Such is the Roman story.

Roman and Parthian Diplomacy

Before looking at the Parthian reaction to Orobazus' negotiations with Sulla, a note must first be made about some of the finer points involved in both Roman and Parthian diplomatic practices and convention. In the minds of the Romans it was expected that at every single diplomatic negotiation meeting, foreign envoys should present themselves in a humble manner before Roman representatives out of respect for

Rome's military might and political superiority. Sometimes, envoys were even expected to display complete submission during negotiations and kneel before Roman military standards, which had cultic status in Roman armies, or before the Roman general on the spot.[13] Such strict, stage-managed display enforced Roman pride and power, and at the same time added greatly to a general's fame and standing back home in Rome upon his return.

Roman diplomacy was therefore a powerful enterprise, and in Rome's dealings with eastern nations that enterprise was expected by Romans to be the prevailing one in all diplomatic dealings. This is reflected in the writings of Valerius Maximus who wrote a short description of the diplomatic negotiations carried out between Ariobarzanes of Cappadocia and Pompey the Great, the gifted young peer and protégé of Sulla's who would go on to leave behind himself everlasting fame where Sulla would not. According to the story, Pompey and the Cappadocian king were busy discussing political matters in an official manner when the king sat on the floor to play with his infant son, and giving the son his own crown to play around and toy with. But it was at that point that Pompey promptly intervened, ordered the king to take his crown off the child, place it on his head and return to his seat next to Pompey in his official capacity whereupon the Roman general then gave him a dressing down and decided the outcomes of the meeting in no uncertain terms.[14] It is a brief anecdote, but nevertheless this little story is a perfect illustration of just how seriously the Romans took their political symbolism. It was the consistent intention of Roman politicians to maintain Roman prestige at all costs and over every other variable which might affect how diplomacy could turn out. Sulla's behaviour, therefore, was in total keeping with Roman diplomatic practices and his famous meeting with Orobazus simply followed established Roman convention.

But the Romans' style of diplomacy certainly did not follow Parthia's convention. In the absence of Parthian literary sources we do not possess any kind of illustrations like Valerius' for what happened on the Parthian side during international meetings. However, there are clear indications of Parthian diplomatic protocols in the surviving Parthian sculptures around their empire. Rock reliefs at Hung-I

Nauruzi, for instance, show a Parthian king, either Mithridates I or II, astride a decorated horse receiving a queue of foreign dignitaries approaching him humbly on foot.[15] In this is a clear signal as to what Parthian protocol entailed. It served to establish Parthian primacy over the course of meetings. And it was a motif that would have a long legacy: at Bisutun a relief carved in the first century AD shows the Parthian king Gotarzes II atop a steed,[16] and at Tang-I Sarvak another relief shows a Parthian of the royal family riding a horse in pride of place next to four foreign envoys walking on foot.[17] The image of a Parthian king on horseback was, then, a powerful image which literally and symbolically set him above all others. Even in other reliefs, where the king is portrayed on foot or on a throne, he is again always elevated or in a clear and unreserved position of power.[18]

Parthian diplomacy, in a similar fashion to Rome's own, was clearly conducted to reflect the Parthian king's own power and the regime which he ruled and at the same time worked with. Through diplomacy, the Parthian king maintained his superiority, privilege, and ultimate power over all foreign representatives, and those same qualities were also expected to be observed on his behalf by all of his envoys at his disposal. Of course, we must take into consideration the fact that such rock-reliefs were commissioned by Parthian kings themselves who had their own public interests in mind, and that therefore they did not necessarily reflect the realities of every single negotiation that took place between Parthians and other peoples. Indeed, the meeting that transpired between Orobazus and Sulla shows that sometimes they did not. But nonetheless it still stands that as far as the king was concerned, his image was everything. Hence, when Orobazus relinquished the central place in his negotiations with Sulla, he was going directly against what his king expected of him. Of course, he may have acquiesced primacy at that meeting simply as a gesture of friendship and goodwill to his new prospective ally in Sulla. But, because of his concession to Sulla at that meeting, Plutarch tells us that when Orobazus returned to 'Arsaces' with good news that the alliance with Rome was secured and the proceedings of his meeting with Sulla, he was immediately put to death by the Parthian king.

The Response in Parthia

But the burning question remains: which king? Plutarch's account is problematic because he only called the king by his official title 'Arsaces'. This title stemmed from the name of Parthia's first king Arsaces, and was a common one used by all of Parthia's kings. Indeed, it was a rare thing for a Parthian king to strike his coin with his actual name in place of this title. In fact their coins nearly always bore the title 'Arsaces'.[19] So, Plutarch might simply have held in his hand a coin of the king in question and recorded the name he saw on it: Arsaces. Added to this confusion is the fact that throughout most of the twentieth century it was the accepted view that this initial meeting took place in 92 BC.[20] However, since then it has been conclusively shown that it actually took place closer to 95 BC.[21] This small change, and a seemingly innocuous one at that, might appear trivial. But it is anything but. That is because despite these conundrums, Parthia's coinage can still teach us so much about this period in Parthian history, and for that reason its mint issues are sometimes called the 'annals' of Parthia. Intriguingly, one thing they do show us is that at the time of Sulla's and Orobazus' meeting, there were actually two kings ruling different parts of the empire at that time. Of the two, Mithridates II had reigned the longest. After coming to the Parthian throne in 124/3 BC, he pursued an aggressive expansionist policy and strengthened the eastern parts of the empire imposing Parthian control, not only over the Saka kingdoms of the Indus valley, but even as far east as Taxila in India itself. Whilst to the west, he also conquered Characene, an area which in ancient times was situated in roughly the same location as modern-day Kuwait, as well as Armenia.

However, Mithridates' reign was not considered a high point by all of his subjects. By 95 BC Sinatruces, the eldest son of Mithridates I and opponent of Mithridates II's expansionist policy, rebelled and took Susa for himself. Therefore, it was probably he, as 'Arsaces' in his own right in Susa, who sent Orobazus up the Euphrates to meet with Sulla. Sinatruces sorely needed any alliance he could find. He needed an alliance with Rome in the west to counter the power of Mithridates who still held the upper hand in Iran and parts of Mesopotamia.[22] But, as a

king and a rebel king at that, he was not interested in swapping obedience to Mithridates with obedience to a Roman, even one like Sulla.
Thus, when Orobazus returned to Sinatruces and gave an account
of the meeting's proceedings to him, Sinatruces, defiant in submitting to others, was enraged. In the king's eyes, Orobazus, whether it
had occurred to him or not, had given away pride of place during his
meeting not to Sinatruces, but to Sulla, and therefore by default he had
shown submission to Rome. It was a sleight on Parthian prestige that
would not be reversed until decades later when another king turned
the tables upon another Roman general, Marc Antony, and made him
the object of submission in his own diplomatic meeting. (See Chapter
Four) But although Sinatruces did not wish to submit to anybody, nor
have Parthian political conventions flouted and disobeyed so publicly,
he was a man of his word, he stood by the alliance regardless.

As for the other Parthian king, Mithridates, his response to Sinatruces' alliance with Rome was characteristic of his own consistently
imperialist policy. He took an Armenian princess as his wife, and thus
cemented an alliance with her nation, and so as to gain a counterbalance to any potential Roman military presence in the region, he
also established an alliance of his own, but with a very different ally:
with Mithridates VI of Pontus – the enemy of Rome.[23]

Cuneiform records from Babylon tell us that Mithridates of Parthia died several years later in 91 BC.[24] He was succeeded by one Gotarzes to the Parthian throne, and we happen to possess some crucial
knowledge of this new king's earlier career that has an important
bearing on our understanding of Parthian politics at this time. At
Bisutun a rock-carving bears the following inscription: "Gotarzes the
satrap of satraps, [of] the great king Mithridates".[25] Since Mithridates
II was called by his title 'the Great' by his subjects,[26] and that the
Bisutun inscription refers to 'the great king Mithridates' we can be
safely sure that they were one and the same person. This obviously
goes on to mean of course that his successor, Gotarzes I, must have
been the same one who served under him as the pre-eminent 'satrap of
satraps'. These are telling facts. Parthian politics was a complex thing,
especially because the King of king's position rested upon the consent
of his court and nobility. Often, when his rule proved unpopular and

14

that consent was withdrawn, the king could be overthrown, and civil war often erupted as a result. In fact, civil wars so often ravaged the Parthian Empire that some Romans like the historian Tacitus even believed that they were an established Parthian tradition.[27] Hence, for the sake of the security his own position as ruler over the nobility (or puppet?), Mithridates' expansionist policy may have been at least partly dictated by those nobles who gave that king the right to rule. Gotarzes, as 'satrap of satraps', was foremost among those nobles and as a result he had a leading hand in that policy's formulation and implementation. That is why when Gotarzes came to the throne he continued the same expansionist policy that had been put into place during the reign of his predecessor.

But Gotarzes' succession did not quell the unrest in Parthia, and years of bitter civil war between him and Sinatruces were still to follow. The two rivals clearly had conflicting hopes in mind for Parthia, and are almost a mirroring of the opposing views held for and against rampant military expansion that were current in Rome. Gotarzes continued king Mithridates' expansionist policies and he too looked to further Parthia's claims in the west: just as Mithridates II had moved the Parthian capital west from Nisa to Hecatompylos with an eye to expansion in the west, so Gotarzes moved it again even further west from there to Ctesiphon. Sinatruces, on the other hand, is not known to have embarked on any foreign campaigns, but was instead content to consolidate Mithridates II's vast conquests made already, and ensure his and Parthia's position through diplomacy rather than expansion. That explains his burning desire to secure an alliance with Rome in the west rather than to contest with its Roman armies for more conquests, even despite his loss of face on account of Orobazus' concurrence to Sulla. Ironically, although in this war Gotarzes proved victorious Babylonian as cuneiform tablets state, it was Sinatruces who was to outlive him.

Gotarzes was to die in c.87 BC surrounded by revolt. Sinatruces was still at large and Orodes I made his own bid for the Parthian throne as well. Remarkably, Sinatruces, although beaten, once again made another attempt to secure the kingship at the ripe old age of eighty years, and this time around, after years of fighting Mithridates

II, Gotarzes, and then Orodes for the throne, he finally won it in 77 BC. Coinage shows that Sinatruces' reign lasted for seven years and by all accounts they were remembered as peaceful ones for Parthia, and ones of mutual respect between Parthia and Rome. Even when he was asked by Mithridates of Pontus for military aid in a war against the Romans, Sinatruces, honouring his old alliance with Sulla and ever the anti-expansionist, decided not to take advantage of Rome's weakness and flatly refused. Coinage also shows that when Sinatruces eventually died the Parthian throne was left to his son Phraates III who ruled until 58/7 BC. But it was this reign which, as Roman literary sources relate, saw Sinatruces' alliance with Rome put to the severest tests by the Roman generals Lucullus and Pompey the Great, and who, like Sulla, were a rule totally unto themselves.

CHAPTER TWO

MITHRIDATES OF PONTUS TO ORODES II

Mithridates of Pontus and Lucullus

WHEN PHRAATES III came to the Parthian throne, Rome and Mithridates VI of Pontus had been at war, on and off, for some eighteen years. Mithridates was genuinely feared by many in Rome as another Hannibal, or Hannibal-like enemy, intent on destroying their city by leading countless distant nations on Italy as Hannibal had done over a century before. The fear was such that even after he had been forced by Roman armies to flee to distant Crimean Bosporus in the northern extremities of the Black Sea, rumours still continued to spread all around Rome that the king was planning to march from his banishment on Italy as Hannibal had.[28] Of course, he could not have in reality, but these rumours are a reflection on the fear an eastern king could instill in the Roman mind. Rome's paranoia of this Pontic king began in 88 BC when he notoriously ordered the mass-killing of some 80,000 Roman and Italian expatriates in the province of Asia. This act of ethnic cleansing appalled and shocked those in Rome, but in the east where Mithridates had styled himself as a cross between a Hellenistic Dionysus and an Iranian 'King of kings', this depraved act actually bolstered his public standing as an alternative ruler to Rome there.

Mithridates' power-base and empire stretched throughout the Anatolian peninsula, the Aegean Sea, and the shores of the Black Sea. With such power and hatred for all things Roman, and a desire to appear noticeably un-Roman to his subjects, his 'ethnic cleansing' of Romans was not just an act of violence – it was an act of divine, and brutal, force.

In order to check Mithridates' anti-Roman actions the Roman Senate commissioned Sulla, who at that time was one of Rome's most accomplished generals, to the east to confront him with a Roman army. Despite Mithridates' best efforts, he could not stop the surging tide that was Roman expansion, and when Sulla arrived in Greece in 87 BC the Romans succeeded in pulling off several emphatic victories on the battlefield against Mithridates' generals there. Smarting, Mithridates sued for peace. It is an historical irony that, as things turned out, this anti-Roman Pontic king would owe the survival of his anti-Roman power to a Roman general: Sulla, who was in desperate need of a quick result in order to return to Rome and there undercut his bitter political enemies jealous of his success, allowed him to retain his Pontic kingdom. It was a rushed decision that Sulla was forced to make under pressing circumstances, for Rome was on the brink of the civil war which would eventually give Sulla ultimate power in Rome; but ultimately it was one that gave the Pontic king ample time and space required to wage further wars on Rome. Yet to save his own public image Sulla had learned something on promoting one's public image from his enemy in the east and sought to outdo him in this respect: Sulla adopted the titles 'Epaphroditus' and 'Felix' (Fortunate) so as to equal, but differentiate, himself from the king's titles' claims of divinity and greatness.[29] But because he had failed to decisively defeat the king, in-so-doing he had proven that it was not he but Mithridates who was the more fortunate of the two.

Mithridates, never one to remain idle for very long while opportunity was knocking, mobilized his forces for another war against Rome. When the Romans learnt of this, they too acted quickly, and dispatched the general L. Licinius Lucullus with an army to fight the king.[30] Lucullus by all accounts was a talented general and by 71 BC he had succeeded where Sulla had failed, driving Mithridates out of

Pontus altogether. In despair, the king fled for his safety to the court of another powerful king, Tigranes of Armenia. Tigranes, like Mithridates, styled himself as another 'King of kings', and controlled an extensive empire in his own right: his power extended throughout Mesopotamia, Adiabene, Media Atropatene, Syria, and Cilicia. Much of his vast empire had actually been conquered at Parthia's expense: Mithridates II had conquered these regions for Parthia beforehand. But after the years of civil war that followed his death Parthia was in such a terribly weak state that Tigranes was quickly able to capitalize and take them over for himself.

When Lucullus tried to secure a handover of Mithridates by Tigranes, the Armenian king flatly refused, and so Lucullus, taking the initiative, prepared for war against him too. It was around this time that after years of civil war in Parthia, Phraates III succeeded to the Parthian throne. As a sign of his Parthian empire's weakness in the Near East at that time, it is noteworthy that Lucullus made no overtures to the new Parthian king for any support for his campaign against Armenia.

With his three legions and a large provincial cavalry force Lucullus swept across Cappadocia and beyond the Euphrates into Sophene, Mesopotamia, and then back to Syria, and Cilicia, and then east once again into Adiabene on the other side of the Tigris. Now that he had cut off Tigranes from his empire, Lucullus next turned north and took on Tigranes himself and sacked Tigranocerta – the new capital Tigranes had built for his new, now crumbling, empire. The exact location of Tigranocerta is something of a mystery: while Strabo placed it between Armenia and Mesopotamia, Tacitus identified it with a site near Nisibis.[31] However, if Tigranes' empire's southward thrust is any indication of his general imperialist policy, then Tacitus' more southerly site is most likely to be the city's correct location.[32]

With the onset of winter there was some respite for Tigranes and Lucullus had no option but to station his army in winter quarters at Nisibis. That was standard Roman military practice. But, by doing so he, like Sulla, for all of his military success, had failed to strike the decisive blow and both Tigranes and Mithridates still remained at large. As things turned out, that winter marked a turning point in the war. Mithridates regrouped his forces, and attacked Lucullus' legates, and he even won several victories on the battlefield against his legions. This disgusted the remaining Roman troops that were still serving under Lucullus, and by 67 BC Lucullus' soldiers were mutinous. As for Mithridates, he was back in Pontus, and Tigranes once again established himself in Armenia and even crossed the Euphrates and added the kingdom of Cappadocia to his empire.

Pompey

Back in Rome, frustration with Lucullus' command was seething, and the Senate promptly decided to replace him with Gnaeus Pompeius. Pompey had recently proved himself a consummate general by virtually clearing the Mediterranean Sea of pirates. He was an intensely ambitious general, and unsatisfied even with this, he was eager to expand his achievements. He jubilantly welcomed the war with Mithridates for two main reasons: firstly, Mithridates had worked with the pirates and Pompey was eager to follow-up on his victory over them by taking out the Pontic king as well.[33] Secondly, he was well aware of the fame and riches a victory over Mithridates would bring him, especially if he were to succeed where other generals had failed.[34] So Pompey arranged with his political friend and ally, the tribune C. Manilius, to propose in the Senate that Pompey take over from Lucullus. The motion was carried, and Pompey set off for the east.[35]

Phraates' neutrality during the war between Lucullus and Tigranes had meant that Parthia went largely unmolested from war, and as a sign of its reemerging strength as a result, when Pompey arrived in the East in 66 BC he immediately sought contact with the Parthian king. The two leaders formed a coalition, and soon a Parthian army was strong enough to march on Armenia and attacked Artaxata, the northern capital of Armenia. Strangely though, the Parthians did not press home their attack and soon withdrew. Perhaps the Armenian army had proven itself too strong a foe against a Parthian force that had been inactive and weak for so long. But it is also possible that there was more civil unrest in Parthia which Phraates diverted his army to confront. As for Pompey, while these events were taking place in northern Armenia, he simultaneously headed straight for Mithridates and defeated him in battle near Nicopolis in southern Armenia.[36]

Defeated, Mithridates fled to the Crimean Bosporus where he was later killed by the hand of his own mutinous troops. Pompey was jubilant, having ridded the region of one of Rome's most hated foes. But the war was only half finished. Pompey still had to deal with Tigranes. Sensing defeat, Tigranes came to terms, but Pompey felt it imperative to impose Rome's control over the Armenian kings' empire just to be certain the king would no rouse it for another war against Rome. As he did so Pompey discovered an invaluable secret the Parthians had kept from the Romans up to that point: the lucrative Silk Route. Stretching from Syria in the west, through Babylonia and northeast along the shores of the Caspian Sea, and then on through Iran, Bactria, India and China, the Silk Route was a trade superhighway for large numbers of merchants and caravans wishing to trade throughout the ancient world. It was a trade artery that Parthia would keep tight control of for centuries and was one that Parthia's kings did not want any prying Roman opportunist like Pompey to discover and exploit for himself. Learning of its existence, Pompey made some use of it, marching his army along its leg from Iberia to Colchis, finding ready supply from passing traders for his troops along the way.[37] A decade later, Marcus Crassus would try to use a Roman army to seize Parthia's wealth for himself. No doubt he was inspired by Pompey's accounts of the wealth passing along the Silk Route into Parthia upon his return to Rome. That return was celebrated with a huge triumphal procession through the streets of Rome and endless fame for Pompey. From that point Pompey reveled in his successes in the east, boasting that he had found the province of Asia the furthest of Rome's provinces, and had left it a central one.[38]

With Mithridates dead and Tigranes properly dealt with, the general made plans to make speed to Rome. Some modern historians question whether it would have been possible for Pompey to have carried Roman arms any further anyhow, but Crassus' impression that a war with Parthia was easily winnable probably reflected Pompey's own opinion too.[39] But first he established four of his legions in Syria and Cilicia as a safeguard. He was keenly aware that the region required an armed presence to deter the rise of any future Mithridates or Tigranes there. But he also perceived the advantages of the division that such a strong military presence would cause there too. Soon Phraates' own position on the Parthian throne was threatened by a contender issuing anonymous coinage but who is generally recognized to have been one Darius of Media.[40] Pompey certainly knew of this division in Parthia and did nothing to discourage it. In fact, he refused to address Phraates by his royal title 'King of kings', choosing instead to call him the lesser title 'king', thus opening the way for other such aspiring kings to stake their own claims to the Parthian throne.

Wishing to reassert his position over Parthia's former territories that Pompey had now taken over, Phraates sent him an envoy with a request that the Euphrates River be agreed a common frontier between Rome's and Parthia's empires. Pompey refused. It was a turning point in history and one that would have repercussions for Rome and Parthia for centuries to come. Had Pompey agreed upon a common border then peace might have prevailed between Rome and Parthia. But Pompey had refused to agree to one, and for that, despite his leadership talents, it must be said that in this case his foresight had failed. But that said, Pompey might have felt he had little choice. He had already conquered a vast area east of the Euphrates and was thus understandably unwilling to relinquish it to anybody. However, Pompey's imperialist pride would prove the possibility of a longstanding peace's ultimate undoing.

In response to Pompey's refusal, Phraates tried to seize some parts of Parthia's former empire that had been lost to Tigranes and then Pompey back to Parthia and invaded Adiabene and Gordyene. But if he had hoped that Pompey would concede to him these kingdoms he was soon to be disappointed. Pompey dispatched his legate Afranius to eject the Parthian host. We have two very different accounts of what happened next. According to Plutarch, Afranius fought Phraates in battle and forcefully drove him back to Arbela beyond the Tigris River.[41] But, on the other hand, the testimony of Cassius Dio says that no fighting actually took place between Afranius and Phraates; Phraates was simply escorted by Afranius to Arbela.[42] This discrepancy in our sources has confounded many, and to add to the confusion are also the facts that: Plutarch, a biographer and not an historian, openly admitted that he sometimes overlooked historical accuracy for the sake of character portrayal,[43] so his written claims are sometimes open to question; while Dio, who was generally anti-expansionist and coloured his narrative to discredit Roman conquest abroad[44] is perhaps not the best authority when it comes to Roman military operational policies. Indeed, on these grounds, we might be forgiven for thinking that maybe neither writer is totally trustworthy on the matter. But thankfully, in this case we can be sure that Cassius Dio's statement is the correct one, for in Plutarch's own narrative of Crassus' later Parthian war, the author conceded that the Romans were still totally unfamiliar with and completely new to Parthian warfare.[45] Thus, it stands to reason that given Dio's testimony and Plutarch's own admission here no fighting could have taken place on this occasion. But Afranius' escort for the Parthian king was a warning that if he did not conform to Rome's own agenda, war was certainly to come.

Phraates was at a loss, but he made one last armed attack on Armenia as a final attempt to regain Parthia's losses. That attack was repulsed by Tigranes however, and Pompey again warned him against any further attack on Armenia. Phraates was finally forced to relinquish his claims for territory there.

In 61 BC Pompey, the ever victorious general, celebrated his triumphal homecoming through the streets of Rome bedazzling and astounding his Roman peers with the wealth he brought back for the occasion [46] It was a vast amount of wealth indeed. The victorious general added 200 million sesterces to the Roman state's treasury and disbursed over 100 million sesterces to his staff and soldiers.[47] But Pompey did not give all of his wealth away – on his return he was far and away the richest man in Rome and seemed to many there that he might have emptied all of Asia of its riches.[48] Those riches were paraded for all to see in Pompey's triumph through the streets of Rome. Such was the power of the spectacle that was Pompey's triumph that he was believed to deserve the epithet 'the Great', and future Romans, like Julius Caesar, would set his outstanding achievements as their own benchmarks.

Pompey's command is critical to understanding Roman and Parthian relations in two very important respects: firstly, by refusing to set the Euphrates River as a common boundary between the two empires of Rome and Parthia, Pompey ensured, albeit perhaps entirely unintentionally, that the disputed territories east of the river were to be fought over by the two powers for the duration of their mutual histories. Certainly, that is what eventuated. So consequently, it could be said that after Sulla's and Orobazus' initial contact, Pompey's refusal to agree on a firm frontier was *the* most important event in Romano-Parthian relations to take place, for its legacy was just so incredibly long lasting. Secondly, Pompey's discovery of the Silk Route meant that from that point on Romans became increasingly eager to acquire goods from the East. The sweep of history contained in this book will demonstrate that they would do this by trade and by war.

Parthian Weakness

Jesus of Nazareth was famously quoted in the Gospel of Matthew as likening the eventual destruction of Jerusalem to a dead body being picked apart by vultures.[49] But this metaphor, made a century after Pompey's triumph, could easily be said to apply to the situation in Parthia during Pompey's command in the East as well. Parthia was a shell of its former glory, and we have seen that it all too easily lay open to the likes of Mithridates of Pontus and Tigranes of Armenia to pick off Parthian titulature and territory for themselves at will. Thus they made vast political capital out of the carcass that was once the mighty Parthian Empire. Both Mithridates and Tigranes had usurped the titles 'Great King' and 'King of kings' for themselves in such a way as to signal that is was they, rather than Phraates, who were the true successors to the glories of the Parthian Empire. However, it was Pompey who proved to be the most victorious carrion-bird in the region. The metaphor is strikingly pertinent given that his contemporaries, both at home and abroad, saw Pompey and his army as vulture-like. In Rome, Lucullus even likened Pompey as a vulture that liked to swoop down upon his own former commands and take all the glory for himself,[50] while a Dead Sea Scroll writer living among the Essene Jews at

Qumran at that time likened Pompey's army to carrion-birds captur-ing city after city with flying speed.[51] However, the carcass was not yet a true carcass. By swallowing his pride, and accepting Pompey's politi-cal will, Phraates had ensured Parthia's survival, and indeed, its revival.

However, he could not ensure his own life. In 57 BC Phraates was assassinated by his sons Mithridates III and Orodes II who then waged civil war for the vacant throne. At first, Mithridates, the eldest of the two brothers, was successful, but he was soon forced to flee the Parthian Empire, eventually finding safe haven in Syria which was then governed by the Roman general Gabinius. Gabinius had been dispatched to Syria with several legions and it was his aim that while there he would make the best use of them he could.[52] Thus when par-ricide Mithridates arrived in his court the Roman found that he now had a valuable pawn-like nominee for the Parthian throne should he wish to invade it. Two years later he led his army into Mesopotamia, but at the eleventh hour war with Parthia was averted. Whatever hopes Gabinius may have entertained for such a war were soon dashed when the all-powerful Pompey advised him with gentle force to lead his army south and restore Auletes to the Ptolemaic throne in Egypt.[53] Gabinius, recognizing that intervention in Egypt would bring him huge wealth anyway, followed this advice. For all his leadership talents and potential use of Mithridates as a pawn in his own game Gabinius was no leader of Rome like Pompey or his closest political friends like Julius Caesar or Marcus Crassus, and the future conquest of the Par-thian Empire was now firmly believed by most in Rome to be the sole domain of one of those friends, the triumvir Marcus Crassus.[54]

Still, not to be idle, Gabinius gave Mithridates permission and the money to launch an attempt to reclaim the Parthian throne. He may have hoped that by doing so he would soften up Parthia for Crassus' coming war. However by 54 BC Orodes had defeated his brother in battle and executed him in order to finally establish his own posi-tion securely on the Parthian throne. However, that kingship was not yet established when within a few weeks of gaining the throne Crassus launched his attack on Parthia. Given the civil unrest in Par-thia between the two brothers, Crassus must have anticipated that the war would prove an easy victory with boundless looting. However, what Crassus had not foreseen was the loyalty a Parthian king, even a parricide Parthian king at that, could galvanize among his subjects. What was to be Crassus' finest hour became Parthia's own.

Roman and Parthian Imperialism

The issue of Roman imperialism as displayed by Pompey is one which historians find difficult to agree upon and define. Of course, by the early twentieth century it was firmly established that as conquerors of Macedon and Greece, the Romans had inherited the imperial provincial mechanisms of the rulers of those lands.[55] But it was left to later scholars to debate how the Romans internally justified and made use of those mechanisms. Galtung led the way in searching out this matter, arguing the sober point that imperialism by nature is generally the product of ruling elites among nations who make dominant and submissive relationships in order to secure their own interests.[56] However, such collective theorizing does not account for the anomalies that frequently occur throughout history, and by recognizing this fact, scholars started looking to the ancient sources themselves for evidence of the nature of Roman imperialism. Increasingly, they began debating the concept of 'defensive imperialism', since it was noticed that the Romans on almost all occasions upon declaring war, did so with the justification of a pretext. So it was argued on one side of the debate that Romans made war and conquered only for defensive purposes, while on the other side it was pointed out that such pretexts were usually mere excuses for all-out conquest – a detail not lost upon the ancient writers themselves.[57]

However, the nature of imperialism has never been a matter confined solely to historians to consider. Other humanities disciplines too have reflecting upon it in depth, such as anthropologist Barroll, who weighed into the debate and raised the point that, culturally speaking, the Roman populace like any other imperialist people generally did not see pretexts as mere excuses for aggressive conquest. Barroll argued that Romans publicly held onto the justice in such pretexts tightly to the point of obsession. But, he added they did this to collectively satisfy their individual private and personal cravings for power and wealth through blatant conquest.[58] This view has some merit, and many historians have since ascribed to it in their own formulations of the nature of Roman imperialism.[59]

However, all such debate seems to over-generalize the internalisations of different Romans with different interests, who as the ancient sources themselves express, had varying opinions regarding conquest. As can be seen by the period we have been discussing in this and the preceding chapter alone, the Romans were more heterogeneous than is often acknowledged. Yet the debate goes to the heart of Roman imperialism by that same debate's own very nature: just as there are many opinions about imperialism in modern times, so there were divergent views about it in ancient times. Certainly, Lucullus and Pompey, and particularly Pompey, used every opportunity to extend their imperialist aspirations, and yet they had their own political opposites who held very different political concerns in Rome itself.[60] Even going beyond this chapter into the next to illustrate this point, Crassus' announcement in Rome that he would invade Parthia was met with some support notably by Julius Caesar, but other politicians at the time including C. Ateius Capito were staunchly opposed to it pointing out that such a war was entirely unprovoked and unjust.[61] Thus, generalising theories about Roman imperialism still require some revising in order to be totally convincing.

Parthian imperialism shared some similarities with that in Rome. As we saw in the last chapter, Parthian kings like Mithridates II and Sinatruces did, as was the case among politicians in Rome, could either be for or against the idea of unprovoked conquest. But during the reign of Phraates there were notable differences produced by Rome's and Parthia's varying fortunes. Parthia was in a far weaker position to Rome and could only try to recapture its former greatness and territory that had existed under Mithridates II. Such weakness would have a lasting affect on the Parthian psyche: for centuries the Parthians would seek repeatedly to recapture its former glories. But not only Parthia's own. Parthian Arsacid kings would often style themselves as both Alexander the Great's successors as well as the Archaemenid Persian kings of the past. Thus the Parthian kings' own titles 'Great King' and 'King of kings' were drawn from Persian models of titulature. Accordingly, Parthian kings aspired to equal Alexander as well as Cyrus and earn the recognition of being a true 'Great' King in their own right and tried to emulate their power and fame. Such aspiration is visible in Phraates' attempts to steal Armenia and the other territories east of the Euphrates from Pompey's control, but it was one that he ultimately had to give up when it became clear to him that such a dream was unrealistic for the time being.

Throughout Roman and Parthian histories, it was often the more warlike voices that found an audience and readership. However, Phraates' eventual decision to consolidate his Parthian kingdom and throne and discard any plans for a wars of conquest he may have had turned out to be of inestimately higher value than the varying fortunes of an aggressive imperialist policy. It allowed Parthia to reemerge as a strong power once again having wisely surrendered its goodwill to Pompey. But such wisdom and goodwill was to be totally lost on Crassus. Still, stability within a strong, small empire like that of Phraates' own would prove to be a more durable weapon against any enemy, even a larger one like Rome.

CHAPTER THREE

THE BATTLE OF CARRHAE

Plutarch as an Historical Source

THE BATTLE OF CARRHAE was a pivotal event in Romano-Parthian history, a precise point in time that would go on to define relations between these two great empires for decades to come. Yet while in Parthia it was remembered for over a century as a famous and celebrated victory against reckless Roman imperialism, in Rome there was despair as the outcome of the battle was a resounding defeat. Moreover, the loss held far-reaching consequences for the res-publica: later generations of Romans often pin-pointed it as the beginning of the breakdown of the so-called first triumvirate - the political pact originally formed between Pompey, Julius Caesar and Marcus Crassus. With Crassus' death at Carrhae, only Pompey and Caesar remained left, and in the space of four years they would engulf the Roman world in a civil war that saw Caesar emerge as sole ruler of the empire. It would be Caesar's fame, absolute power, and expertise on the battle field that would underpin and define the role of all Roman emperors that followed.

When we turn to the battle itself there are two important points we must firstly bear in mind; and both pertain to the nature of our main ancient literary source, Plutarch. Firstly, we must consider Plutarch's own self-confessed literary purposes. As a native of Greece,

Plutarch naturally inherited a deep admiration for Greek tragedy, and such admiration is reflected throughout his biography of Crassus. It was one of his last works, and each one of these last works is invariably tragic in tone and theme.

The fifth century BC play by Euripides, the *Bacchae*, is the standout tragedy that Plutarch evoked in writing of Crassus' demise culminating in his death at Carrhae. Just as Pentheus' fall from grace was staggering, so too was Crassus' own.[62] While the tragedy genre was not Plutarch's own invention, clearly he chose to make it his own. The reason so was to convey to the listening and reading audience a moral lesson, as well as an example of the doomed person – the characteristics of whom one should not emulate. At its heart is the message not to ignore providence, as the doomed have done. Thus, when omens and curses which had accompanied Crassus' setting off for his ill-fated Parthian war were discarded by the general, it bode ill for Crassus, as well as his army and indeed Rome's own future. At least, so Plutarch would have us believe.

Another model of tragedy Plutarch drew upon which was just as influential on his biography of Crassus as Euripides' plays, was that of the Sicilian expedition written by the Athenian historian Thucydides, a younger contemporary of Euripides'. Like Crassus' own campaign, the attempt by the Athenians under the general Nicias' command to conquer Sicily proved a total disaster. So, not surprisingly, Plutarch chose to parallel Crassus with Nicias. As a history enthusiast, Plutarch, like countless other historians, could not resist this Thucididean influence.

But it was not just Crassus who supplied moral fodder for Plutarch. His representations of Parthians in Crassus' biography are examples of treachery, hypocrisy, and licentiousness that Roman writers often liked to associate with the barbarism of the east – one that inherited, like Rome, classical Greek and Hellenistic culture, but one that warped that inheritance into a reversal of the wholesomeness and modesty of Roman civilization. Thus the din of Parthian war-drums, like that caused by the Trojans in Homer's *Iliad*, and the mock-triumph by the Parthian army following their victory over Crassus was an inflection of all that was thoroughly Roman.[63] Hence, following their defeat,

Romans felt a growing hunger and imperative to avenge Crassus, and seek retribution against an enemy that aroused hatred and fear within their own ordered, wholesome, and familiar Roman world.[64]

All of these literary and cultural nods would have been picked up by Plutarch's peers,[65] and so, through his interwoven turns of evocations, Plutarch was able to convey numerous layers of meaning which were at once both pedagogic and entertaining, maintaining his readers' interest and leaving them in no doubt as to the writer's justification for the importance of composing such a biography.

But so far we have looked only at Plutarch's literary style. This brings us to the second issue that we must bear in mind when approaching Plutarch and it is partly based upon his style: it is his reliability as a historical source. We have seen that Plutarch was not shy in using artistic license when it suited him. Some have argued that such license has irretrievably coloured Plutarch's narrative to the point that his overall reliability is questionable at best. Such an argument, however, is perhaps too skeptical of a source as familiar with history as his peer critics who would no doubt have condemned him in no uncertain terms for connivance, if that were indeed the case. But that said, the reliability of any ancient source is crucial to the study of history, so some skepticism is not out of place in approaching Plutarch's writings or any other ancient writer's.

But for all of Plutarch's literary nods and preoccupations, his account of Crassus' Parthian war remains our most detailed and important source. It reflects the growing ambition and political independence of figures such as Crassus, so characteristic of the age of the first-triumvirate.[67] Even the juxtaposition of Roman and Parthian cultures is not an entirely bad thing either. It reflects the Roman mood of Plutarch's day, which he had, like many Romans, inherited from the period following the fallout of Crassus' spectacular loss. It is tinged with the animosity one would expect from a culture with a gloating enemy like that of the Parthians. The sense of cultural superiority found in Plutarch's life of Crassus is probably also a genuine part of the Roman psyche following the defeat, affected by an enemy in Parthia that itself felt that its own cultural and military superiority over those of the Romans had been proven on the battlefield. The sense of tragedy was palpable, not only for Plutarch, but also his immediate Roman audience, and it was shared by many as the Romans searched for answers to what was indeed a great defeat. Plutarch's literary layers, then, do not render his account of the war useless, but inform us about the multifaceted response in Rome to their loss on the battlefield at Carrhae which had crystallised by the time Plutarch wrote. Thus, although it is somewhat dramatized and embellished, Plutarch's biography of Crassus is of inestimable value in its descriptions of historical facts and its sense of social despondency felt in Rome after the battle was well over, both immediately following and long afterwards.

Origins of Crassus' Parthian War

In 60 BC Rome's three most powerful political personalities, Pompey, Julius Caesar and Marcus Crassus, cemented the political union known famously today as the 'first triumvirate'. The union served primarily to further all three parties' political ambitions. In order to do so, the triumvirs decided that Caesar would campaign for one of the twin offices of the annual consulship, and once in power, force into legislation the political ends and means of all concerned. Caesar himself, least powerful of the three, benefited greatly during his consulate upon election, and not merely for the fact of being consul, because he was able to secure a five-year proconsular command in Gaul. Situated immediately northwest of Italy, Gaul provided Caesar with a base not only to conduct war and conquest over its inhabitants, but also one from which he could bear influence over affairs in Italy itself.

When the end of Caesar's command approached in 55 BC the three parties recommitted themselves to their triumvirate alliance, and together with a large number of Roman Senators, who had clearly recognized where power now lied, they dictated the new political status quo. The results of this recommitment were certainly far-reaching for Rome's future relations with Parthia. Together with a further five-year extension for Caesar's Gallic war, Pompey and Crassus both decided that it was now their turn to hold the twin offices themselves while Caesar remained in Gaul, and that they should also receive new military commands as well. So Pompey secured a command in Spain. Crassus on the other hand made his mind up on a Parthian war.

In a certain way, Crassus' war was designed to establish him a standing as a military commander on an equal footing to Caesar and Pompey who were both now the most famous military generals of their day. Such fame beckoned many in the Roman elite, and indeed senatorial position, which all three triumvirs held it should be remembered, was based upon military office and wealth, and that wealth was often procured from military victories. Up to that time Crassus had indeed successfully put down the dangerous slave revolt led by the infamous Spartacus, but in Rome his victory was seen less as a war against a foreign enemy as it was against an enthusiastic rabble. So, he sorely needed a victory like Caesar's and Pompey's own to cement himself as a true leader of Rome, both by reputation and fact.[68] But it was also more than just that. According to Plutarch, in Rome the fame of Lucullus' and Pompey's successes in the East was so great that Crassus could not resist trying to emulate and even surpass.[69] At the forefront of the searching for success in the east was the torch of Alexander the Great, whose victories, fame and reputation led the way for Romans such as Crassus to follow. Pompey had styled himself as 'the Great', and Caesar too sought to equal his achievements.[70] Even Gabinius had considered conquering the east beforehand (see Chapter Two); now Crassus, believing victory in the East would be as easy for him as it was for Pompey, became obsessed.[71] Roman armies had not yet fought Parthia in battle, and Crassus and his military staff were satisfied that victory against it would be as certain as those won in Armenia. History, however, shows that he would be proved wrong.

Marcus Licinius Crassus, at the Louvre, Paris.
Wikipedia.org

In Plutarch's biography there is a deep-running theme that the sense of foreboding associated with the outset of the campaign was mistakenly ignored by Crassus much to his and Rome's peril. But even if such a statement is seen as an over-dramatisation it still stands that there were indeed negative precursors to the event. According to Plutarch, when Crassus had announced his intentions in the east, C. Ateius Capito, who held one of the august offices of tribune of the plebs, opposed the idea outright correctly pointing out that Parthia was in fact an ally and had done nothing to provoke war. However, in the age of the triumvirate political ambition overawed institution and Crassus prepared for his campaign nonetheless. But Ateius kept up his protest. He even ordered the arrest of Crassus himself. Fortunately for Crassus' ambitions though, the order was not followed by the other tribunes. It was then that Ateius publicly cursed Crassus, invoking several obscure but greatly feared deities to achieve the curses' purposes. But, although Ateius' political cause might have been just, the Roman public would not tolerate the calling upon of underworldly beings for the sake of a Roman such as Crassus, and accordingly they cleared the way for Crassus' setting out from Rome to the east when his consulship end at the end of that year. Thus, Ateius' protests turned on the protester and endeared Crassus' unjust cause to a populace now thrilled at the prospect of a great conquest under Crassus' leadership.

However, it must be said that this account of Plutarch's has been rejected by some as entirely spurious. It is alleged that the author had confused Ateius' opposition to Crassus with Atinius' cursing of Metellus following the defeat of P. Licinius Crassus in 131-130 BC as described by the historian Livy.[72] But that was clearly not the case. Plutarch's account is replete with knowledgeable details, and given that Livy's life overlapped with that of Marcus Crassus, it is more likely that Livy drew inspiration from this later event and projected it upon the earlier one of the two in his own historical work. He may have even witnessed the actual cursing by Ateius itself. He certainly would have conversed with many who had. Sensing their impressions from such an event it probably seemed evident to Livy that the drama of it all warranted a place in own narrative of Roman history especially where similarity of names could evoke acclaim among his contemporary readers. In any event, other pre-Plutarch writers confirm his account of events, including Velleius Paterculus.[73] Later, Appian and Cassius Dio would do the same.[74]

Conditions for Crassus' Campaign

Crassus, having set off from the port at Brundisium, proceeded to Greece and from there sailed to Asia Minor. He then marched through Galatia until he reached the Euphrates River. However, his following acts show that he was entirely unprepared for a war in Parthian conditions. The terrain of the Middle East was tyrannical to events in any war there. In the searing heat of the Parthian Empire, fighting was not only for the battlefields but also conducted on the walls of their great cities that fed and watered their defenders and sheltered them from the blazing Middle East sun.[75] Even today harsh weather conditions are a major issue in Iran. For four months of the year the winds are so strong and destructive that archaeological excavations can not be carried out even by professional archaeologists there. All that they can do is cover and screen their digs and hope that winds and looters do not carry it all away. In fact, weather patterns can be so extreme in Iran that a particular 86 meter stretch of wall at one Parthian fortress is visible only after the rainy season when the annually accumulated salt and sediment is washed away. But when those rains stop the winds return again blowing huge amounts of salt and dust over it again it is completely reburied every year until the next rainy season.[76]

Because of such extreme weather and dust the Parthians relied upon their cities for refuge and protection from the harsh elements outside. This meant that for the most part daily life centered within cities. This also meant that there were always Parthian troops stationed on walls of every city. Moreover, conditions dictated that fast moving cavalry proved the ideal method of fast travel from city to city across the windswept Mesopotamian plains. Thus Crassus would have to, if there was any hope of conquering Parthia's empire, conquer city by city in the face of cavalry forces.

A number of Parthian cities have been excavated by archaeologists and those settlements after so many centuries still bear silent witness to the heavy strategic importance the Parthians placed in them. Archaeologists working at Yazdegerd for example have uncovered thick walls, towers and bastions, and large city gates there to serve for both defense and attack.[77] Often Parthian cities, like Merv, Hatra and others, were laid out not in the rectangular Roman fashion, like the shape of Roman military camps along the lines of which Roman cities were built,[78] but rather featured city centers around which was a circular residential sprawl. That was a legacy of the Assyrian military camp shape,[79] and goes to show one main difference between Roman and Parthian cultures – they had inherited very different cultures - one from Europe, and the other from Asia.

However those cities served more than just a purely military purpose. They were centers of Parthian society. At various Parthian sites archaeologists have found detailed and elaborate murals, stucco carving and paintings on the walls of the cities' public buildings that were once administrative structures, prayer halls, palaces, and fire-temples once used for the worship of fire – a central part of Parthian religion.[80] These finds show us that Parthian cities were social hubs as well as military bases armed to the teeth. If anyone was to conquer the Parthians, they would have to capture their cities, that is, if they could survive the harsh elements surrounding them first.

Crassus Invades

Setting out from Syria, Crassus began to take cities. He had obviously realised early on something of their importance to Parthia and was intent on making them submit to Rome and, more precisely to his immediate concerns, himself. But with each city or town that he captured Crassus found that he now had to garrison each one if their allegiance to him was to continue after he marched onwards into Parthian territory. Thus, a slow depletion on his total manpower served the Parthians well, since with every one of Crassus' sieges it provided them with ample time to prepare to eventually meet him in battle.[81]

In response, Orodes dispatched a number of envoys to meet with Crassus to ask the rhetorical question as to whether he was acting on his own judgment in making war with him, or Rome's decision. When Crassus answered with the rhetorical wit to match it, saying that he would give his reply in the Parthian capital Seleucia, one of the envoys laughed and said rather flatly but also with flare that hair would begin to grow on the palm of his hand first.[82] It is a curious tale, and displays the confidence that Parthians may have felt by and large in the face of Crassus' attack upon them. Of course, Plutarch did not inform us as to his source, but the final reply made was certainly fulfilled by Carrhae. But perhaps a bit too well. It may well be the case that in this exchange is an embellishment made after the fact so as to justify it. We can only guess at Crassus' and his staff's response. But it may have had some historical basis: it was certainly a bold conversation between Crassus and the envoys and thus a memorable one in light of events that followed. Something factual along the lines of Plutarch's account might therefore have taken place, although we have only Plutarch's account as witness.

Yet if the realisation that the demanding conditions for war with Parthia were harsher that he had anticipated, he was soon stung into proceeding deeper into Parthian lands. An embassy from Artavsdes, king of Armenia, arrived in Crassus' camp to pledge the welcome support of 6,000 cavalry with 10,000 more to come. Crassus had been informed that the Parthians' main weapon of attack was in its cavalry, so given that his force was comprised mainly of Roman legionnaires he embraced the Armenian offer with glee. But the envoys offered Crassus more: they also suggested that Crassus consider staging his invasion from Armenia, which being mountainous, was more suitable for an infantry marches into Parthia than the plains of Syria and Mesopotamia. Now, Plutarch did not divulge his source of such insider's knowledge, but it certainly has something of a historical ring to it – Parthian armies had found it difficult to penetrate Armenia in the same way that Roman infantry armies, like Pompey's, had in the past. But, even if this episode is reliable, the Armenian suggestion was not an acceptable one to Crassus. He had already garrisoned many of his own soldiers within numerous towns along his path and he was not prepared to give them up simply in order to take up any Armenian suggestion to start his campaign all over again far to the north of where he was.

While all of this was happening Orodes had kept busy mobilizing an army and putting the empire on a war-footing. Marching into Armenia, he created a diversion there which ensured that Artavasdes' cavalry would remain there to defend it and never reach Crassus. As for Crassus, Orodes had decided to deploy Suren, a gifted and innovative general who bested Crassus in the approaching battle in every manner. Suren's force of some 10,000 cavalry was outnumbered by Crassus' legions 4 to 1, but it seemed to Orodes and Suren sufficient to defeat the enemy regardless. This force was itself of Suren's own mustering from his vast estates around the Parthian Empire. Without a professional army, like that which Rome possessed, Parthian kings often conscripted armies from their nobles' estates. As a result, the king, if he were to win any war, had to have the loyalty of his nobles. This arrangement added another dimension to the title 'King of kings'. In a sense, the Parthian nobility were semi-monarchical and had a powerful hand in the running of the empire which the Parthian king had to accommodate if he was to get his way on matters pertaining to the running of the state. Thus by answering Orodes' call to war, Suren was following convention. But in the battle to come, Suren proved that he was no conventional general. His decisions to lead a force entirely made up of cavalry, to convey vast amounts of camel-loads of arrows as ammunition for that force, and to have especially made armour-penetrating arrows carried by those loads, were in themselves each a statement that he had studied Crassus' movements from afar and had decided upon a concerted plan to defeat him in battle by other means than infantry.[83] He was not going to play into Crassus' hands. On the afternoon of the 9th June, 53 BC, the armies of Crassus and Suren came within contact of each other near the town of Carrhae.

The choice of this location for battle by Suren was a well-thought out one. Carrhae was where the royal highway from the west forked, with one road leading east through Adiabene to the Tigris, and another leading south along the Euphrates to Seleucia.[84] Crassus had decided to march down the latter road, but Suren was intent on dictating the course of the war and headed him off before the Roman army could advance any further. As with the forthcoming battle itself, Suren had taken the initiative that would dictate the outcome of the whole war.

The Battle of Carrhae

The battle of Carrhae is often described as being a clash of cultures, or a confrontation between two vastly different civilizations, and in a sense both of these descriptions are correct. The battle was the first time that Roman and Parthian armies had met in conflict and is a perfect case of how vastly different military machines in the ancient world could perform against each other on the battlefield. Indeed both Roman and Parthian civilizations comprised of very different military traditions: Rome's being based upon its legions and Parthia's upon its cavalry to highlight one glaring difference. In fact the power that a dominant culture could exert upon populations was well recognised in Crassus' own day. His contemporary, the poet Pubilius Syrus, famously hailed the "sway of custom" as "most tyrannous".[85] But in this poet's statement is the clear indication that Romans, and by implication all humans, are able to reflect upon and consider others' customs, and indeed one's own, for him or herself, and in so doing make calculated decisions about which facets of those customs one wishes to partake of or reject. When we look at the battle of Carrhae itself the contrast between cultural convention and individual calculation is manifest within both Crassus on the one hand and Suren on the other.

When the two sides made contact for the first time they immediately prepared for battle. Crassus, following traditional Roman battle tactics, drew up his army in battle formation. But since it was already late afternoon when initial contact was made both sides withdrew to make camp. Crassus himself ordered that his army to build a camp-site next to the nearby Balissus River. Plutarch saw these movements as a reflection of indecision on Crassus' part and inability to bring the enemy to battle.[86] But the reality was rather different. Crassus had seen the surrounding barren landscape firsthand and must have thought that by securing the closest supply of water for his own army, which was how all Roman commanders operated, he was denying that same source to an already thirsty and exhausted Parthian foe.[87]

Crassus planned to offer battle the following day, when the Parthian host, being denied a water source, would be parched and dehydrated, and thereby unable to fight a battle. Or so he thought. In fact, Suren had stocked a thousand strong baggage camel-train to supply his force with weapons, food and water. So he had no need to secure a position by the river and could afford to lull Crassus into a false sense of security and bring him to battle the next day.

At dawn the following day both commanders drew up their forces and battle began. Its sights and sounds were a clear sign that two very different armies were fighting that day. In contrast to the Romans' war-horns the Parthians kept marching order in time to war-drums, and while the legions wore traditional Roman armour the Parthian cavalry were arrayed in their own style of brightly shining protective coverings. The battle proper started when Suren gave the command to his thousand strong horse-lancers to charge. They were easily repulsed by the densely formed up legions, and Crassus in turn gave his own order for pursuit. But Suren's lancers were too swift to be overtaken and instead they galloped around the Romans and encircled them. Then Suren discharged his main strike weapon in his nine-thousand strong horse-archers, which he had drawn up behind his lancers, hiding them from Roman view. As the Roman legions charged, he ordered them to attack.

Roman armies were well trained and were used to fighting cavalry. But up until this point they had only fought full-scale engagements against cavalry forces that used swords or lances, and so Crassus had not calculated upon meeting such a large host of horse-archers. As the battle transpired Crassus showed that he did not know how to engage them effectively. So, when the enemy horse-archers attacked, Crassus was surrounded and at a loss, and all he could do was repeatedly order his legions to charge again and again. The result was a Roman bloodbath. For the first time a Roman army had fallen victim to the Parthian shot.

The Parthian Shot was a battle tactic employed by Parthian cavalry archers, wherein they would feign retreat enticing the enemy to pursue, and then they would fire arrows behind them at the unaware charging adversary. Suren employed the tactic repeatedly and consistently at

Carrhae with devastating effect. Such a battle ploy was held in contempt among Romans as unmanly. Plutarch himself voiced popular Roman disgust at the tactic in his account of Crassus' life, saying that it was somewhat akin to simply "running away" so as not to come to close grips with the enemy in the heat of battle.[88] However, for the Parthians, it was their main strength, and indeed, it was their most famous and successful battle tactic.

The tactic grew out of the fact that the Parthians never maintained a full-time professional force but relied instead, during wartime, on conscript armies drawn by kings and nobles from the citizen populations of their satraps. As a result, Parthian generals had to employ the use of maneuvers familiar to civilians who made up those armies. They found the ideal one in the Parthian Shot. The Parthian Shot was a widely used maneuver employed in hunting by peoples around the Middle East, and was adopted by the Assyrians, Persians and Greeks for that same purpose. Evidence of this is found in numerous sculptures, including an engraved Assyrian cylinder dated to the eighth to seventh centuries BC in the British Museum which portrays such a manner during a hunt.[89] Therefore, the shot was a maneuver that those who were to be conscripted into Parthian armies would have been extremely adept at performing on the battlefield. Parthian generals were thus able to bring to bear against an enemy a tactic that was not only familiar to Parthian civilians themselves, but one that had been employed for centuries among the various subject nationalities that made up their empire. Because Parthian armies relied so heavily upon the shot, some have argued that the Parthians were by and large unimaginative when it came to military developments and that their military lacked the flexibility to adapt to changing circumstances.[90] These are astute observations and are true to a certain point, but we must remember that the reason why Parthia did not often alter their military arrangements was because it already worked so well under Parthian conditions. Parthians would never be able to seriously threaten Rome, but time and again Roman commanders like Crassus, and later Antony, learnt the hard way that neither could Parthia be conquered even by a professional Roman army.

At the beginning of the Parthian horse-archer charge, Crassus had placed much confidence in the durability of his soldiers' shields and armour to withstand the attack. He may have even been delighted that after the repulsion of the enemy's lancers, their only answer was in arrows. But they were no ordinary arrows. Suren had expected the Romans to be armoured so he had especially designed armour-piercing arrows made in such a vast quantity that his army would not run short of them in battle. So the arrows kept flying. With legionnaires falling around him, and his repeated charges repulsed, Crassus expected the enemy's arrows to run out soon giving him the perfect moment to turn the battle around and launch his own attack. But, stocked with almost endless ammunition, Suren had already made sure that that moment never came.

Desperate and losing, Crassus' son Publius launched his own charge at the enemy. But that was to prove a fatal move both for him and the Roman army. He was cut down and his head decapitated and thrown back at the Roman line. According to Plutarch it was the sight of this which finally broke the Romans' fighting spirit.[91] Crassus' orders to charge from this point on carried little effect and when Suren renewed his horse-lancers' attack, the battle was all but over. Bunched together by the enemy lancers, the Romans stood as an open target for the enemy archers. The massacre continued until nightfall.

Defeated, Crassus fled into the town of Carrhae. Again Suren attacked him by laying siege to the town, and again fighting continued until sunset. It was all over for the campaign and finally Crassus conceded, seeking terms of defeat from the Parthian general. Suren agreed to meet him but when Crassus rode out of the town to meet with him he too, like his son, was cut down and decapitated. The losses suffered by the Romans were immense. Even if the loss to Rome of one of its most powerful politicians, and his son, were not enough, in the battle itself 20,000 Roman legionnaires were killed and another 10,000 taken prisoner.

Crassus' head was taken to Orodes who had set up court in Armenia by Artavasdes' invitation. Artavasdes, now a Parthian ally, was a Greek drama enthusiast and a playwright himself, and happened to be entertaining the Parthian king at court with a performance of Euripides' *Bacchae*. At the climax of the tragedy when the decapitated head of the main character, Pentheus, is revealed, Crassus' own head was also exhibited to a thrilled audience that included the Parthian and Armenian kings themselves.[92] This is the account given by Plutarch, and by his evidence alone it all appears too coincidental that Crassus' head was shown at the exact point of the play when Pentheus' own was. Consequently, our first impulse is to regard it as a fabrication. But upon closer inspection it is clear that Parthian affairs were often highly managed and staged for maximum effect. Diplomacy, politics, and ceremony were highly structured issues which demanded highly structured public performance. As a result, the appearance of Crassus' head at that point in the play was also deliberate and symbolic. It sent a message to all that just as Pentheus had fatally ignored the will of the gods, so too had Crassus. Just as Pentheus was punished for his act of hubris, so was Crassus, and by none other than the Parthian king himself. Thus it was an official statement that any threat against Parthia would be dealt with, and likewise any scheme, or plot, to harm the sacrosanct body of the king, no matter how short his reign or dubious his legitimacy to rule was, would not be tolerated. Although Plutarch could not bring himself to state these truths openly, it is still clearly implied throughout his whole *Life of Crassus*. Plutarch's account of the life of Crassus, therefore, is not a work warped by constant expression of tragic genres, but was rather a well informed one that ended in such disaster that the incident involving the performance of the *Bacchae* became inspiration to moralise throughout it. The facts of the disaster of Crassus' Parthian war were well established, and Plutarch did not ever seek to undermine them intentionally. But the sad outcome of Crassus' life was such that a moralizing parallel along tragic lines was irresistible to the author.

Aftermath of the Battle

Suren's fate did not befit his service to his king at Carrhae. After the battle Suren staged a triumph in mockery of all that was Roman to Seleucia. It was widely acclaimed by Parthians exultant over their defeated Roman enemy. But, jealous of Suren's fame and threatened by his emerging popularity among his subjects, Orodes quickly had him executed.[93] Yet Suren's fame lived on in Parthia long after Orodes had died, and was remembered as the victor at Carrhae and the one who put a stop to Rome's naked aggression.

Coin of Orodes II. Legend: 'King of kings, Great Arsaces, and Founder'.
From mint at Seleucia on the Euphrates.
Reverse: An archer with a bow.
Wikipedia.org

In Rome, however, the battle took on a very different guise. With the elimination of a triumvir, Caesar and Pompey soon found themselves in competition until the point when they would embroil the whole Roman Empire in a civil war. In 49 BC Caesar marched south from Gaul and marched on Rome and after several battles Caesar emerged victorious and became sole ruler of the empire. Thus Carrhae was seen by many Romans as a turning point in their city's history when Rome descended into autocracy and chaos. But the effects of Carrhae were even longer lasting and far-reaching than just that. It marked a shift in Roman affairs not only politically, but also economically, and militarily. So, while to Parthians it remained a sign of superiority over Romans in battle, to Romans it served as inspiration for future wars of vengeance.[94]

CHAPTER FOUR

CARRHAE TO ACTIUM

Cicero and the Parthian Threat

RASSUS' CRUSHING DEFEAT at Carrhae did not just herald a military defeat in Rome. It also signaled that political change would soon sweep across the Near East, and so it transpired. Armenia soon prepared to invade Cappadocia, Syria revolted against Rome, and to Syria's north Cilicia also threatened to rebel.[95] Added to this extremely volatile mix was the looming presence of Parthia, and Orodes was in no short time extending Parthian economic influence over the whole region. Parthian traders opened up new markets in places like Palmyra, a city in Syria's east that was to go on and have a major standing as a commercial leader in the Middle East and beyond as will be shown in chapter seven. All this allowed goods from as far east as China to be traded by Parthian entrepreneurs in Roman Syria. That would mark the beginning of a trend that would cause Romans to become obsessive about the procuring of Eastern fabrics and other Eastern luxury goods through trade. But that obsession still lay in the future.

Meanwhile in Syria, Crassus' lieutenant Cassius had collected what remained of his original forces and invested Antioch in haste to meet the expected massive Parthian counter-attack. However, that attack did not come. The Parthian army, which had always been a conscript military force, had actually been disbanded after its victory over Crassus, and Suren had been executed by Orodes. Thus, what was Suren's finest hour succumbed to Orodes' own paranoia, and Parthian jubilation was cut short. It has been pondered by many historians as to why no special commemorative coins were issued in Parthia in celebration of the victory at Carrhae. The reason is that Parthian coinage was the sole domain of Parthian kings and usurpers. Orodes did not wish Suren to be portrayed, in public especially, as either.[96]

Ridden of Suren, Orodes felt he could make his move in his own good time. In 51 BC he conscripted a new army and placed it under the command of his own son Pacorus and the seasoned general Osaces, whose fighting prowess and experience in military matters served as good reasons for Orodes to dispatch him and keep a close eye on the young prince. To meet the threat Cicero was commissioned as governor of Cilicia with the charge of stabilizing the region through his tact and influence, and to take control of the two legions in that province and keep it at the ready if need arose as it was expected to.[97]

We are fortunate enough to possess many of Cicero's own letters which he wrote during his governorship, which means that we have the luxury of a rare window into conditions on the ground at that time. They convey a real and palpable fear of the Parthian threat on the writer's part, a threat made all the more nerve-racking by its prolonged postponement.

Finally, in September Pacorus crossed the Euphrates with the Parthian army and marched on Antioch.[98] Cassius, who had served under Crassus and survived Carrhae, was still there waiting for the arrival of his replacement Bibulus and an expected Roman relief force. But, as Bibulus was frightened of the Parthians he and his forces were slow to arrive and Cassius had to prepare to defend the city himself as best he and his soldiers could. To give him support Cicero marched from Cilicia into Syria and opened a second front. But it was unnecessary. The Parthians were unsuited to siege warfare and withdrew.

But that did not put an end to the fighting. According to Cicero's dubious boasts, Cassius was so emboldened by Cicero's arrival on the scene that he took heart and led his soldiers out after the enemy, forced them to give battle, and then carried off an emphatic victory.

Osaces even sustained a fatal wound in that battle and died la
a result of it. Of course, while the basic details of these events ar
doubt credible, Cicero's boasting and self-congratulations are larg
not – a fact not missed by his own peers.[99]

To counter this setback the Parthians regrouped just outside Cy
rhestica in Syria and waited eagerly for the expected arrival of king
Orodes himself. He had sent ahead to Pacorus notifying him that he
was going to henceforth lead the army onto victory.[100] But he never
came and by August 50 BC Parthia's forces had withdrawn from Syria
entirely. Understandably, a very relieved Cicero could not believe his
luck, and was at a total loss as to how to explain the Parthian flight.
He himself could only put it down to the hidden will of some god.[101]
His loss for a reason was shared by other Romans as well. Later, the
Roman poet Horace put it down to the fact that unrest was beginning
to surface between Pompey and Caesar and that Orodes had decided
to let them fight it out in civil war and intervene at a more opportune
moment.[102] Although Horace somewhat over-dramatises his claim
through the medium of poetry, it was a claim which nonetheless had
a lasting legacy among many Romans.[103] But Horace's claim was made
with the benefit of hindsight, and ignores the fact that Orodes did
actually consider making a pact with Pompey at the outset of the
civil war.[104] It also fails to consider how conditions in Parthia had an
impact on Orodes' decision to withdraw. Certainly, on the face of it,
it looks like the Parthian Empire was strong at this time. Its economy
was thriving with mints churning out millions of Orodes' coins,[105] and
the Parthian army was already encamped in a part of Roman territory
that was severely lacking in defenders. In fact, things appear so good
for Parthia, and Parthia appears to some so unbeatable had she wanted
war at this point, that one current view is that Cicero's intelligence
was poor and that their was never any Parthian threat, only a series of
small looting raids into Syria.[106]

But scratch the surface of the Parthian Empire and real reasons
for the withdrawal come to the fore. Just prior to the withdrawal, not
only were several Parthian satraps on the point of open revolt, but they
were even plotting to overthrow Orodes and replace him with his own
son Pacorus. Of course, Pacorus had no hand in this plotting. He was

would continue to prove himself to be Oro-
for years to come. But Orodes was a parricide
that he lacked the luxury of communications about
Osaces who was now dead, the king had no reliable
and to warrant his own appearance amidst a seemingly
my in Syria. Nor did he wish to give Pacorus the chance of a
over the Romans that would give him the power the king had
feared in Suren. So, instead, Orodes recalled his army from Syria
and dealt with the rebellious satraps.[107] Thus ended the Parthian threat
that Cicero, Bibulus, and so many others in Rome's eastern provinces
had so greatly feared.

The civil war between Pompey and Caesar was protracted and shed
much Roman blood. Eventually Caesar emerged victorious while Pompey
was decapitated in Egypt after fleeing there following his defeat at Phar-
salus in Thessaly. But despite the chaos, Roman power in the east was
restored and by 45 BC Caesar had prepared to use it as a spring-board to
launch his own Pacorus-like non-event invasion into Parthia from.

Julius Caesar's Parthian War

Julius Caesar had begun plans for a Parthian war at an early stage.
The death of Crassus, Caesar's fellow triumvir, was a severe shock to
the Roman world, and left Caesar and Pompey behind as Rome's two
most powerful figures. The tense rivalry that ensued between these
two men finally escalated into civil war.[108] But all of that lay in Rome's
unforeseeable future. However, the loss at Carrhae did foment a feeling
among Rome's generals that Crassus' death had to be avenged. Caesar
was one such general, and he showed signs of vengeful designs on
Parthia as soon as news reached him in Gaul of the heavy loss at Carrhae.[109] In fact, Caesar was so intent on playing some part in Rome's
vengeance upon Parthia that not long before he and Pompey made war
on each other Caesar was actually prepared to send one of his own
legions, and another that had been on loan to him from Pompey, to
Syria for an expected Parthian war.[110]

After Caesar emerged victorious over Pompey he was left as Rome's
most powerful man. But he was not content with just that. By 45 BC

he had begun serious planning for the conquest of Parthia. Such plans were initially greeted with enthusiasm and Cicero and many other Roman Senators ostensibly voiced their approval publicly.[111] But their outward appearances hid an acute fear and consternation. Caesar's position as sole ruler frightened its members, who were forced to bow and scrape to Caesar's every whim in terror of the man who alone held the future of the Senate in the palm of his hand. It was the common hope of all Senators that Caesar would restore them to the position of power they had enjoyed before the civil war - Cicero himself voiced that particular concern to Caesar.[112]

However, when Caesar ignored all such motions and began planning for his Parthian war instead, and thus demonstrating to all that this war was more important to him than the welfare of the Senate, the Senators were outraged. It had finally dawned on them that their powers would not be restored any time soon. On the 15th March 44 BC Caesar was killed by a Senatorial plot and his plans for the coming war came to naught.

But before he was assassinated during the Senate meeting, Caesar's venture in the east bore all the hallmarks of potential success. According to Suetonius, Caesar had planned to escape Crassus' fat by tentatively marching through the hilly and infantry-friendly terrain of Lesser Armenia, and after taking time to observe Parthian tactics descend into the plains of Mesopotamia.[113] For such a venture sixteen legions and 10,000 cavalry were mustered and sent ahead to Macedonia, where, with Caesar's heir Octavian, they were to await his arrival.[114]

However, Caesar had not only mustered an army. He had also roused religious zeal to support the military cause for the duration of his absence. The last months of Caesar's life is still the topic of much historical debate, particularly in regard to whether Caesar really desired to become king or not. Yet resolution to this debate is found in the context of his future Parthian campaign, a huge undertaking with huge ramifications. In fact, it could even be said that in order for one to comprehend Caesar's behaviour leading up to his Parthian War one must first understand something of the importance of it at the time. Such was its importance to Caesar. When Caesar announced a forthcoming Parthian war there was circulated a Sibylline prophecy that stated that only a Roman king would ever conquer the Parthians. It was a curious prophecy and one that invited widespread consideration about Caesar's own position and power. But it was certainly no coincidence that at the Roman festival of Lupercalia on the 15th January 44 BC, precisely one month before Caesar had planned to leave Rome for the East, many partakers of the celebrations, including Caesar's own second-in-command Marc Antony, actually tried to crown Caesar as king.[115] Caesar, knowing full well that there were many Senators and Senatorial supporters that still deplored the institution of monarchy, refused their approaches on that day, but his hopes of becoming king remained nonetheless.[116] Consequently, on the fateful day of the 15th March, on the eve of his setting out for the East, Caesar called a meeting of the Senate to confer kingship upon himself. It was a bold move. He would be first king since the Senate's overthrow the last king in the late 6th century, and being proclaimed king by the Senate would have ensured his legitimacy to rule as that overthrow had the Senate's. Then, he hoped that day to immediately remove himself from the scene by setting out for Parthia while the Senators were left to stew in their humiliation. But he would never embark. As the meeting began Caesar was stabbed to death bu furious senators.

Therefore, in light of all this solid evidence it is almost impossible to escape the conclusion that Caesar really did desire kingship. Although he had refused Antony's offers, the reason for such was not that he did not wish to be king, but that that was not the appropriate means for becoming king.[117] For Caesar, only confirmation by the Senate would suffice.

But why king specifically? Wasn't sole ruler enough? He had already been voted dictator for life by the Senate – a power that was kingship in all but name.[118] The answer once again lies in Caesar's planned war with Parthia. He had no desire to relinquish his autocratic power to anyone, but his autocracy was becoming increasingly unpopular in Rome where the Senate had traditionally made decisions for centuries. Sensing the mood, the dictator experimented with another title besides king for a short while. When members of the Roman public began to hail him as king, Caesar was often heard to reply "I am not king, but Caesar!" It was a cute remark indeed, but it contained a deeper meaning, even if it could not be easily gleaned by ancient historians a century and a half later: Suetonius believed Caesar was deflecting suspicion of his plans to be proclaimed king; Plutarch that he was reacting in horror to the title.[119] But in the context of the coming Parthian war the comment's deeper meaning is exposed. Just as every Parthian king that followed their dynastic forebear Arsaces bore the title Arsaces, so too was Caesar dreaming of a dynasty that would bear his own name as its title. One should not be too surprised by this. Every emperor to follow the dictator used the title 'Caesar' as was perhaps Julius' original intension, and in any case other nations closer to Rome also used such convention: hence in Egypt the dynastic successors to Alexander's general Ptolemy adopted the title 'Ptolemy'. Caesar's own recourse to use such a title is that he knew well that Parthian kings possessed the allegiance of their armies in spades, even after numerous civil wars, and setting up a rival kingship would have gone a long way in breaking that up. Caesar hoped that it would be just short step for Parthians to swap their allegiance, both phonetically and politically, from 'Arsaces' to 'Caesar'. One should not be too surprised at this either. Alexander had himself adopted Iranian customs in order to cement his position over his Iranian subjects even though he knew that that could potentially isolate him from his Macedonian officers.[120] Julius Caesar was doing nothing different, although his timing certainly was different: whereas Alexander had waited until he had conquered Iran before he adopted Iranian custom, Caesar was simply experimenting with them before he had set out on his own conquest of Iran. The Parthian context, therefore, sheds an interesting light onto Caesar's last days and his political movements leading up to his massive forthcoming conquest of the East. However, because Parthian history goes neglected by comparison with Roman history, the Parthian context of Caesar's final days is too often missed. One thing we can be certain of: it was not missed on Caesar.

But for all of the power and glory that the name of Caesar evoked, his position proved to be a tenuous one as his assassination shows. In fact, Caesar's power rested upon one thing alone: goodwill. To sustain the goodwill of the troops and populace Caesar needed a charisma that appealed to them collectively and personally. He found a convenient rallying cry to achieve such ends in a war with Parthia. He had already put the Roman world through one civil war, and in order to maintain his charisma and popularity Caesar needed a true Roman victory, one not over another Roman general, but against a worthy foreign adversary. Parthia fitted that bill. In other words, what was originally devised a war to avenge Crassus' death became for Caesar a means for political relevance and survival.[121]

In planning to invade Parthia in itself was a means by which Caesar could invoke the fame of Alexander to enhance his own legitimacy to rule in Rome. The most powerful and successful of all Macedonian kings, Alexander was the greatest of all in Roman eyes.[122] By setting himself up as a new Alexander, Caesar was playing a master-stroke that if pulled off would establish his sole hold on power, a dynasty, and popularity. That popularity was of immense value to Caesar at this point. For his conquest of Parthia to succeed, and his kingship to attain real legitimacy, Caesar had to make certain that there would not be a popular uprising in his rear that might embroil him in yet another civil war. So Caesar decided the emulate the example of Alexander's kingship; and by appealing to the Sibylline prophecy, whose coincidental and all too convenient appearance casts serious doubts as to its professed authenticity; the dictator calculated that the goodwill of his troops and subjects would be bolstered sufficiently enough so that, as king, the glory of Alexander would be associated with him and him alone.

Here was a chance for a Roman to equal the great king himself, a chance that so excited Caesar and his Roman supporters. But Rome's Senators were appalled. So on that day in March, instead of being proclaimed king, Julius Caesar was assassinated by Brutus, Cassius and a number of other Senators in the middle of the Senate's last meeting before Caesar was scheduled to embark for the east. It was a clear sign by the Senatorial conspirators that the modesty of the republic was preferable to the excesses of kingship, and that they would tolerate only a mutual power base over an autocratic one like Caesar's.

But, though Caesar was dead, he had invoked the fame of Alexander, and that fame was to live on, and was one that Marc Antony could not resist. It was only a matter of time before Antony would attempt to set off on his own Parthian war and establish an eastern empire to rival Alexander's own.

By all accounts Caesar's grand plans were appropriate for a great general. But plans they were to remain. Later, people would embellish upon Caesar's designs on Parthia, and by the 2nd century AD Caesar's final imperialist wishes were enhanced to rival Alexander's own that he had planned before his untimely death centuries before. Plutarch even believed that after conquering Parthia, Caesar then wanted to conquer all the shores of the Black Sea, then march west along the Danube, conquer Germany, return to Gaul, and finally enter Rome bathed in splendour for a homecoming triumph.[123] So even though the envisaged Parthian war did not eventuate, Caesar's greatness lingered on with Alexander's. Indeed, it lasts to this day. For high empire historians there is the burning question: what would the Roman Empire have looked like if Caesar's Parthian War proved a success? At the same time, historians of the republican period might themselves ponder what would have become of Caesar if he had ultimately decided against a Parthian War and restored the powers of the Senate, and how the res-publica might have handled the resulting power-vacuum. But these dreams and questions will remain just that; thoughts of what could have been had Caesar lived on. But that is perhaps appropriate given the lasting memory and greatness that Rome's finest of statesmen and generals has left all who follow.

From Caesar to Orodes

Immediately following the funeral of Julius Caesar both Brutus and Cassius were forced to flee Rome. Roused by a moving eulogy, the crowds that attended the funerary ceremonies began rioting, calling for the assassins' blood. In their absence the Roman Senate allotted the province of Macedonia to Marc Antony and Syria to his political ally Dolabella thus placing the legions that had been collected by Caesar for his Parthian war effectively in their hands. But the republicans were not to be outdone. Upon leaving Italy, Brutus made straight for

Macedonia and Cassius set off for Syria. Thus it was they who secured Caesar's armies, not Antony; and now that the Roman Senate was faced with such vast opposition in the eastern regions it had no choice but to ratify the assassins' commands in their respective provinces over Antony's and Dolabella's claims there.[124]

But while Brutus and Cassius remained in the east, Antony and Octavian (the nephew of Julius Caesar and the main beneficiary in his will) began to consolidate their own positions with an eye to overthrowing the republicans. Together with Lepidus, Rome's other most powerful politician at that time, the three formed their own triumvirate: the 'second triumvirate' as it is called. They would soon prove themselves ruthless political animals. Desperately short of funds for another civil war, since the western provinces were totally exhausted from the previous one, the triumvirs carried out a series of proscriptions and property confiscations throughout Italy. It was a terribly harsh policy, and one that resulted in the execution of Cicero himself. But as the three had to find the necessary funds to meet their aims somehow they felt bloodshed and confiscations were appropriate measures regardless of the grief they caused.[125]

But in the midst of such heartache and loss there occurred a public display which reflected the Romans' zeal for a real war, not against other Romans, but against foreign foes. What makes this display most notable is that it was given by a woman. When the triumvirs announced that 1,400 of Rome's richest women were to have their properties confiscated, those women voiced their protests to Octavian's sister and Antony's mother and wife. But while they initially found some sympathy in the first of these two matrons, Fulvia, Antony's wife, turned them away. Outraged, a group of the women, led by one Hortensia, the daughter of a Senator and esteemed orator, pushed their way through thronging crowds all the way to the magistrate's tribunal in the forum. There Hortensia delivered a resounding speech in protest of the confiscations. That in itself was risqué, for in Rome politics was the sole domain of men. Of course, many Roman women held great influence in Rome economically, artistically and in certain religious affairs, but in the rigid male-dominated spheres of military and politics feminine involvement was frowned upon by most of their male peers.[126]

But not sparing such scruples, Hortensia delivered a speech in the forum that went down in history as eloquent and a wonderful reflection on her father's oratorical instruction. In fact it was so celebrated that it was even written down to preserve it,[127] and Livy himself drew upon the whole episode when he wrote his historical narrative of the repeal of the Oppian Law in 195 BC, which had originally been passed during the second Punic War ordering Roman women to be taxed to finance Rome's war effort.[128] He was not the only Roman historian to be captured by the speech. In the second century, Appian also drew inspiration from it in writing up his account of Hortensia's delivery. Crucial to her specch as reported by Appian is the plea to the triumvirs to make war not upon other Romans, but upon another more fitting adversary - like Parthia:

"Let us have a war with the Gauls, or with the Parthians, and we shall rival our mothers when it comes to saving Rome. But may we never pay taxes for a civil war or aid you against each other."[129]

The triumvirs' reaction to this plea was typically hostile, for they would not be told what to do by any woman, however refined. But they by all accounts admired her bravery and were moved a little by her love for her countrymen and women. But, brave though Hortensia might have been, the triumvirs still held out for more funds, and so they struck on a compromise – only 400 of Rome's richest women would be taxed but added to their number would be all men that possessed over 100,000 sesterces. Despite Hortensia's best efforts to curb the triumvirs' armies away from their fellow Romans and towards foreign enemies, the lack of firm checks upon Rome's most powerful and ruthless men meant that such efforts were simply an inconvenience to the triumvirs. Her words obviously were the voice of reason. But they had no appeal to the ambitions of the triumvirs.[130]

While the triumvirs made preparations for the coming war and people like Hortensia cried out for a Parthian war in the city of Rome, in the east Brutus and Cassius were making their own preparations by forging an alliance with Parthia. Initially the alliance was only a nominal one when a group of Parthian cavalrymen joined Cassius in Syria out of an admiration for his brave exploits there following Carrhae. But Cassius hoped for more from Parthia and dispatched his lieutenant Labienus there with orders to obtain substantial Parthian military support for the republican cause. There he met with Orodes, who agreed and provided him with a very large army as well as his own son Pacorus to lead. But the decisive battle at Philippi in Macedonia came before Labienus' return. In the battle, Antony and Octavian emerged victorious, and with Brutus and Cassius now both dead, the triumvirs were left in control over Rome's legions. As to why the republicans did not wait for Labienus' arrival is something of a mystery. But Appian, upon investigation, found that both Cassius and Brutus had a change of mind about using Parthians to fight their battles because they became uneasy about the idea of Parthians becoming accustomed to Roman military affairs; and feared that they would later exploit them for their own imperialist use to Rome's future cost.[131]

When Labienus finally arrived in Syria with Pacorus and his vast forces they swept across the entire eastern region as far as Asia Minor.[132] To meet the threat Antony, who at that time happened to be busy at Alexandria with his partner Cleopatra, dispatched his lieutenant Ventidius with an army into Syria. Ventidius proved himself an extremely gifted general. After chasing Labienus out of the Anatolian peninsula and into Syria, both generals waited for reinforcements for the coming battle, and when they eventually arrived on exactly the same day both made preparations for the fight. Their spirits could not have been different: while the Parthians roamed the local plains at will and ignored Labienus who as a Roman and not a Parthian was not a popular leader; Ventidius immediately ordered his legions to encamp atop a high hill nearby which they carried out in complete confidence in their commander's abilities. The next day, the Parthian army, despite Labienus' strict orders to the contrary, rushed up the hill's slopes in such a condensed body that there was no room for maneuver once they reached the top. It was then that Ventidius, who had calculated on such recklessness, gave the prearranged signal for his legions to charge. Bunched up and unable to flee, the Parthians were mercilessly cut down.[133] The result was a clear signal that while Crassus' legions might have been unsuited to the plains of Mesopotamia, Parthian cavalry was not suited to fighting in the hilly terrain of Roman Syria.

Routed, the Parthians fled for Cilicia to the north, and Labienus was captured. Ventidius immediately followed, but knowing that his legions could not catch up to the enemy, he sent Pompaedius Silo ahead with a body of cavalry after them. At the narrow pass at Mount Amanus in Cilicia Silo encountered a Parthian force under the command of Phranapates who was a lieutenant of Pacorus. After several inconclusive engagements between the two forces Ventidius' forces eventually arrived and decided the issue. In the hilly terrain that so favoured heavy infantry trained in close hand-to-hand fighting like Rome's disciplined legions, the Parthian cavalry was quickly defeated and Phranapates was killed together with a large number of his men.[134]

But there was still Pacorus to deal with. He had returned to Parthia before the first battle took place, so as yet he had not familiarized himself with Ventidius' leadership skills or the discipline of his legions. But now he was back in the Cyrrhestica district in Syria collecting another vast army to fight the Romans. Ventidius set out immediately from Cilicia and at Gindarus in Cyrrhestica the two leaders and their armies finally met on the battlefield.[135] Ventidius opened proceedings. But with no open violence. Instead he employed mind games. By pretending to fear Pacorus, he withdrew before them as they crossed a nearby river, and lulled Pacorus into a false sense of security. But Ventidius had defeated Parthian armies already and he knew that all he had to do was employ the same successful tactics in this case as he did in others. Given the enemy commander had not met Ventidius in battle before, the Roman commander knew that Pacorus was totally unfamiliar with his tactics. So, using his tried and trusted methods, Ventidius encamped his army atop another nearby hill and waited for the Parthians to make the next move. Pacorus, eager for a quick victory, and showing contempt for Ventidius who he thought was a timid leader and scared of his Parthian army, ordered his men to charge the camp from all sides. But like the first battle it too proved a disaster. As had happened before, the Parthian cavalry charged en masse without any room to maneuver and once they reached the top of the hill found themselves so bunched up they were simply unable to move. When he saw the state the enemy was in, Ventidius ordered his men to charge, and obeying his orders they killed Pacorus and many of his men unable to flee due to the surging pressure that pushed them on from behind rank after rank.[136]

Victorious, the Romans soon regathered Syria and their other eastern provinces, and for their efforts Ventidius and his army marched through the streets of Rome in splendid triumph over the Parthians – the first of its kind over that nation.[137] Rome was jubilant with the triumph, and most there believed that Carrhae had been avenged: the Parthians had been defeated in a war and Pacorus, the prince and Parthian general had been killed like Crassus was.[138] But many Romans still clamoured for more, including Antony himself, who did not wish the final word on Carrhae and Parthia to go to anyone but himself, certainly not to a mere lieutenant – even one as talented as Ventidius. No, that final word was to be his alone. Or so he believed.

As for Parthia, in the same year as Ventidius' victory over Pacorus, 38 BC, king Orodes died of old age and grief for his son. His son Phraates IV succeeded to the throne, and immediately had all of his remaining brothers executed so as to not invite any possibility for another civil war which one of them might have led.[139] Observing the dynastic upheaval in Parthia at the hands of an inexperienced king, Antony decided that the time was certainly ripe for a Parthian war all of his own. Hortensia's pleas had at last been heeded by a triumvir.

Antony' Parthian War

Marc Antony had planned his Parthian War for quite some time, motivated by the following factors: 1) As punishment for having thrown support behind the republican cause, 2) Vengeance for Carrhae, and 3) the immensity of power a general would accrue if victorious over an empire like that of Parthia's own. But to meet with any success, preparation and timing were critical. To address the former, Antony mustered 60,000 Roman soldiers together with 40,000 allied soldiers comprising both infantry and cavalry, together with the promise by Octavian that more of his own troops were to come (a promise that Octavian would not keep). It was to be the largest force Rome would ever put into the field against Parthia and its collection alone naturally took quite some time. Being so huge, it would prove very hard to maintain, and lack of provisions proved the main reason why Antony's war ultimately failed. However, before that failure came about, Antony appeared to have perfect timing when he embarked on his war. Orodes was old and approaching death, and all Antony had to do was wait until his passing and the succession of an inexperienced new king to begin his thoroughly planned onslaught.

In the meantime, while he waited for events in Parthia to unfold, Antony settled affairs in the eastern provinces to ensure that while he was elsewhere in Parthia his rear was secure. He established Darius in Pontus, Amyntas in Pisidia, Polemon in Cilicia, Herod in Idumaea and Samaria, and a number of other kings in regions throughout the eastern provinces.[140] The consolidation of these provinces was central to Antony's designs to eradicate the last vestibules of Parthian military presence there, and his choices to rule them were calculated and shrewd. Like the others, Herod (later known as 'the Great') owed his position to Rome. A gifted leader with a promising future, Herod was ousted from Judaea by the Hasmonaean Antigonus with Parthia's support. Desperate, in 39 BC he fled to Rome and was proclaimed king of Judaea by the Senate which had recognized that his pro-Roman allegiance could come in very handy there indeed. But it would not be until two years had passed that Herod would capture Jerusalem with the backing of Antony's legions. Finally, to solidify his legitimacy Herod married Mariamne, a granddaughter of the Hasmonaean High Priest who had preceded Antigonus, Hyrcanus, thus admitting him to the upper echelon of Jewish society. With that, Herod's place in his kingdom, and Antony's rear for the coming Parthian war, were finally secured.[141]

While Antony made these final arrangements, Orodes died and was succeeded by his son Phraates. Phraates, although new to the throne proved himself as ruthless as any Roman triumvir, executing his brothers so as not to invite any thought of future competition for the throne. Such harshness disgusted many Parthian nobles, and a number of them actually defected from Parthia and fled to Antony in Syria. Among them was the high-ranked Monaeses. Antony was quietly jubilant. In Monaesaes he had been presented with a potential Roman nominee for the Parthian throne once victorious in war.[142] But to mask his intensions Antony chivalrously sent him back to Phraates. It seemed a kind gesture, but in fact it suited Antony's need for a pretext for war - Monaeses was told by Antony to make a request to Phraates to return Crassus' standards.[143] When he refused, Antony marched his swollen army to the Euphrates.

In Rome, there was panic. Politicians there quickly realized that if Antony proved victorious he would sweep all before him with his freshly conquered manpower and wealth. Octavian, unwilling to risk his life against an all-powerful conqueror, refused to send him any of his own troops and announced that he would relinquish all of his political powers upon Antony's return. Others like Pompey's son Sextus Pompeiius planned to quit the empire altogether and flee to a foreign land.[144]

But as soon as Antony reached the Euphrates, he was inauspiciously forced to change tactics. Instead of marching down the main highway to Carrhae as Crassus had done and then onto Ctesiphon, he turned north for Armenia with the express aim of invading Media from there. This alteration in Antony's line of march has mystified many historians. Some believe that as Antony relied on Armenia's alliance, and in order to secure that alliance the price he had to pay was to make war upon Armenia's eternal enemy, Media, whereupon he could then attack Parthia itself.[145] Others maintain that upon getting a better appreciation for the hot climate at that time of year, Antony opted to march through Armenia which was cooler and more comfortable for his legions.[146] But Cassius Dio offers the most likely explanation for the tactical change: that is that Antony was faced upon reaching the river by such heavy Parthian numbers that passage was simply impossible.[147] Certainly, Antony's preparations were no secret to anybody,[148] and by taking a long time in making those preparations so openly he allowed Parthia to make its own to meet him in war.

After arriving in Armenia, Antony then invaded Media making straight for the city of Praaspa, the royal Median capital. But the resulting siege was anything but a success for the Roman general and its invulnerability proved one reason for Antony's failure. Praaspa was near impregnable and heavily defended, and as the siege dragged on Antony still had to maintain his vast army that was still largely unused - the enemy Parthian army still happened to have been returning to Media from its defenses on the Euphrates' eastern bank. Thus, with a decisive battle and a swift end to the war nowhere to be seen, Antony was left to keep up a doomed siege and supply his army in the meantime. With provisions running low Antony had to feed his army the horses' barley. Phraates seized his opportunity to offer terms of peace, and Antony quickly agreed. Sorely in need of a quick end to the war, Antony dispatched several envoys to conclude the treaty. But if Carrhae had rankled Romans, so too did the humiliation incurred at the diplomatic hearing conducted by Sulla decades earlier (see chapter One) still rankled the Parthians. So when Phraates received the envoys, he sought about reversing that humiliation. Seated upon a large golden throne, the Parthian king made sure he took centre-stage as Sulla had done, and then he set about reprimanding them in harsh tones and no uncertain terms, only after which he decided to grant their peace. Antony was most alarmed at the king's proud manner, but his hands were tied.[149] The war already decided, Antony gave the order to march his army away.

What Antony did next has puzzled historians throughout the ages: he left his siege equipment behind. Phraates, sensing a fine chance to put another nail in Antony's coffin, ordered the Parthian army that had finally arrived back from the Euphrates to destroy it all, all 300 wagon loads of it as well as the tiny force Antony had dispatched to guard it, and they did so without much fuss or effort. If only he had kept it Antony could have laid siege to other cities and so find provision for his large hungry army, but without it he had no means of doing so. Plutarch claimed that the general's lapse in judgment stemmed from his longing for Cleopatra, but that was no doubt a literary ruse on Plutarch's part to add extra scandal to the fiasco.[150] In modern times some have suggested that perhaps Antony simply underestimated Parthian tactics to deal with the small force he had deployed to guard the equipment.[151] A more likely explanation is that Antony had simply panicked. The Parthian army of 40,000 horsemen had now arrived on the scene, and his men, owing to the Parthians' scorched earth tactics, were drastically weakened by starvation and of no use for battle. Consequently, he calculated that the siege equipment would only slow his retreat back to the safety and supplies of Armenia.[152] Winter was nearly upon him, and Antony knew that in such conditions siege warfare was made even more difficult, so he probably made the sacrifice in order to speed his army's progress back to the much friendlier territory of his ally Armenia.

But worse was to follow. Unwilling to share in Antony's defeat, his Armenian contingents discharged themselves and fled for their homeland.[153] Then famine and disease began to consume the Roman army.[154] In one last attempt to save face Antony demanded Phraates to return Crassus' lost standards. But Phraates flatly refused and ordered his swift-moving Parthian cavalry to harass the slower enemy all along its march back to Armenia. Finally, when Antony arrived there with what remained of his forces he was left to count the cost. Out of 100,000 soldiers he had lost 20,000 infantry and 4,000 cavalry, mostly from the effects of hunger and disease – almost as many as Crassus had lost.[155] Not surprisingly, Antony's Roman soldiers were furious with the Armenians for their treachery in leaving them behind when they were needed most, and urged their general to attack them. But Antony, knowing full well that he and his army was still reliant upon the Armenians' provisions, had to swallow his own pride and try calming his soldiers down. However, it came at a cost: so when extra funds arrived from Cleopatra he paid his men for their services and loyalty out of that sum as well as his own pocket 400 sesterces for each soldier – a hefty sum, but one that ultimately succeeded in restoring the goodwill of the legions.[156]

Antony's hopes for conquest had turned into damage control. To deter alarm and dissention back in Rome, he tried to withhold all news of the defeat from finding its way there. But somehow word spread faster than he could keep track and the news of his defeat reached the Roman capital. It breathed a sigh of relief. The fears of Octavian and Sextus were put to rest, and once again Roman politicians once again found the courage to hope for a greater stake in Roman affairs now that their source of fear in the east had failed in conquering the world.[157]

Then, some luck for Antony. In the east Parthia and Media fell out. According to Cassius Dio it was caused by a dispute over the spoils looted from Antony's army.[158] But deeper dissention among Phraates' subjects owing to his overbearing manner was also a factor.[159] Fearing for his position the Median king, Artavasdes, made overtures to Antony, and they concluded an alliance against Phraates. Thus in peace Antony had achieved what he had failed to bring about by war: the detachment of Media from Parthia and its allegiance to himself. To take Parthian pressure off his Median allies, and to satisfy his own desire for retribution against Armenia at the same time, Antony opened another theatre of war, arresting the Armenian king, also named Artavasdes, and taking control of Armenia. But that was as far as Antony would go and he quickly made his way back to Alexandria. Plutarch ridiculously claimed that Antony feared that Cleopatra would commit suicide if he did not return soon,[160] but in fact for the moment Antony was content to play a waiting game with Parthia, and in any case he was eager to celebrate his homecoming to Egypt with a Roman triumph.[161] As Rome's general in the east Antony needed to justify his position with victories, and a quick triumph seemed to Antony to go some way at least to covering over his failure in Media. So although a triumph in Alexandria, rather that Rome itself, was small consolation for having been defeated at the hands of the rising star Phraates, it seemed necessary to Antony to stage one there in order to counterbalance that other rising star, in the west, that of Octavian.[162]

The triumph was a lavish celebration indeed as Antony's soldiers paraded through the streets of Alexandria. But at its culmination Antony made a pronouncement even more breath-taking. In the so-called 'Donations of Alexandria' the general announced to the gathered throng that Cleopatra would henceforth be known as the Queen of Egypt, Cyprus, Libya, and Coele Syria, and have her son by Julius Caesar, Caesarion as her consort; that her son by Antony, named Alexander, would be king of Armenia, Parthia and Media, and that he had actually been betrothed to the Median king's own daughter; and that their other son Ptolemy was to be king of Phoenicia, Syria and Cilicia.[163] It was a grand and well thought out vision for the East indeed, and Antony planned to have them realized by embarking upon future wars of conquest to bring these 'Donations' in the east about.[164] But it came to nothing. Phraates soon put down the Median rebellion, and regained control over Armenia immediately after Antony mistakenly decided it safe to withdraw his troops from there.[165] Thus the Roman army's immense sacrifices under Antony's leadership bore little legacy to commend it.

When news of the triumph and Donations were made public in Rome there was outcry. Roman triumphs were a distinctly Roman affair and transmitting it to Alexandria was considered akin to a betrayal of all things sacred to Rome.[166] It is also true that the very idea of a monarch ruling Roman territories was still sharply inimical to Roman sentiment; and added to that the notion that young children born to Antony and his foreign Queen wife would also be a part of that rule the whole of Rome was outraged.[167] But that was not all. As husband to the Queen and father of her children, Antony was moving to assert himself as king-like over the entire East including Rome's own eastern provinces. The Romans were furious.

Sensing an opportunity to weaken his rival further and enhance his own position, Octavian made his move. In the months that followed Octavian set in motion a scathing propaganda war defaming Antony and Cleopatra at every turn. But with the Parthian front now quiet, Antony too had space to turn on Octavian.

In 31 BC the decisive sea-battle took place off the west-coast of Greece near Actium. In all, over 600 warships took part in it. Roman sources, which became typically hostile to Cleopatra after the battle, claimed that when the Queen and her 60 Egyptian warships fled the battle that sealed her and Antony's doom.[168] But the battle was in fact over well before that. When Octavian's admiral Marcus Agrippa extended his left wing so as to out-flank Antony's right, Antony had no choice but to extend his own right wing to deter the much-feared envelopment. But that left a glaring gap in his battle line of ships between its centre and right. Then Arruntius, who held Octavian's centre, immediately made for the gap and began to sink Antony's ships and destroy Antony's whole formation. It was then that Cleopatra fled for Egypt, and Antony followed her.[169] They had seen that their side had already lost because they knew that Alexander the Great had used similar tactics to expose the Persian armies' centre repeatedly, and just as happened at Gaugamela, so too happened once again at

Actium. Cleopatra and Antony knew it. Nothing was left to them but the chances of flight.

With Antony's fleet routed or destroyed, Octavian had asserted himself master of the Roman world, and just as the Parthians had supplanted the Seleucids in Asia, so too had the Romans brought an end to another Hellenistic dynasty, the Ptolemies of Egypt. It is a striking paradox that through using a battle maneuver that won Alexander an empire, Octavian had brought to an end the rule of the longest-running successor kingdom of that same king. But make no mistake, that did not signal the end to Alexander's imperialist vision. Octavian saw himself very much as Alexander's heir, and besides battle tactics, he utilized numerous aspects of Alexander's own rule to support his own hold on power. Among those was control over information. Octavian, having seen the importance of propaganda in bringing down Antony, soon realized that information control was the key to maintaining his position and bringing down other would-be-rivals.[170] But for the moment all that lay in the future. There was still Antony and Cleopatra to bring down entirely and once and for all. Octavian pursued the two to Egypt.

CHAPTER FIVE

AUGUSTUS

Political Power-Play After Actium

IMMEDIATELY AFTER ACTIUM, both victors and losers made haste to secure for their respective military causes a Parthian alliance. Cleopatra, for one, sent as a gift to the Parthian king the head of his enemy Artavasdes with the request to move the main theatre of war against Octavian to the Persian Gulf.[171] But Octavian, not to be outdone, also made overtures to the Parthian king, restoring to him his daughter Iotape in the hope that the king might throw his military weight behind him.[172] For a while the situation hung tenuously in the balance, but when Antony and Cleopatra died soon afterwards, the matter was over. All that remained to be seen was a formal peace agreement to be ratified between Octavian and Parthia.

However, the roles in these events were soon reversed when Octavian found himself the object of courtship by both Phraates, and Tiridates, a new contender for the Parthian throne. After Octavian had pacified Egypt, he traveled to Syria, and things looked as though he would soon side with one or the other. Back in Rome, this change in Rome's fortunes was welcomed enthusiastically and the anticipation leading up to Augustus' next move excited many there, who, like the poet Horace who bewailed the recent civil war, believed that Octavian's and Cleopatra's courtship of Parthia had been unfairly

exploited by the king intent on weakening Rome for his own imperialist interests.[173] Of course, Horace had obviously over-dramatised these
comments,[174] but the fact that they appealed to a wide audience, who
still felt that due to Antony's death the contest with Parthia was left
unfinished, shows its deep-seatedness.[175] All such bewailing had probably been encouraged by Octavian himself while he was lingering in
Syria. Of course, it is sometimes believed that Augustus was generally
an exponent of peace rather than war,[176] but history teaches us that the
many wars of conquest fought right throughout his principate indicate
that while he might have espoused *pax*, he also sought *imperium*.

But Octavian was a very different kind of political animal to Antony. He was content to withhold his support for either side in the
dispute and by raising each one's hopes to play each off against the
other. Accordingly, when Tiridates was defeated by Phraates in battle
he allowed the vanquished permission to settle in Syria. It was an
extremely shrewd move. Although Tiridates' influence within Parthia
itself was taken away from him, and thus one party of the civil war was
neutralized, which brought peace to the Parthian Empire, Octavian's
gesture held within it another, more subtle, purpose. Not only did
Octavian secure for himself the goodwill of the Parthian populace,
but since he still held in his possession a handy nominee for the Parthian throne he could use him to intervene militarily, and politically,
in Parthia if Phraates proved a threat to Roman security. But just as
he welcomed Tiridates, so too did Octavian welcome Phraates' own
offers of goodwill, receiving a delegation and from the king as well
as one of his own sons. But such a gesture on the Parthian king's
part also hid another agenda. Phraates' hostage-giving had a two-fold
purpose: while it forced upon Octavian an alternative nominee for
the Parthian throne to Tiridates, it also removed a potential threat to
Phraates' own rule in the person of that son. So, after bitter civil war
Phraates had secured his position, and as bringer of peace for Parthia, he had demonstrated that he was a guardian of peace equal to
Octavian. But despite Phraates' own role in bringing this peace about,
Octavian publicly claimed it as his own design, and boasted that the
settlement was as great as any resounding military victory. Wishing
to make political capital out of his pride, the Roman Senate voted him

honour upon honour, and Octavian, the wager of civil war, became Augustus, the leader of Roman interests in one swoop.[177]

But the bitter memory of Carrhae still loomed large in Roman minds. As can be seen in Horace's odes that were published in 23 BC, there still clearly remained a lingering hatred felt by many Romans for Parthia. But while Horace had moved on from his claim that Parthia rejoiced during Rome's civil war, he nonetheless still seethed with displeasure that Carrhae had not yet been properly avenged. Defeated by an enemy whose main maneuver in the Parthian Shot was akin to a retreat, Horace mourned the fate of the prisoners of war, imagining them to have now lost all remaining hints of their manly and wholesome Roman culture.[178] Such imaginings in Horace's poems were no-doubt intended for dramatic affect, but they were real enough in the poet's eyes for another war.[179]

Such calls for war were not only Horace's own. They were made by many others in Rome too. For that reason in 23 BC Phraates sent a delegation there to reestablish the peace. When the Senate referred them to Augustus, the emperor welcomed them and returned Phraates' son to them. This return contained a multiplicity of purposes. First and foremost it was a sign of official goodwill. But underneath this amicable venire were two other, and very political, ulterior motives. Firstly, it secured a place for a quasi-Romanised influence in Parthia's affairs in the form of the prince; and secondly, it served as a bargaining chip for Augustus to in turn request the return of the Roman standards captured at Carrhae and other battles. As insurance to get his way, Augustus retained Tiridates to make a play for the Parthian throne if Phraates was to refuse. If pulled off, it would settle cries for a Parthian war in Rome, and again support his claim as a peacekeeper at the same time – a sorely needed reputation after the civil wars he had fought. Phraates, sensing that he was up against a consummate political tactician in the emperor with vast resources at his disposal, agreed to the request, and as a sign of peace he promised the return of all prisoners of war into the bargain as well.[180]

Peace established – that was how it must have seemed to many at the time. But that was far from being the end of the power-plays. Even two years after the agreement the return of the standards and prisoners was still forthcoming. Running out of patience with the seemingly untrustworthy Phraates, Augustus began making preparations for war. He already possessed Tiridates, and in Rome there lingered much unresolved bitterness towards Parthia. Even the poet Propertius, who openly stated that he had little personal interest in taking part in the war himself,[181] could not help being swept up in the excitement for war. He planned to watch the triumphal procession of the victorious Roman army that would follow it,[182] and wrote that he looked forward to the day when Parthian trophies would be carried off to Rome in vengeance for the Roman standards that had been taken to Parthia.[183]

But even during Rome's mobilisation, Phraates continued to hold out. So, Augustus, deciding enough was enough and that Roman pride needed defending, dispatched his general Tiberius, the future emperor, with an army into the heart of Armenia, while he himself set out for Syria. Arriving in Armenia, Tiberius showed off Rome's military might to all and sundry, and performed the coronation of Tigranes who had only recently emerged victorious after a bitter civil war fought there. Meanwhile, Augustus arrived in Syria, thus creating two separate fronts for Phraates to contend with at once. Finally, Phraates realized he had no option but to return the standards and the prisoners. But the actual return ended up being something of a backhanded compliment to Augustus, for he returned them to Tiberius in Armenia rather than the emperor himself.[184]

Augustus, however, did not take the slight to heart, at least not publicly. He had ultimately won a hard-fought political battle with none other than the king of Parthia, an able politician himself, and was thrilled with the outcome. Satisfied, the emperor called off the war and withdrew from Syria,[185] and relished in this victory which he claimed as a sign that he was a true leader of a united empire and first politician for Rome as well.[186] Where his predecessor Antony had failed using war, Augustus could claim that he was successful in peace. Tiberius too joined in the celebration for his part in the standards' return. According to Tacitus he would later tell Germanicus that he had achieved "less by force than by diplomacy" in Germany.[187] The same could equally apply in this case with regard to Parthia.

All of these self congratulations were well deserved many Romans like Horace accepted. Horace himself celebrated the occasion, portraying Augustus in his poetry as stripping what was rightfully Roman from Parthia's clutches.[188] Of course, while such portrayal was based more on imagination and zeal rather than actual facts,[189] it reflects the kind of jubilation that many Romans, not only Augustus, felt at the time.

Symbol and Meaning

Such celebration was also displayed on the statue of Augustus from Prima Porta. This particular statue, the most famous of all statues of Augustus, was commissioned by Augustus himself about this time, portraying the emperor in a decorated cuirass. The cuirass itself shows a Parthian dressed in a tunic handing over a Roman standard to a figure, probably the god Mars, wearing Roman military armour.[190]

The meaning behind the benign appearance of the Parthian on the Prima Porta statue conveys a more sinister meaning than upon initial impression. This same representation of youthful and clean-shaven Parthians wearing simple tunics has been found right around Rome and the empire in statuary and ornamentation.[191] In an ivory frieze from Ephesus dated to 120AD, captive Parthians are shown, all with a shared likeness in flowing tunics and trousers standing in front of a triumphant Trajan. Likewise, a 3.5cm glass gem dated to 20 BC-20AD shows identical Parthians in the same flowing garments kneeling before Victory. Also, in Pompeii a 74cm marble table leg from 50-70AD also shows a youthful Parthian in flowing apparel.[192] These sculptures, in light of various artistic portrayals found at Pompeii, tell us much. Not only do they reduce the Parthians to a single stereotype, but it was an extremely derogatory stereotype at that. These sculptures of Parthians bear striking resemblance to artistic impressions of *cinaedi* actors and performers found at Pompeii, with their flowing tunics, clean-shaven faces, arranged hair, and youthful appearance. Such actors were nothing short of entertaining prostitutes. As Juvenal wrote, these people were

Augustus Statue of Prima Porta, at the Chiaramonti Museum, Vatican.
Wikipedia.org

infamous for giving themselves over to be anally penetrated by their lovers.[193] In Roman society, such a quality was scorned and was denoted not only as sexually demeaning but indicative of weakness. As Beard put it, it was by the act of penetrating alone, and never that of being penetrated, which correlated with proper manliness and wholesome enjoyment,[194] whereas the act of being penetrated was that correlation's direct opposite – a sign of unnatural passiveness. In fact, the words 'passive' and 'pathetic' are derived from the Latin term *'pathicus'*, often used as an interchangeable word for *cinaedus* by Romans, and one that draws derogatory association with 'Parthia' in sound and form. Thus, by denigrating all Parthians to such an unmanly stereotype, the Romans were in effect portraying them in a similar manner in which they often characterized Cleopatra: depraved, dangerous, and open to abuse.[195] Parthia was a new feminine threat: a new race of Cleopatras receiving residual and longstanding hatreds for the danger she posed. As a result, far from celebrating friendship between Rome and Parthia, the Prima Porta statue shows that there remained a deep hatred and disdain for Parthians by the Roman elite, who saw them as effeminate, submissive and weak barbarians. As Augustus had commissioned the statue's creation, he clearly shared that same disdain, and by the portrayal of the *pathicus-* Parthian on the cuirass, he even endorsed it.

**Close up of a Parthian returning a lost standard, on the cuirass of the
Augustus Statue of Prima Porta.**
Wikipedia.org

In this one statue is also exhibited the new formula to be followed
under the Roman Empire: any victory for a Roman general was a
victory for the emperor. Matters on the ground ultimately had little
bearing upon that arrangement, in which the emperor was now sole
imperator and princeps who held all military glory for himself. All
triumphs would also be his. It was only a matter of time before he
assumed the right to be worshipped. Of course, such worship did soon
begin in Pergamum and Nicodemia in Bithynia,[196] and it is interesting
to note the Parthian context for such ruler-cult. It is often presumed

that in the East such worship was solely the legacy inherited from the ruler-cults of Hellenistic kings starting with Alexander.[197] But such precedents were by that time well-past and were not as alive and present in the East as ruler-cult in Parthia. Since the reign of Mithridates II Parthian kings were recipients of ruler-cult, including Augustus' own contemporary, king Phraates himself. Coins bearing the inscription 'God Manifest' for Parthian kings were standard issue[198] and it would be unwise to entertain for the notion that such a fact had no bearing on Rome's own self-professed image too. Notably it was in the eastern provinces where Augustus allowed ruler-cult – in the west the genus of Roma was still the object of worship, not the emperor. This tells us that there was greater need for ruler-cult in the east that went beyond diplomatic niceties and nods to the past. Augustus was not simply giving way to a groveling populace, or invoking examples from Hellenistic history for enjoyment. Rather, Augustus was attempting to be seen as an equal to the Parthian god-kings whose empire lay closer geographically to Pergamum and Bithynia than Rome, and therefore he had to be honoured there as a god as well.

So we come to a startling paradox in Augustus' assumption of ruler-cult: that although Romans conspicuously and proudly set themselves apart from Orientals like the Parthians, and considered themselves superior and manlier on the battlefield, their hatred for Parthians did not stop their assumption of Parthian cultural assets when it suited them. That may seem the height of double-standards to us today, but that was a typical facet of Roman culture which identified itself in respect and comparison to foreigners. Foreigners were often in the forefront of Roman minds when Romans contemplated their own cultural identity. They needed an 'otherness' to compare their own self to, and the Parthians were the ideal 'other'. In short, without foreigners, Romans would have lost something of their own sense of culture.

In light of all this Roman stereotyping of Parthians it is useful to compare to it the imagery which the Parthians projected of themselves and others too. The most famous Parthian statue is a 190cm high bronze statue from first century BC from Shami in the Bakhtiari region now on display at the Muzeh Melli in Tehran. It shows a bearded and mustached figure wearing a belted jacket not unlike those worn as part of modern karate uniforms, suspender-like trousers, and carrying several daggers. It was a very different image of a Parthian compared to the stereotype in Rome and was typical of Parthian sculpture being replicated in other Parthian sculptures too. A small marble statue from Parthian period Susa also on display at the Muzeh Melli in Tehran appears to be a faithful copy of the Shami statue, as does a limestone stela from Ashur, exhibited in the Archaeological Museum in Istanbul, which also shows a bearded male wearing half-trousers and a belted jacket. It was this appearance, rather than that propagated in Rome, which was the common Parthian costume, and it was even used by Parthian royalty. An eroded relief at Sar-i Pol-I Zohab near the main Baghdad-Kermanshah highway in western Iran shows a Parthian king believed to be one of the Parthian kings named Gotarzes in such costume (the first Gotarzes was a rival king to Mithridates II who found mention in Babylonian tablets in 91 BC, and the second ruled in his own right from 38-51AD).[199]

So, we might ask, which side was right and what did the Parthians actually look like? Fortunately, we can tell that the Parthians' own sculptural imagery was closer to those in Rome. In 1993 a group of miners working in a salt mine cave in Chehrabad in the Zanjan province of northwest Iran came across a grizzly discovery: the bodies of six men. But these were no ordinary corpses. When the miners reported their find to the authorities the bodies were forensically tested and were found to date to the late 2nd – early 3rd century AD – the Parthian era. The best preserved of all six corpses, the so-called 'Salt Man 1', bears a striking resemblance to the images of Parthians in Parthian sculpture. Long haired, and sporting a beard, a golden earring, three iron daggers, leather boots, and half trousers, Salt Man 1 stands in stark contrast to the stereotyped image of a Parthian on the Prima Porta statue.[200]

But just as the Romans stereotyped the Parthians, so too did the Parthians stereotype other peoples as well. Parthian sculptures often depict Parthian kings in ascendancy and superiority over foreigners; and although early sculptures were added to and adapted to changing rulers and circumstances, the ideal of a Parthian king taking pride of place over foreigners remained strong.[201] In all depictions of Parthians with foreigners the message is all too clear: the Parthian elite considered themselves superior to all others, and among those others were included the Romans.

However, just as the Romans needed an 'otherness' like that associated with Parthia to compare their own identity with, so too did the Parthians look to Rome to formulate their own identity. Indeed, as opposed to the Romans, the Parthians imagined nobility and manliness the domain of horseback riding and believed it to be one thing that set them apart from the legionary infantry reliant Romans. This is illustrated throughout Parthian sculpture and also by the testimony of literary sources. Josephus, in his *Jewish Antiquities*, relates a story of king Artabanus III of Parthia (See Chapter Six), and how when upon learning of a plot within the Parthian nobility to assassinate him, he fled from Parthia to the court of king Izates of Adiabene. When he came to that king he approached him as a supplicant seeking political asylum humbly on foot. But, whereupon Izates learnt that this particular supplicant was none other than Artabanus himself he gave him a nearby horse straight away, pledged to the Parthian king his allegiance, and wrote to the nobles who were privy to the plot to reinstate their king, which they did.[202]

So it would seem that in some areas the Parthians were as fervent to differentiate themselves from Romans as Romans were from Parthians. The result was similar too. By keeping Romans in the forefront of their minds to be the model to be most unlike, the Parthians inevitably adopted some Roman cultural facets. In the areas of art and architecture, they used Roman techniques and trends alongside those of the Near East and Orient. It is certainly a strange paradox that the manner in which the Romans and Parthians believed set themselves apart, and indeed the act of believing in that separation itself, actually made them the same. Consequently, when it became apparent that the other had an upper hand in some regard the two peoples would vie to keep up with that other, while at the same time adopt their rivals' customs for their own purposes and advantage. However, many lessons that were available to be learnt from their imperial rivals would be lost upon those many Romans and Parthians who chose simply to keep abreast from one another. So the stereotypes remained entrenched, as did the rivalry between two peoples who were prepared to fight in order to outdo one another in all respects.

On the Fringes of Empire

The paradox seemed all too obvious to outsiders who dealt with both peoples on a regular basis. Along the shared frontiers allegiances could, and did, alter so long as nations along those frontiers saw neither Rome nor Parthia as inherently different to the other. Often, those nations even had pro-Roman and pro-Parthian factions in them who sought to influence their wider populations that just wanted to get on with their own private lives. But they could ultimately not escape being drawn into the politics of the day in some way or another, and even the birth of a baby could, in 7 BC, turn into a bitter local political dispute between Roman and Parthian protagonists.

According to the Gospel of Luke, Jesus Christ was born during an empire-wide census taken by the emperor Augustus. English translations of this Greek manuscript erroneously render that it took place "while Quirinius was governor of Syria".[203] That implies that the census in question was that taken by Quirinius, but his later census of 6 AD covered Syria alone, not the empire. However this English rendering is probably a mistranslation. In the original Greek text, the word rendered "during" in English is *prote*, which more accurately means "before".[204] With that in mind we can ascertain exactly which census Luke was referring to. Augustus did, in fact, order an empire-wide census registration of allegiance that took several years to carry out. Papyrus found in Egypt indicates the registration was carried out there in 9 BC, and inscriptions from Cyrene, Spain and Paphlagonia record that it took place in those places in 7 BC, 6 BC, and 3 BC respectively.[205] Augustus' own *Res Gestae* also states that it was carried out in Rome in 8 BC.[206] As for when this empire-wide census was carried out in Judaea, we have the evidence given by Josephus at hand. According to that historian it was completed a little less than a year prior to the end of the governorship of one Saturninus.[207] Since Saturninus was governor of Syria, and thus Judaea as well, from 8 BC to 6 BC this would mean that it had to have taken place about a year before 6 BC. Given that the census normally lasted a year in each province[208] that means that it must have been conducted throughout Judaea for much of the duration of 7 BC. No doubt such lengthy details forced Luke to describe the census with greater succinctness as simply the one that took place "before Quirinius was governor of Syria". His audience would no doubt have appreciated Luke's use of brevity over endless detail and have quickly recognised exactly which census the author was referring to.

So, sometime in 7 BC, the infant Jesus was born in a stable in Bethlehem in Judaea as is universally known. But what is of real note for the purposes of this book is the visit of the 'wise men' from the east who visited the infant at Bethlehem and its political context. That is hard to do given the embellishments made to the story over the millennia, but possible nonetheless. One such embellishment is that there were three so-called wise men. Throughout history various peoples in Mesopotamia and Persia have claimed that the three came from their localities. When the Venetian traveler Marco Polo visited Saveh he was even shown three tombs which locals said contained the bodies of Beltasar, Gaspar and Melchior who they claimed were none other than the three wise men.[209] Of course, there is no mention as to their number in the Gospel of Matthew, our main ancient Christian source, although there is the possibility that the number of gifts that they offered to Jesus, three, may indicate that there were indeed three of them. Those gifts: gold, frankincense, and myrrh have themselves been the subjects of debate as to their function and meaning. Some Christian theologians believe that the gold was given in honour of Jesus' right to kingship, frankincense in recognition of his divinity and for prayer, and myrrh as an aid to his embalming to respect his death.[210] But, some disagree with this view, and suggest that perhaps given frankincense's medicinal properties it was intended to heal the child if he was ever faced with health problems.[211]

The comment in Matthew's Gospel that these wise men followed a star to find Jesus' whereabouts has in particular been the topic of lively debate. Some have pointed to the fact that Halley's Comet was visible in the sky in 12 BC and another comet-like body was observed by Chinese and Korean stargazers in 5 BC. Given that comets were often described by ancient writers as having stopped over certain cities, just as the 'star' had when it stopped over Bethlehem, it is thought that the 'star' must have in fact been a comet.[212] Certainly, the suggestion has some merit, for Romans like the poet Virgil called comets stars. Virgil himself called the comet that appeared after Julius Caesar's death in 44 BC "the star of Caesar".[213] Others, however, take the comet notion much further and claim that the star in Matthew's Gospel is actually a work of fiction inspired by sightings of Halley's Comet in 66AD which coincided with the visit to Nero in Rome of another easterner, Tiridates of Armenia. Exponents of this hypothesis argue that by inserting a reference to a star in his own narrative Matthew was pointing out to readers that Jesus was as great as Nero.[214]

But the wise men were not Christian theologians, medical practitioners, Chinese or Korean stargazers, Roman poets and they were certainly not modern atheistic source-critics. The original Greek term for these wise men in Matthew's Gospel is in fact 'magi'. This identification, I believe, is the key to understanding their journey and the 'star' itself. The magi were a Zoroastrian priestly class from Persia which had a history and standing as lore and occult knowledge keepers stretching back to the origins of the Medeo-Persian Empire in the 6th century BC.[215] In that same century they came into very close contact with Judaism which was carried east by the Jews who were deported there under the Babylonians. Although the Persian king Cyrus the Great allowed the Jews to return to Jerusalem again, many Jews like the prophet Daniel already had made lives for themselves in Persia and decided to stay there. The Jews and Persians exchanged many religious teachings during that time,[216] and Daniel himself learnt many Babylonian rites and received formal religious instruction.[217] The magi, in turn, learnt from Jews like Daniel the ancient prophecy of Moses that a Messiah would come to the Jewish people accompanied by heavenly phenomena: "a star shall come out of Jacob; a scepter shall rise out of Israel".[218]

So what was the 'star' of Jesus' birth? The answer is to be found not in modern hypothesizing but in the magi themselves. The magi were not astronomers, but as keepers of Persian lore and occult knowledge, they were astrologers. In this lies the key to the star. According to astrological lore among the ancient Jews that the magi were familiar with, the planet Jupiter was called the King's star and Saturn the star of God's Messiah. Jewish astrologers also recognized the zodiac and believed that each sign represented a different country. Importantly, the sign of the 'Fish', known today as Pisces, represented Palestine and for that reason the sign was often called the 'House of the Hebrews'. Now, according to astronomical calculations, on precisely the 12th April in 7 BC, in the very same year as the census was being carried out in Syria and Judaea, a conjunction of Jupiter and Saturn appeared in the sign of the Fish in the east, and continued for the duration of that year until it finally set in the west. In December the conjunction would have been observed from Jerusalem to the south in the direction of Bethlehem.[219] This celestial phenomena that progressed from east to west, and its astrological meaning to the magi that a Hebrew king and Messiah was appearing in Palestine, perhaps best explains why, when they arrived from the east in Jerusalem in search of Jesus, they asked locals there "Where is the one who has been born king of the Jews? We saw his star in the east and have come to worship him."[220]

Of course, it has been noticed that in Babylonian astronomical records now on display in the British Museum and dated to 7 BC only brief mention is made to Jupiter and Saturn appearing together in Pisces.[221] This has led some to suggest that the conjunction did not mean a great deal at all to the Babylonian astrologers and others in the Middle East. However, our impressions of events today are often not the same as those millennia ago. The Parthians were never prolific writers, and nor were they meticulous historians – no Parthian works were ever referred to by ancient authors.[222] Therefore, this simple mention of Jupiter and Saturn appearing in Pisces is actually in itself a true indication that such an event was of real importance to the Babylonians, and that in its recording it had to have had great value to the scribe who wrote it down after all.

However, when news of their arrival in Jerusalem reached Herod, events took a turn for the worst. Religion and politics went hand in hand in Jerusalem as they did right throughout the ancient world, and the search of the magi for Jesus soon brought Roman and Parthian interests into conflict. Herod had certainly not forgotten that he has wrestled his throne with Rome's backing from his Hasmonean rival

Antigonus who himself had Parthian support.[223] So, the magi's wish to worship another candidate for kingship in Herod's realm incited the king's fear and anger. Added to this was also the well-known fact that Herod was not himself of royal Jewish lineage, and that the Hasmonean line which he overthrew traced its genealogy back to king David. Jesus, born in Bethlehem the hometown of David,[224] and of David's lineage, would usually have been tolerated by Herod like all the other subjects claiming descent from Jewish kings. But, being worshipped by Parthian magi, Jesus was not any baby.

Herod's response to the news was brutal. He told the magi to identify the baby's location for him and made plans to kill them afterwards. The magi found the baby. But he was not in the stable. He was in a house. Apparently the magi arrived in Bethlehem some time after Jesus was born when Joseph and Mary had secured more comfortable lodgings. There they worshipped him and presented their gifts. But although they had planned to return the way they came, they were warned in a disturbing dream that it was unsafe, and so the magi, who respected dream interpretation as part of their religious tradition, took a different route and returned to Parthia safely. Enraged that the magi had slipped through his fingers, Herod next turned his attention on Jesus and ordered the execution of all infants aged up to 2 years in and around Bethlehem. Fortunately for Jesus, Joseph too had a disturbing dream which he interpreted as a warning of danger, and so he, Mary and Jesus, beat a hasty path to Egypt. In doing so they escaped Herod too.[225] The legacy of Daniel's famous dreams interpretations had come full circle.

Given that Matthew's Gospel is our only record of this 'slaughter of the innocents' in Bethlehem, the whole account given by him has been questioned. In fact, various historians argue that the story as a whole was of Matthew's own invention for the purposes of portraying Jesus to be a worthy successor to the kingly Herod as well as satisfying some desire around the fringes of the Roman Empire for political importance.[226] But such theories do not take into account the harsh political conditions Herod lived in or the deteriorating character of Herod himself in his final years.[227] Even Josephus recognized that Herod was a brutal character living in a brutal age and that he was very capable and willing to carry out such atrocities. According to Josephus, at the time of this same census six thousand Pharisees refused to take part in the registration whereupon they were fined. But when they refused to pay the fine Herod executed all of their ringleaders and all others associated with them including members of his very own family. Josephus recorded that this was all part of the king's well-known paranoia and distemper which plagued him during the last years of his life.[228] Matthew's account, therefore, in light of such facts should not be disregarded so quickly. Indeed, if anything, its historical setting during the last years of Herod's life actually confirms that it holds a real ring of truth.

As a result, Matthew's treatment of the visit of the magi serves as a rare historical window into how pro-Roman and pro-Parthian interests could impinge upon frontier regions like Judaea. So often history is all about the doings of the elite, but in this case we can see how those elite affected lower levels of society. Even on a global level, international politics could, and did, intrude upon provincial populations and make local rulers handle them with ruthless and decisive action. Judaea was one such province. But although conditions were different from province to province throughout the Roman world, Judaea still remains one striking example of how Roman and Parthian interests could influence provincial politics and local governments, not to mention negatively interfere with local populations.

Phraataces, Gaius and Augustus

In 2 BC Phraates was murdered by his own son Phraataces and Musa, his wife. That was outrageously scandalous in itself but more scandal was to follow. Immediately after seizing the throne for himself, Phraataces married Musa, his own mother.[229] The marriage was abhorred by Parthians and Romans alike and it begs the question: why did they marry? Some have seen in it religious observance of Zoroastrian kin-marriage teachings.[230] However, the most telling clue is found in the character of Musa herself. Musa was by all accounts a true political animal. Given as a concubine to Phraates by Augustus in 20 BC, she was famous for her intelligence as well as her obvious beauty, and soon endeared herself to the king becoming his wife and bearing a son, Phraataces. By the time this son had reached the age of ten years, she had already begun clearing a path to the throne for her son, convincing her husband to send four of his elder sons, two daughters-in-law, and four grandchildren to Augustus as hostages. Phraates, who had suspected in his family sedition, complied, but his suspicion was misplaced – it was Musa who was in fact planning to overthrow the king.[231] Finally, when her son reached eighteen years of age, Musa and Phraataces killed the king, and the way to the throne was finally opened to Musa's son.

In these events Musa's famous intellect is clearly evident, and it is with those events in mind that we must evaluate her notorious marriage to her own son. She and Phraataces certainly had ambition, and the promotion by a queen of her own son to the throne was not confined to her alone. Augustus' own wife Livia had furthered her son Tiberius' promotion at every turn to such an extent that ancient writers believed she had even employed poison on repeated occasions to do away with his rivals.[232] But although Livia's fame far outshine's Musa's today, both women probably had an impact on Roman court politics: in Agrippina's promotion of her own son Nero that is certainly apparent. But in Agrippina's case Musa's example carried the most weight as she too showed marked public displays of inappropriate affection towards Nero once he became emperor. Although ancient writers put them down to the wanton morals of the emperor and his mother, it is now agreed that Agrippina showered her son with affection in order to remain relevant to the emperor and win his favour and the power that brought with it.[233] Musa had no doubt resorted to the same ruse for the same reason, establishing her own power through marriage ties with her son, the king. In an age when women had far less opportunities for advancement, sexual favours were one means, however unpalatable, to secure power. Certainly, Phraataces learnt much about political ambition from her. Upon securing the Parthian throne, the new king began pursuing his own imperialist interests providing military support for the pro-Parthian faction in Armenia. But if he had held any high hopes and grand designs for Parthian prestige there, they would soon be dashed.

It has sometimes been suggested that Augustus's recourse to diplomacy to secure the lost military standards in 20 BC shows that he never really considered all-out war with Parthia.[234] But Augustus' hostile response to Phraataces' intervention in Armenia proves otherwise. Granted, Horace's odes published in 13 BC show that he was content to live in peace, but his poems also seethe with a bitter hatred for Parthia as an enemy nonetheless.[235] He was not alone. In addition to Horace's poems, Virgil's monumental epic, *The Aeneid*, published only six years earlier, also contains an aggressively negative stereotype of Parthia as a traditional eastern enemy of Augustus and all Romans. That is obvious in his depiction of the battle of Actium – in Virgil's mind a battle between west and east and good and evil – on his 'shield of Aeneas'.[236] *The Aeneid* famously celebrates Latin myth and lineage, and places great importance in their great leader Augustus against all external threats, and it is in the emperor that victory over Rome's enemies will ultimately come about.[237] Livy also wrote with a similar thematic vein throughout his historical narrative, remarking that it was Rome's destiny to conquer every one of its enemies and go on to rule the whole earth.[238] Such sentiment Augustus clearly shared and encouraged: the emperor's own hand in the production of such works for the sake of a reinvigoration of his tarnished image from civil wars is now widely accepted.[239] So it would appear that on these grounds alone the emperor still considered Parthia an enemy, albeit a somewhat containable one through skillful diplomacy.

However written evidence is only part of the picture. Besides the literary sources, monumental buildings dating from that time show clearly that Augustus was planning the conquest of Parthia; if not by him then certainly by one of his successors. Most notable among those monuments which display Augustus' intensions for Parthia is the Temple of Mars Ultor, dedicated in the centre of the Augustan Forum in 2 BC with much celebration.[240] The temple was decorated with scenes of examples of Roman virtues from history, and Roman victories in foreign wars. It was planned back in 42 BC by a young Octavian when he prayed to Mars for victory just before the battle at Philippi. Victorious, Octavian calculated that such a temple would bring closure to civil war. However, when the standards were handed over in 20 BC the temple adopted another purpose: it would also house the standards and act as a statement that Mars would always have the ultimate word against foreign enemies. The first and foremost among those was Parthia.[241] Augustus proclaimed upon its dedication that the temple would be a focal point for all military ventures. Among its functions were that victors would present their spoils of war there, equestrians hold festivals there, and that young men joining the legions should formally and ceremoniously present themselves within its precincts. But that was not all. It also became the symbolic launching point for all future foreign campaigns, and served as a rallying space for war and the instilling of military pride among Romans, whether they were simply onlookers, or the actual performers in its rites.[242]

Thus, with so many rallying mechanisms and symbols in place, when Phraataces incited rebellion in Armenia, Augustus' response was sharp. He deployed intelligence gatherers into the heart of Parthia to survey its preparations, among them Isidore of Charax who later wrote a description of Parthia's trading stations from one end of its empire to the other which acted primarily as protection for commerce.[243] Next, Augustus whipped-up public excitement by staging a mock sea-battle on an artificial lake near the Tiber between 'Greeks' and 'Persians'.[244] Those two peoples had come to symbolize in Roman minds the eternal battle of West versus East, and by invoking their past wars the princeps was hailing the start of a new one against the East. Finally, satisfied with his preparations, the emperor commissioned his grandson Gaius to take command of the war, encouraging him to outdo Alexander the Great by conquering Armenia, and then Parthia and Arabia.[245] Gaius was sent off from the Temple of Mars Ultor, with his army, for the east, amidst rapturous applause.[246]

But for all of that celebration, and Augustus' efforts to mobilize Rome for war with Parthia, that war was averted. Sensing real danger in Gaius' deployment, Phraataces immediately pled for peace. The king even gave Armenia to Rome as part of the deal. When Gaius arrived in the east, the agreement was made official. On an island in the middle of the Euphrates River Gaius and Phraataces finally met, but it was not in battle. Rather, it was a display, at least a public one, of imperialist harmony. Velleius Paterculus, serving as military tribune under Gaius, left behind a description of the meeting and it clearly shows that diplomacy between these two ancient superpowers had certainly come a long way since the time of Sulla. This time, for the sake of sparing offence on either side, such conferences were thoroughly planned and stage-managed. Nothing was left to chance that might undermine the outcome. According to Velleius, while Gaius and Phraataces negotiated on the island in private, both Roman and Parthian armies were drawn up in full array on opposite banks of the river as exhibitions of respective military pride. Then, once matters were decided upon formally, Gaius dined the young king on Rome's side of the river, and then Phraataces dined the young prince on Parthia's.[247] The result therefore was that Rome's superiority was duly recognized and that its claim to Armenia was confirmed, but both sides maintained their prestige.

However, the workings and implementation of that peace proved difficult because Phraataces's interference had already deeply damaged Armenia, and both sides needed to handle the situation there carefully. Phraataces' nominee for the Armenian throne, Tigranes III, had overthrown Artabazus, who was Rome's nominee, but Augustus agreed to recognize Tigranes so long as Parthian soldiers completely withdrew from that country. Phraataces complied with his terms, but when Tigranes died soon afterwards, political instability returned and threatened to involve Parthian and Roman intervention once again. This time Rome intervened and Augustus installed one Ariobarzanes, a Mede, upon the Armenian throne. Parthia honoured this decision on the emperor's part in what was now technically Roman territory anyway, but exacerbation again swept through it when Ariobarzanes proved unpopular and the Armenian nobility rebelled against Rome. But the outcry throughout Parthia for Phraataces to intervene proved useless. Phraataces expected the Romans to respond quickly with deliberate force in Armenia and he did not wish Parthia to be another victim to Roman arms once they were finished there. Indeed, Rome's response was swift and Ariobarzanes was soon reinstalled. For a while things were settled, but when Ariobarzanes himself died soon afterwards it might have looked as though peace was unattainable. Fortunately though, the king had provided an heir, and when his son Artabazus was crowned peace did finally return to the troubled kingdom.

Thus both Rome and Parthia had shown themselves true to their word in respecting the treaty ratified by Gaius and Phraataces. But by 4 AD the balance of power that these two young rulers had established had come to an end. Gaius and his younger brother Lucius had died prematurely, and Phraataces had been assassinated. Given that Musa is never heard of again it is most likely that she was killed at that time too.[248] The upheaval throughout Parthia was almost tangible, and when the new king, Orodes III, who was responsible for overthrowing Phraataces, was himself assassinated only a few years later, Augustus took it upon himself to restore order there.

Since the reign of Phraates the Roman emperor had kept four of his sons in Rome as insurance for Parthia's goodwill. Now, to restore that goodwill, and to show his own to Parthia in return, Augustus dispatched Vonones I who was one of them to Parthia to secure the throne there for himself. This act signified that Rome was no longer just a force in the Mediterranean basin, but a contender on the world stage. Understandably, Augustus took great satisfaction in that fact as well as his hand in it, and boasted proudly about giving the Parthian Empire its king.[249] But his success proved short-lived. Vonones appeared too Roman and too foreign to the Parthians and they could not accept him as their king, and civil war erupted. It would last two whole years. Finally, Vonones was defeated and overthrown.[250]

The new king, Artabanus IV, would prove himself a longer-lasting monarch, and this in itself was clear proof to Parthians that they did not need a Roman emperor, or a Roman nominee to run their empire for them – they could handle matters for themselves. In this milieu that sought to reassert Parthian imperial interests over Rome's, Artabanus at the outset of his reign showed himself to be a king very prone to aggression against Rome. At the same time the Roman Empire had also undergone decisive change. With the wiping out of Varus and his three Roman legions in Germany in 9 AD, the thirst in Rome for imperialistic gain slowly began to dry up. The Varian disaster had shocked Rome deeply, and Augustus himself was even witnessed by his staff roaming through his palace crying out "Quinctilius Varus, give me back my legions!"[251] The shock hit the armies too. Once a source of fear and invincibility, Roman armies were not shier and more cautious and no longer hastened for battle. Even the seasoned general Tiberius, a popular military hero and Augustus' heir, became so scared of sharing Varus' fate that he kept his legions permanently stationed along the Rhine.[252]

In 14AD, after a reign lasting some forty-four years, Augustus breathed his last leaving the empire to Tiberius, the son of Livia. Augustus had striven hard to extend the empire wherever possible and his generals indeed succeeded in conquering many nations in Spain, along the Rhine, the Nile, and the Danube. But by the time he died such expansion had grounded to a halt. On his deathbed he had instructed Tiberius not to extend the empire any further, and advised him to consolidate what had been conquered already rather than embark on any further risky foreign campaigns. Just as Phraates and Phraataces had beforehand learnt that diplomacy could be wielded effectively against great odds, so too Tiberius now had to admit its advantages. But Artabanus was a new ruler with new ideas. With an eye for territorial gain, he would have to discover the advantages of diplomacy for himself, but given Artabanus' character, that would take time.

CHAPTER SIX

TIBERIUS TO NERO

Vonones I to Germanicus

U PON AUGUSTUS' DEATH his adopted son and heir Tiberius
became emperor. The principate, as Augustus had devised it,
was still a fairly recent institution even if very few Romans
even remembered what life was like under different forms of government. That is why Tiberius acted tentatively first-off and made every
effort to emulate his predecessor's example. But despite those efforts,
Tiberius' principate was to prove a very different one to Augustus'.
When it came to the responsibility for the eastern provinces Tiberius
was happy to delegate to his governors and diplomatic representatives,
who were left to grapple with what they judged were conducive to
Tiberius' wishes.

For Tiberius' principate and his dealings with Parthia, we are fortunate to possess the narrative of a first-rate historian in Tacitus. But
being first-rate does not mean that Tacitus' *Annals* are not without
bias. It was Syme who famously wrote that through his generally negative portrayal of Tiberius Tacitus was in fact making spiteful political invective upon Hadrian. A deep longing for a return to the military glories of Trajan, so Syme theorized, coloured Tacitus' writing,
and made Tiberius appear as gloomy as the historian's impression of
Hadrian's arising from that emperor's defensive imperial policy.[253] As

for Tacitus' lengthy accounts of Parthian history and politics, that was due Syme believed, to the thrill and excitement of Trajan's Parthian adventure lingering in Tacitus' own mind.[254]

Syme's is an imaginative theory and it is one that still captures the attention of historians to this day. However it has its shortcomings, for Syme did not consider that Tacitus' portrayal of a benign Tiberius could have rather been intended to increase the glory of Trajan, not decrease Hadrian's. Nor did he properly entertain that Tacitus' enthusiasm for Parthian affairs was a reflection of the social climate in Trajan's own day leading up to his war with Parthia. Moreover, Syme also missed that Tacitus' negative portrayal of Tiberius was similar to other writings of his own peers including Suetonius' biography of the emperor and Juvenal's satires.[255] That is why it is more sensible to conclude that Tacitus' presentation of that emperor was not of his own device, rather it was the prevailing legend during the time he wrote – i.e. during Trajan's reign. (For more on Tacitus as a source on Hadrian see Chapter Eight) But legends aside, Tacitus was right to acknowledge Tiberius' preference for peace over expansion. Ever since the Varian disaster Tiberius had pursued a more defensive strategy under the principate of Augustus, and that was a policy he continued to hold after he became emperor, apparently under Augustus' own instruction. Tiberius, not one to shirk his predecessor's policies, or his own mind, complied to the full.[256]

However, despite Tacitus' all too real animosity for such a policy, it was not one shared by all of Tiberius' own contemporaries in Rome. The historian Velleius Paterculus simply adored the princeps,[257] and he was not alone. Others like the astronomer and poet Manilius also admired a more peaceful approach.[258] Of course, Tacitus was quick to state that Tiberius closely monitored the content of writers' works, and that he even reserved the right to use the law of treason to punish hostile authors. Hence, in 22AD Clutorius Priscus was condemned for treason, as well as Gaius Cominius and Aulus Cremutius Cordus in 25AD.[259] But despite Tacitus' venom, such charges were relatively rare and the above condemned writers had bitterly attacked Tiberius, the sexuality of his own mother, and the peace of the empire, and had even shown delight in Drusus' approaching death throughout their condemned works.[260] They could not go unpunished. But still, despite these authors' open spite for the emperor and his harsh response, it is impossible not to recognize the genuine admiration felt for the princeps in the pages of Velleius. As a general Tiberius was admired by the armies, and Velleius himself served under him in Germany during the principate of Augustus. His brief account of Roman history is palpable with the armies' love for Tiberius and his celebrity status,[261] and that love for Tiberius could not have changed overnight upon his assumption of power. Whatever his policies, and whatever his contemporaries' criticisms, many honoured Tiberius' celebrity.

The political climate in Parthia was very different. Vonones I, Augustus' nominee for the Parthian throne, had been overthrown by Artabanus III and the Parthian nobility. At the heart of the discord was the Roman manner of Vonones himself. Brought up in Rome as a hostage he did not share the Parthians' traditional tastes for horses, hunting and riding; and so it appeared to many Parthians that they were being treated more like a Roman province with Vonones at its governor than the proud victors of Carrhae.[262] The Arsacid Artabanus, on the other hand, was a far more popular personality and had been brought up with horses and the nomadic life of the Dahae. That made him far more Parthian-like in manner and custom, and therefore far more suitable to be a Parthian king. So it was believed by the Parthian nobility.

When Vonones and Artabanus met in their first battle Vonones carried off the victory, but this contender's success was only short lived. Artabanus remained at large and his nationalistic cause and Parthian manner endeared many to him. As a result he soon had an army that swelled once again. Thus in the two contenders' second and final battle Artabanus won such a resounding victory that Vonones was forced to flee to Armenia for safety and asylum. But, just as Artabanus had thrived after his initial defeat, so too did Vonones' fortunes change after his loss: soon after arriving in Armenia Vonones was offered the Armenian throne. Making the most of this opportunity, Vonones unsurprisingly accepted the offer and was crowned king.[263]

But Artabanus was not content to allow his rival a reprieve or the luxury of using Armenia as a base for a future attempt on the Parthian throne, so he mobilized his army for war with Armenia. Tension increased when Quintus Caecilius Metellus Creticus Silanus, the Roman governor of Syria, tried to defuse the powder-keg by deposing Vonones and retaining him in Syria. Artabanus knew that as a pawn in the Roman governor's hands Vonones stood a chance of making another serious bid for the Parthian throne with Roman backing. He had already been put on the throne by Augustus, and Artabanus no doubt feared a repeat under Tiberius' rule. So, it appeared to all that war was imminent and that the balance of power Augustus had created in Rome's favour was unraveling. To salvage the situation Tiberius had to act fast. His solution: his nephew Germanicus was dispatched to the east to settle things down there. With that the unfolding tragedy turned into a political theatrical performance with Germanicus centre-stage. Eastern commissions for Roman princes had always been occasions for displaying Roman pomp and pageantry, and Germanicus took the unsettled situation in the east as an opportunity to tour Greece and the Anatolian peninsula as he made his way to Syria.[264]

From Syria, Germanicus proceeded straight to Armenia and gave orders for Gnaeus Piso, an experienced general and governor who Tiberius appointed to accompany the younger prince, and who was at that point in Syria, to follow him from that province with the Roman forces stationed there in order to make a show of military strength in Armenia in due course. These preparations exude with Tiberius' own hand in planning. Diplomacy backed up by military threats was a favourite device of sorts for the emperor. In 20 BC his own military presence in Armenia had secured the return of Crassus' captured standards, and Gaius Caesar's arrival in the east persuaded Phraataces to come to terms with Rome. Therefore, it followed that just as Tiberius had crowned an Armenian king while he was in Armenia on a previous occasion, so too did Germanicus crown an Armenian king while he was there.[265] The obvious choice had already presented itself. Prince Zeno was the son of king Polemo I of Pontus, and since he and his father owed their positions to the goodwill of Rome Germanicus knew that he would be useful to Rome's interests in the region.[266]

As for the other interested stakeholder in the region, Parthia, Germanicus certainly ran the risk of offending Artabanus by his arrangements in the buffer-state. Hence he eagerly waited for Piso and the Roman legions to arrive in support. But just when matters looked like escalating into a major war Germanicus' theatricals brought about an unexpected happy result: as it turned out Artabanus was overjoyed with the prince's arrangements in Armenia. That is because Zeno, being brought up an Armenian who enjoyed horses and hunting as Artabanus and the Parthians did, was seen by Artabanus as an advocate for Parthian interests in the region as well. So, Artabanus agreed to Germanicus' coronation of the young Pontic prince and the tension that had been mounting was defused.[267]

The coronation itself took place in the Armenian capital of Artaxata and Zeno was given the new name Artaxias III to mark the location and event.[268] As for the Roman show of force, it never materialized, for Piso never left Syria with the legions. He rightly saw, as Germanicus must have, that such an exhibition would only have been an affront to the Parthian king and lead to war. Therefore, to maintain the peace, Piso refused to obey Germanicus' orders.[269] Of course, Piso had seen the wisdom of Tiberius' own diplomacy backed by force before he became emperor, but he also saw that Germanicus was going a step too far. By risking a full-scale war with Parthia Germanicus was breaching Tiberius' non-aggression policy. Certainly that was nothing new for Germanicus. His war in Germany had to be cut short by Tiberius just previous to his eastern commission, and the emperor knew that if Germanicus should prove victorious on the battlefield against Artabanus his own position might come under threat by the more impetuous and popular young prince. Piso, as a result, should not be too hastily accepted as the deviant figure that history portrays him, but should rather be recognized as an unflinching servant and devotee to the interests of the emperor over all else.[270]

Missing an opportunity for war in this way, Germanicus turned his attention towards consolidating Rome's territories, perhaps with an eye for returning at some later date and finishing what he had wished to start with Parthia. Cappadocia was made into a province and Quintus Veranius was appointed governor, and its taxes on all goods were halved, reduced from 1% down to ½%.[271] Commagene was also attached to the Roman province of Syria. To appease Artabanus, but only for the time being, Germanicus also removed Vonones from Syria to Cilicia. It was a token gesture. Artabanus had in fact requested his surrender, but Germanicus was intent on showing that this Roman nominee, although out of the political picture for the moment, could be produced from nearby Cilicia should Artabanus ever err.

But, for the moment hostilities were put off, and just as Roman prestige was maintained, so too was Parthia's, and peace reigned for almost another two whole decades. But ultimately, final credit for the peace must go to Artaxias and his new Armenian subjects. As a trusted provincial employee of Tiberius' beloved imperial administration and at the same time an advocate for Parthian national pride which had swept Artabanus into power, the Armenian king kept his western and eastern neighbours at arms length and at bay with total success. So long as both Rome and Parthia were of the belief that it was their own interest that Artaxias was maintaining in Armenia both were happy to leave things as they were there. It is to Artaxias' credit that he recognized this and exploited it to full effect so that peace was unbroken until his death in 34AD.[272]

Tiberius and Artabanus

When Artaxias died the capstone that had preserved the peace by holding the structures of power in place was removed, and with that, those structures came crashing down. Almost immediately, Artabanus, without conferring with Rome, installed his son Arsaces upon the Armenian throne. It was a brazen act that signaled defiance and imperialist aspirations in Parthia's western frontier. These aspirations had been brewing for some time. After a number of victorious campaigns against various neighbours around Parthia's peripheral borders, Artabanus began dreaming of emulating Cyrus and Alexander and of reconquering their territories along the Euphrates and further west beyond that. Insulting Tiberius' age and abilities as a leader, the Parthian king began to seek to undermine his power and assert his own throughout Rome's eastern provinces.[273]

But Tiberius, although old, had not lost his ability when it came to dealing with Parthia. Following the tried and true methods of his predecessor Augustus, Tiberius sought a Roman nominee who could himself undermine Artabanus' own hold on power. That was difficult since the king had eliminated most of the male members of his family. So he produced Phraates, a son of Phraates IV who had been given to Rome as a hostage under Augustus, and equipped him with an army to invade Parthia and wrestle the throne there.[274] But the wrestle was not to be. Upon arrival in Syria the prince died. However Tiberius was not to be outdone, and another Arsacid prince, Tiridates, the emperor decided would make a fine replacement.

As preparations were being made in Rome for the dispatch of Tiridates to the east, the emperor turned his attention towards the situation in Armenia. Having a Parthian prince on the Armenian throne was hazardous for Rome since it lay open to pro-Parthian influence, which under Artabanus was now notoriously anti-Roman as well. To deal with matters there Tiberius embraced ingenuity and invited Mithridates, the brother of king Pharasmanes of Iberia, to attack Armenia and take it for himself. It was an admission by the emperor that the lives of Roman soldiers would not be risked in the east, but the use of a foreign nation for Roman agenda appealed, and indeed proved itself a useful strategy in the long run: later emperors would make full use of such a method in their own quests to contain Parthia. Not surprisingly, having seen a perfect opportunity for conquest, Mithridates quickly accepted Tiberius' offer and led his army into Armenia with the emperor's blessing. The Iberian prince took Artaxata and overran the countryside thus becoming the Armenian king.[275]

In response to these events in Armenia Artabanus dispatched his son Orodes with an army to fight off the invaders. Upon arrival Orodes discovered that the Iberians had been accompanied by Albani and Sarmatian allied forces and he promptly set about enticing them to his own side in preparation for battle. In this he had some success and in the battle that followed there were Albani and Sarmatians fighting on both opposing armies. Despite being a fiercely contested battle, Orodes had to concede defeat when in the chaos of the fighting a false rumour began to circulate through his army's ranks that he had been killed and the cause was lost. The desperate forces of Orodes withdrew, and Orodes was forced to return with his dejected army back to Parthia. Artabanus was furious. He mobilized for a full-scale war against Mithridates.[276]

But Artabanus' attention was quickly diverted elsewhere. In Syria Lucius Vitellius had been appointed by Tiberius to take matters in the east in hand, and when Tiridates arrived there the Roman general gave him a military escort to the Euphrates. There he was met by Parthian nobles who had grown tired of Artabanus' arrogance. So Artabanus gave up on Armenia for the moment in order to attend to this new trouble on his frontier. But Vitellius was not content to let the king regroup. He knew Artabanus was an able general and leader and did not wish to give him any opportunity to fight back. Therefore, he incited even more rebellion among the Parthian nobility. The result was such that Artabanus was cut off from his support base. He fled for his life. But it was while he was in exile that the untiring king at last found his own opportunity to regroup. Enlisting the military support of the Hyrcanians and Carmanians he waited for the right moment to reclaim the Parthian throne.

Meanwhile, Vitellius had returned to Syria satisfied that Tiridates' standing among the Parthian nobility was secure. But that sense of satisfaction was to prove to be part of Tiridates' downfall. Certainly, to begin with things went very well for the prince and he was even welcomed in Seleucia itself.[277] But just when things were starting to look good for his prospects Artabanus made his move. Rallying his forces he returned the favour to Tiridates and the Romans, and in his turn, incited mutiny among Parthia's nobles and army against them. Clearly, the same cries for Iranian nationalism that had propelled Artabanus to the kingship were still strong. Indeed, they were strong enough to sweep him into power once again. So just as Vonones had been despised as a foreigner and a Roman enemy, so too was Tiridates, and Artabanus was welcomed back into Parthia with open arms.

However Tiridates, too, was not one to give up power easily and he took himself and what was left of his forces west to the Euphrates where he sent requests to Vitellius for Roman military support. But Vitellius, sensing that Artabanus' position was already strong and not wishing to decide the issue with him in battle himself, refused to commit Roman legions to the prince's cause. So Tiridates, left without any sort of substantial army had no option but to flee to the safety of Syria a miserable failure.[278]

Thus ended the power-play between Tiberius and Artabanus. When Tiberius died on the 16th of March 37AD the world lost one of the Augustan regime's most loyal exponents. But one could be forgiven for thinking that little had changed in the realm of politics: the Parthian king still retained his Parthian Empire, and Rome its own. Only Armenia had a change in its royalty. But not so great a change. Mithridates' predecessor Artaxias was a foreigner who owed his position to Rome and the new king was no different. To cement a new status quo, or rather an agreement upon the conventional one, Artabanus and Vitellius met on the Euphrates, just as Gaius and Phraataces had done. The Parthian king's son Darius was also given as a hostage as a sign of goodwill. Again, the gesture was a shrewd move. Although he had voluntarily supplied Rome with a potential nominee for the Parthian throne, recent events had shown that such nominees were ultimately unsuccessful in the face of a strong Parthian king. As a result, what often appears to many observers as a clear win for Rome and Tiberius' administration in particular,[279] was actually a major victory for Artabanus and Parthia. A potential threat to the throne in the person of Darius was removed from Parthia, and with his Romanisation ensured, his foreign manners would soon deem him too foreign in the eyes of the Parthians to rule. Thus, his throne was made secure.

At this point we come to the end of Tiberius' principate and it is fitting to return to where we began in our treatment of Tiberius and Parthia with Tacitus and his aims in describing Parthian political affairs. According to Tacitus himself, he had well recognized that battles and the changing fortunes of leaders was what really entertained his readers, and for that reason he apologized to his audience for the inglorious and uninteresting lack of expansion of the Roman Empire under Tiberius.[280] But Tacitus was excited about Parthia's affairs, and that must have ranked high in his reasons for describing their volatile politics and military coups as he did. Syme even recognized that there is an element of respect for Parthia in Tacitus' tone, if somewhat patronizing, but he could not explain why.[281] Perhaps the reason can be found not in any conspicuous respectability within the

Parthians themselves, but in Tacitus' own admiration for the drama, excitement, and ultimately violence, that their politics and military ventures exhibited.

Although Artabanus' imperialist dreams had been dashed, he still retained his empire, and his throne, and he had outlived his rival Tiberius. Only time would tell if Tiberius' successor, Gaius, known to history as Caligula, should prove Tiberius' equal as much in policy as he notoriously did in moral bankruptcy.

Caligula

When Gaius, more commonly known as Caligula, succeeded his adoptive father Tiberius as emperor, there was sheer delight and jubilation in Rome. According to his biographer Suetonius, the popularity of Gaius' paternal father Germanicus still resonated throughout the empire long after his death, and so when Caligula became princeps it was like a 'dream come true' for many Romans and their subjects.[282] His first act regarding Parthia certainly seemed to confirm his potential as a leader that so many Romans had invested in the young emperor. On becoming emperor the young Gaius ordered Vitellius to conclude a peace treaty with Artabanus. It was an amicable act but one not entirely without at least some selfish motivation. Gaius understood that the reinstatement of peace would add to his own popularity, which would bode well for his rule, and secure his position of power. But Artabanus concurred to Gaius' aspirations and agreed to meet with Vitellius on an island in the Euphrates River. There the two set about negotiating a peace treaty.

However, during the negotiations Artabanus' Iranian manners were met with condescension by the Romans and their ramifications would be felt for years, especially for Vitellius. As negotiations were coming to a close Artabanus prostrated himself before the Roman Eagles and standards, and several statues of the deified Caesars.[283] In Vitellius' eyes this was a clear indication that the Parthian king had submitted entirely to Rome and that only he had made that possible. The obvious contrast between this act of honour for Roman military standards on the one hand, and the hostile seizure of Roman standards at Carrhae in times gone by, sparked in the Syrian governor's mind that he had played a part in a turning point in Roman history, and that he alone had reversed all shame in the East. Accordingly, Vitellius began bragging about his importance and power, boasting that he had forced the Parthian king into total submission.[284] But Vitellius had missed the meaning that such an act like that of prostration had in Parthian eyes. Proskynesis, in its many forms, including that of prostration, was a common practice in the East and a mark of honour for others' station in a similar way to bowing still does today in Japan. Artabanus had, in fact, performed it on many other occasions but in no way believed that by doing so he was submitting Parthia to anybody.[285] The king was just showing good Iranian manners, and no doubt it was met on this occasion with genuine acceptance among his Parthian dignitaries present at these diplomatic proceedings too.

The emperor was jealous. It was on his own orders that the treaty had been forged and yet all the credit was clearly being snatched away by his governor. Gaius had him recalled and even planned to put him to death for sedition, so when Vitellius arrived in Rome he fell at the emperor's feet and groveled for his life. But it was more than just any grovel. In this one act Vitellius was mimicking the prostration Artabanus had performed on the Euphrates, and just as that act had been thought of as submissive so too in this one was a transference of homage from himself to Gaius. Pride restored, Vitellius was allowed to live and on account of his subservience to the emperor became one of Gaius' most trusted confidants. But it came at a cost. To ensure his position, and indeed his very own life, Vitellius was forced to be the emperor's permanent sycophant for the duration of the rest of Caligula's life.[286]

But warm relations between Rome and Parthia were soon tested. Both Suetonius and Dio recorded a strange incident that, as it happens, reflects a warlike design that the emperor had on Parthia. According to these ancient writers, Gaius ordered the construction a long bridge made of water vessels fastened port to starboard all the way from Puteoli to Baiae over the Bay of Naples. Once completed, the emperor, bedecked in ornamental armour, then rode an armoured horse across it for a whole day. But that was not the end. On the next day he was carried across it once again, only this time he was in a chariot. Suetonius believed, as do many modern historians, that Gaius' mental instability lurked behind such a seemingly megalomaniac display, or perhaps that it was made to inspire awe and fear in Britons and Germans to the empire's north.[287] But in this one odd event is perhaps a display that the emperor was marking out his intentions for Parthia. Not only was his chariot driver on day two one Darius, an Arsacid hostage, but Dio recorded that the emperor even claimed to have been wearing the breastplate of Alexander the Great, and that while crossing the bridge he hurled insults at the ancient Persian kings Darius and Xerxes, the famous fifth century BC enemies of classical Greece.[288] The message was a clear one, if somewhat misunderstood by our sources: Caligula had set Persia's successors, namely the Parthians, in his sights, and he as a new Alexander, was showing to all and sundry that he held aspirations of further conquest in the East. He even had the blessings of an Arsacid, his own chariot driver.[289]

To all initial appearances, Caligula's actions seem to be a display of megalomaniac nonsense.[290] Certainly, that is how they appeared to Suetonius and Dio. But the princeps had good reason to send a warning-shot to Parthia. According to Josephus the Parthians had been inciting sedition among the Jews in the eastern provinces for some time, and with them Herod Antipas, tetrarch of Galilee and Perea, had been colluding for a rebellion. There was still a sizable Jewish population throughout the Parthian Empire and Babylonia itself had only recently been administered by the Jewish brothers Asineus and Anileus.[291] The Jewish presence would be felt for a long time to come as well, and on the eve of the first Jewish War with Rome there were many in Jerusalem who hoped for military support from their Judaic brethren beyond the Euphrates, and even from Adiabene beyond the Tigris.[292] Although such support was never forthcoming, the fact that it had been considered at all shows the high standing Judaism had within the Parthian Empire. That Antipas had involved himself in plotting a rebellion at this early stage shows that he had envisioned a Jewish nation that pledged its allegiance not to Rome, but like Asineus and Anileus, to Parthia.

When news of this sedition came to the attention of Herod Agrippa, governor of Batanaea and Trachonitis and keen supporter of Roman interests, he informed the emperor and Antipas was immediately ordered into exile. As a reward, Agrippa was given all of Herod Antipas' former territories. Thus despite his deteriorating mental health, Gaius had exhibited that he still possessed some powers of political ability when it came to matters involving Parthia. In one sweeping ostracism all Parthian intrusion was checked, and by rewarding Agrippa in the way that he did he demonstrated that allegiance to the emperor brought with it great benefits. However Parthia needed to be dealt with, and that is probably why at this point Gaius ordered the construction of his famous bridge across the Bay of Naples and rode across it as a menacing display of power to warn off Artabanus and instill a warlike spirit among his onlookers. But plans for war, or indeed any further symbolic lessons Gaius may have contemplated for the condescending benefit his subjects, were dashed when Gaius was assassinated in late January 41AD and succeeded by his uncle Claudius. Gaius' plans for war were thus postponed and the manifold meanings of the Bay of Naples bridge lost and thus inevitably distorted over time.

Claudius

By the time Claudius had become emperor the practice of delegating provincial and foreign matters to the men on the spot in the form of Roman governors was already well established. Long gone was the Augustan method whereby governors were dispatched with direct and detailed orders of what to do, and in its place governors were free to act as they saw fit so long as maintained Rome's imperial interests. Consequently, their caliber was tremendously important if those imperial interests were to be successfully and properly upheld. During Claudius' principate there was a succession of governors in Syria and each needed to take steps to curtail Parthia's agenda in the region. They would each perform with varying, yet lackluster, ability.[293]

Claudius had inherited from his predecessor chaos in Armenia since Gaius had arrested and imprisoned its king, Mithridates. So he had to act fast to check an escalation, and he immediately reinstated him and began making friendly overtures to the other major power in the region, Parthia.[294] But by 47AD that stability was ruined when King of kings Artabanus died and civil war engulfed Parthia, pitting one of his sons Gotarzes II against another, Vardanes. Upon Artabanus' death Gotarzes was quick to seize the throne and began exterminating his family, as was almost a tradition among the Arsacids, in order to eradicate any future threat to his power. But the Parthian nobility opposed his choice as king and produced Vardanes, who had hitherto survived his brother's proscriptions, who then rallied support to back him as king in place of Gotarzes. Thus Gotarzes' paranoia was justified, although misplaced: he had killed the wrong family members and the true threat to his throne, Vardanes, had survived to challenge him.

Immediately both brothers collected large armies and met each other for a showdown on the battlefield. In the battle that ensued Gotarzes was routed, but unperturbed, he fled north to the Dahae and Hycanians to raise a new army. While he was busy doing this Vardanes, as Crassus and Antony had found beforehand, was faced with the ominous task of imposing his rule over the empire. After initial successes Vardanes knew that he had to take the capital Seleucia if his reign was to succeed, but the city held out and the new king had to lay siege to it. But as Vardanes was detained by the rigours of the siege Gotarzes moved south once again with his new army and attacked his brother's positions, and routed him and his troops.

Vardanes, however, seems to have inherited his brother's optimism and initiative, and he fled east to Bactria, where he in turn raised yet another army to launch his own counter-attack. After gathering a large force there Vardanes marched west, and the two brothers for all intents and purposes were seething to decide the issue of the Parthian throne once and for all with their foreign armies. The fact that their forces were foreign and that they were being used to decide the future of Parthia as an entity reflects the weakness Parthia had found itself in as a result of prolonged civil war. It had suffered in battle and siege, and its inability to decide the issue one way or the other ultimately created a power vacuum that others were only too eager to fill. But as the brothers' armies drew closer news reached the two contenders that a certain number of their so-called followers were plotting to assassinate them both. Fearing they would soon loose their lives if they did not act immediately, Gotarzes and Vardanes made peace. Vardanes who was left to remain within Parthia itself and was given permission by his brother to avenge his previous humiliation before the walls of Seleucia and persist with the siege there, but it was Gotarzes who gained the lion's share by holding onto real power by being given Hyrcania and its armies.

However, this truce was not to last long. By having been given ample breathing space Vardanes was able to rebuild Parthia's military forces and in a rapid succession he reduced a number of northern neighbouring nations, thus restoring its confidence, discipline and effectiveness. Then he announced a tour of Armenia. Although Tacitus believed such a visit an innocent holiday tour,[295] such a belief was perhaps a little too naive: Josephus recorded that Vardanes had in fact planned on reconnoitering the political situation in Armenia as part of his plans of invasion.[296] Such a move would have provoked a war with Rome, and Gaius Vibius Marsus, the Roman governor of Syria ordered the king to leave Armenia alone or else he would face a war. Vardanes, finding that his innocent façade was seen for what it truly was by the governor, obeyed the order and Armenia was left to be. But this back down was a loss of face to many Parthians, including Gotarzes, who decided to act and overthrow his brother and he once again marched south from Hyrcania to face him in one last and decisive battle. However, Vardanes had done much to restore the Parthian army, and when the two brothers met on the battlefield it was Vardanes' Parthians who proved themselves superior in the fighting to Gotarzes' Hyrcanian forces.[297]

It was a great victory and had secured Vardanes' place upon the Parthian throne. Or so he thought. Due to his overbearing pride on account of his victory the king became increasingly unpopular and was assassinated while out hunting. Thus Gotarzes, who had somehow survived his defeat on the battlefield, was restored to his throne once again.[298] But if initiative had run through both brothers' veins, so too did their sense of extreme pride, and when Gotarzes started showing his own signs of proud despotism the Parthian nobility implored the Roman emperor for the return of Meherdates, another descendent of Phraates IV, so that he could take over Parthia. Claudius, eager to emulate and equal the great Augustus himself was only too happy to comply, and he commissioned the new governor of Syria, Gaius Cassius Longinus, to escort Meherdates to the Euphrates River at his own discretion. It was a bold move on the emperor's part, but Cassius knew that such an act would no doubt reignite civil war in Parthia and lead to all out war with Gotarzes. Cassius therefore prepared to obey the princeps' intentions through training and readying his Syrian legions for a coming Parthian war. But when Cassius arrived with Meherdates at Zeugma on the Euphrates, which was the most convenient place to cross over, he was not met by a hostile army but instead by a welcoming party that included Carenes (a Parthian satrap), king Abgar V of Edessa and other members of the Parthian nobility.

Meherdates, however, showed none of the kind of initiative that Gotarzes possessed, and instead of making straight for Parthia itself, the nominee dallied for the winter in Armenia. So, when in the following spring he started his march south with Carenes and their combined forces and pitched camp on the fields of Gaugamela to wait for the coming battle with Gotarzes, the Parthian king was ready for the fight. Sensing a lost cause Abgar defected to the king's side and with him marched on Gaugamela with their combined forces. Battle was soon joined and lasted a full day and by all accounts was evenly contested. However, late in the day, when Carenes led his cavalry against his opposing enemy battle line it fled and Carenes, in overexcitement, pursued it so far that he was cut off from his own line in the main battle. A large gap in Meherdates' line then opened up and Gotarzes' army closed ranks, poured into it, and proceeded to massacre the unprotected flanks at either end of that gap. While Meherdates was killed in the onslaught, Gotarzes' army had routed the enemy.[299]

But the victory was short-lived. Gotarzes died soon afterwards. Although Josephus stated the king was assassinated, given there were no reprisals or any civil wars of vengeance following his death, Tacitus' statement that he died of an illness must be correct.[300] With his death Parthia's civil war came to an end, and when the new king Vonones II, who had previously been sub-king of Media Atropatene, came to the throne, a period of peace was ushered in. Vonones' reign was only a short one though, and yet even though he died soon after becoming king his legacy for peace in Parthia was long-lasting. His successor,

Vologases I, proved himself a powerful leader and king, and also a benefactor of peace just like his father Vonones.

In Armenia though, events took a sharp turn for the worst when the Iberian prince Radamistus, son of king Pharasmanes of Iberia, had his own uncle Mithridates king of Armenia assassinated and then overran the deceased king's country with Iberian soldiers.[301] Clearly, the prince had calculated that his timing was perfect since Vologases had only just come to the Parthian throne while in Syria there was a new Roman governor, Gaius Ummidius Durmius Quadratus. So Radamistus must have calculated that his designs on Armenia would be unchecked by either newcomer. However, he had grossly misjudged the ability of Vologases and the energy of Quadratus. Immediately, Quadratus ordered the prince to evacuate Armenia and prompted Julius Paelignus, governor of Cappadocia, to invade it. But for all of Quadratus' zeal and position his orders were ignored by both Radamistus and his Romans. The Iberians refused to evacuate and Paelignus' army deserted their governor in the middle of Armenia surrounded by hostile Iberian forces. Consequently, Paelignus was forced to crown Radamistus king of Armenia in a lavish ceremony.

Quadratus, understandably, was furious, and accordingly dispatched Helvidius Priscus with an army from Syria to invade Armenia. But Priscus never made it there. Quadratus ordered his return midmarch because he had received the news that Vologases himself had entered Armenia with an army and did not wish to provoke a full-scale war with Parthia. Vologases, ignoring Paelignus' crowning of Radamistus, crowned his own brother Tiridates king of Armenia instead, thus dashing the Iberian prince's legitimacy to rule as well as flouting the prestige of the Roman governor of Cappadocia in one swoop. But then plague hit the Parthian army and Vologases was forced to withdraw. Radamistus once again took control of Armenia. It was a chaotic climate there indeed, but one that was not beyond all hope. Just as the Parthians had shown that they could recover their fortunes and reemerge as a strong power, so too did the Armenians. They rebelled against Radamistus and forced him to flee Armenia for his life back to Iberia, and they regained their independence once again.[302]

This account of racy events makes for a heady brew, although it is slightly one-sided, being derived from Tacitus' momentous *Annals*. The Annals is an ancient masterpiece of literature, but the question must be posed as to whether or not it is a trustworthy account. The answer of course is that it is certainly a reflection of the importance Tacitus placed in it, but needless to say that does not mean that it is a perfect reflection on Roman and Parthian relations as they existed during the sixty or more years before Tacitus wrote the work. Tacitus no doubt included in his narrative of Claudius' reign Parthian and Armenia civil war to excite the reader just as he had also done in the case of Tiberius.[303] But these events expressed far more about Tacitus' own purposes than mere excitement. They were a warning against the evils of civil war universally, whether they be in Parthia, or Armenia, or indeed in the Roman Empire,[304] and they were a warning against the dangers of despotism be they foreign or at home, especially the type embodied by the Julio-Claudian emperors.[305] Claudius had aspired to equal the great Augustus, but Tacitus was letting it be known loud and clear that far more effort was required on the part of Rome's emperors if they truly wished to achieve parity with him.[306]

But questions aside, Tacitus' narrative has far more finesse than all other ancient treatments of Claudius' relations with Parthia. In a time when most Roman historians treated the histories of other nations as dead relics, Tacitus enthusiastically breathed fresh life into Parthian politics in a way that is much admired by historians to this day.[307] All this when other Roman historians, like Suetonius and Cassius Dio, made next to no mention of them at all. However, Suetonius did make one brief remark in his biography of Claudius which reveals that we must be careful not to project Tacitus' kinetic narrative onto all aspects of Rome's dealings with Parthia during Claudius' time as emperor. According to Suetonius Claudius actually allowed Parthian and Armenian dignitaries to sit with Roman Senators in the orchestral section of the Theatre in Rome.[308] Such a privilege reflects a political warmth that is wholly missing in the cold events in the *Annals*. But of course, once again, we should not, as with Tacitus, conclude that Suetonius' account is a perfect source on Roman and Parthian relations in totality. Suetonius deliberately sought repeatedly to undermine

Claudius' military and political achievements and only made brief mention of his conquest in Britain – a conquest Cassius Dio later described in detail as a momentous event in Roman history.[309]

But Dio also acknowledged, like Suetonius, that relations had thawed since the time of Augustus, although he perhaps unknowingly illustrated that point in the description of a particular spectacle put on by Claudius: a mock sea-battle. Augustus had also staged one, but while his sea-battle was fought between Greek and Persian fleets, Claudius' one was fought by Sicilian and Rhodian fleets. The shift from an east-west rivalry towards a far more central theme reflects a deeper tone inherent in Claudius' policy, whereby military action in the east was being curbed towards the west where there was far more potential for easy victories.[310] That curb explains why Claudius appointed such unworthy governors in the eastern provinces, and why he chose to promote men of real ability in the western provinces. That is not to say that the unsettled situation in Armenia and Parthia was of no concern to Claudius whatsoever. The events there as recorded by Tacitus could not have been of no accord to the emperor. But, by delegating to such a caliber of governors in the east, Claudius was trying to show the Roman world that Armenia and Parthia were not where Rome's future lied. However, when he died in 54AD and Nero became emperor in his place, this new princeps would embark upon a very different foreign policy to Claudius', one that brought Rome, Armenia and Parthia to the brink of all-out warfare.

Nero and Corbulo

Peace was not to last in Armenia for long. Immediately upon Claudius' death, Vologases took advantage Nero's youth and inexperience a leader and invaded the buffer-state. His doubts about the new emperor's ability were shared by others too, among them many Romans.[311] But act Nero did, and he promptly ordered the mobilization of all of the eastern provinces' legions and placed them under the command of the man on-the-spot, Quadratus. He then ordered Quadratus to invade Armenia while Rome's allies Agrippa II and

Antiochus Epiphanes IV of Commagene were to cross the Euphrates further south. It was the classic use of diversion by the opening of a second war-front that had been used so often in the past by Roman leaders, and it was to feature heavily throughout, and indeed characterize, Nero's whole principate.

But fighting was put off as Vologases withdrew and marched his army back to the east to deal with a rebellion led by one Vardanes. However, Vologases still held out for the opportunity to exploit Nero's inexperience, and so he planned that once the rebellion was dealt with Vologases would return to Armenia in full military capacity.

Meanwhile, the response in Rome to Vologases' withdrawal was that of the kind of celebration associated with total victory and an end to war. The Senate decreed thanksgiving celebrations, and Nero basked in the satisfaction that his youth had not stood in the way of competency as an able ruler of an empire. But there was even more to celebrate in Rome when Cnaeus Domitius Corbulo was appointed by the emperor to take over affairs in the eastern provinces and Armenia. Corbulo was a gifted and experienced general and his choice is an indication of just how important proper handling of affairs in the East was to Nero.[312]

At that time Armenia was on the brink of another civil war with pro-Roman and pro-Parthian factions dividing the population there, and Nero rightly felt the situation had to be taken into hand. But what delighted Romans even more was Nero's decision to utilise Corbulo himself. Corbulo was a very ambitious Roman general, and his promotion to a command in the East was greeted in Rome as a welcome sign that Nero would reward ability as well as military ambition.[313]

Upon Corbulo's arrival in Syria Vologases made overtures of peace and handed over to the general a number of hostages from the Parthian royal family. This gave the overt appearance that Vologases was submitting to Rome and giving the emperor a number of potential nominees as insurance should the Parthian king infringe upon that trust. But the Arsacid king was also removing potential threats to his throne, and thus while strengthening his own position he was also leading Corbulo into relying upon the notion that he could rely on his apparent goodwill. But nominees had failed dismally in the past, and

Vologases knew that if he could force Rome into repeating its mistakes, Parthia's power, as well as his own, was guaranteed.

So, several years later, once the rebellion under Vardanes had been crushed, Vologases returned from the east and laid out plans to install his younger brother, Tiridates, upon the Armenian throne. Vologases had hoped that would curb the young prince's desires for power in Parthia proper and by doing so deter civil war, and at the same time extent Parthia's empire to the west. But opposition remained in the form of Corbulo, who wished to uphold Rome's own imperial agendas for Armenia. Lucullus and Pompey had taken Armenia in the past and it was this general's wish to recapture their conquests and glory in service to Rome and the emperor. Such was the psychological temper, or rather distemper, that pervaded each side and brought them to war.[314]

But neither side was ready to rush hastily into battle. For a whole year both Vologases and Corbulo trained and prepared their armies for the rigours of the coming fight. Finally though, once he was satisfied with his legions' discipline, Corbulo marched north from Syria into western Armenia, and at the same time Vologases and Tiridates entered it from the east. Immediately the Parthians attacked every city or town that was pro-Roman in policy, and despite Corbulo's repeated efforts to bring the Parthian Vologases to battle to preserve what remained of pro-Roman enclaves in Armenia, Vologases repeatedly refused. The hilly terrain of Armenia once again suited the Roman infantry for battle, and Vologases knew that engaging them in a set-piece battle might have spelt the end for Parthia's cause. So the king engaged the enemy using the kind of hit-and-run tactics that his Parthian soldiers were familiar with and by doing so evaded Corbulo's army's clear strengths in close battle formation.

But Corbulo was not to be outdone so easily. After some effort on his part, he persuaded Pharasmenes, king of Iberia, to ally himself with Rome and open another front by launching an attack on Parthia. More was to come. Corbulo also managed to form an alliance with Hyrcania and by his encouragement a rebellion was raised there against Parthia.[315] It was a serious blow to the king. Hyrcania's army was still extremely effective and had been used by Parthia's own kings in the past. His plans for Armenia once again frustrated by rebellion in the east, Vologases had no choice but to leave his brother alone with a portion of his total army to fight Corbulo while he himself again turned east to crush yet another rebellion. But Tiridates was not the leader or general that Vologases was, and once his brother left he immediately made overtures to come to terms with Corbulo. The two leaders agreed to meet on neutral ground where they could deploy some troops as insurance against betrayal, partly uneven to suit Corbulo's infantry, and partly flat to suit the Parthian cavalry. It was a tentative signal that diplomacy would, from that point on, be conducted in order to appease both Roman and Parthian concerns on an equal basis. It was a huge step. Only if it could have been pulled off, that is. As it happened however, neither Corbulo nor Tiridates trusted the other, and despite all reassurances from both leaders, they withdrew without actually meeting and so the war dragged on.

Corbulo renewed the fight with fresh vigour and energy. Immediately following the non-event that was the intended peace-talk with Tiridates, the Roman general began taking Armenian and Parthian strongholds and settlements. The major cities Volandum and Artaxata were captured, and the latter was even razed to the ground, an exhibition of Roman siege-craft. Tiridates quickly realized that he had no way of stopping this brute show of Roman strength and he conceded defeat, fleeing with his army east into Media Atropatene. Although it was not total defeat for Parthia, in Rome, when news reached the city that both Vologases and Tiridates had fled before Corbulo's men there was sheer jubilation: Nero was hailed victor, and more thanksgivings were decreed by the Senate. It was also decided that a victory arch should also be erected in honour of Nero on the Capitoline Hill in Rome, ranking this victory as equal to any one of those of Rome's past. The arch no longer exists, but by all accounts and descriptions it was a display of Roman artistic genius. Complete with Corinthian columns and niches, the arch was of a bold design that was so ahead of its time that none like it would be built until half a century later. It was a statement that Nero's famous love for the arts would lend its support to many facets of Roman life, including the military aspect.[316] But it was also more than just that. It was in itself evidence that while Roman citizens would continue to fight wars, and also that the emperor would shirk his subjects' hardships and enjoy the glory of their labours through the design and enjoyment of artistic pastimes they were refused. It was that, at the moment of Nero's triumph over Parthia, which displayed the emperor's power. But at the same time it showed off his vanity too, his ignorance of the hardships that Roman armies faced, and the self-glorification that Nero felt was owing to himself alone. In time the remorse that these things provoked in Rome's armies would lead to the emperor's own downfall.

But while Rome celebrated, Corbulo pressed on, imposing Roman rule throughout Armenia. He was welcomed into Tigranocerta and a number of other cities, but found resistance at other places like Legerda. However after another successful siege it too surrendered, along with most of Armenia. Corbulo's army now had practically free rein over the Armenian countryside, and since Vologases was still detained by his Hyrcanian war, and Tiridates dallied in Media, that seems set to continue. Sensing that the time was right to do so, Nero dispatched his own nominee for the Armenian throne to Corbulo for instatement there. His choice was one Tigranes V, a Cappadocian prince. When he duly arrived in the east Corbulo equipped his with a force of 1,000 Roman soldiers and other auxiliary units so that he could defend his hold on throne against any future Parthian threat that might eventuate.

However, when Tigranes misused his army he invited a Parthian invasion. In 61AD Tigranes marched into the Parthian kingdom of Adiabene set on conquest.[317] Vologases was furious. In haste he crowned Tiridates king of Armenia and then ordered, and indeed begged, him to assert himself militarily and take it over from Tigranes. But despite this bold act of Vologases', Tiridates remained unsuited to the task. Sensing this, and rightly surmising that his Hyrcanian war was almost won, Vologases himself returned to the west, invaded Armenia and pent up Tigranes within Tigranocerta. Only when the resulting siege showed signs of failure did Vologases enter into peace talks with Corbulo.

In Rome, the Arsacid king's failure resulted in public celebration in the hope that now finally the war was all but over. But in Parthia, Vologases and his brother laid out plans to recover Armenia once and for all at an opportune moment. It came the following year. During that year Lucius Caesinnius Paetus was appointed to take command of Armenia while Corbulo retained Syria. It was Nero's decision but this arrangement was actually at Corbulo's own request. Now that the Hyrcanian war was now decisively won by Vologases it was important to open a second potential front against Parthia from somewhere other than Hyrcania, and Syria suited Corbulo's designs. Thus, in case of a war Corbulo could attack Parthia from Syria, while Paetus could attack from Armenia. But this device proved Corbulo's greatest military error.

Paetus was an impatient and impetuous leader and Vologases rightly calculated that the new commander, unused to Parthian fighting tactics, would prove easy prey. Immediately, Vologases invaded Armenia at the head of a huge army, bought Paetus to battle, and routed him. Paetus survived fleeing to the fortified city of Arsamosata, but his cause was lost and he quickly came to terms with the king agreeing that all Roman forces would evacuate Armenia. It was a rash move on Paetus' part, but it also reflected the prevailing desire for peace in Rome. There it was realised that even the gifted Corbulo could never entirely prevail over the Parthian Empire. Also, the war had dragged on longer than anticipated by either side, and Nero was eager to bring a war to a close that he had claimed victory over years before. In Parthia too, where it was all too clear that Parthia's armies could never entirely prevail against Corbulo, the mood was also for peace. So, in the midst of this stalemate, when Corbulo asked the Parthian king to evacuate all of his forces from Armenia as the Romans had agreed to, Vologases happily complied, so long as Tiridates, not Tigranes, was recognised as king of Armenia by Nero. Corbulo agreed, but suggested that Tiridates accompany a Roman force to Rome where he would then submit to Nero publicly and be crowned by Nero himself. Tiridates and Vologases agreed to the terms.

Tiridates in Rome

After settling his affairs in Armenia and Parthia, Tiridates set off for Rome, escorted by a Roman army and a Parthian cavalry bodyguard.

As Tacitus observed, Tiridates was technically a prisoner, but he was still nonetheless intent on making an ostensible display of his power and position as a king.[318] Thus what was an extradition turned out to be a kind of triumph.[319] Or rather a mock-triumph. Despite the fact that both Roman and Parthian escorts symbolized a new level of cooperation between Rome and Parthia,[320] a triumph was essentially a Roman institution that also symbolized Roman identity. That is why, when Antony led his triumph through the streets of Alexandria there was such outrage back in Rome.

But when Tiridates finally arrived in Rome in 66AD, any rankles were swept away in the excitement of what was to follow. Nero proclaimed that the city be decorated for the occasion, and it was: with lights, garlands, and so much gold that that particular day entered the common vernacular as the 'golden' day.[321] The use of gold in such display was no mere accident. Nero consistently espoused that his reign as emperor was a golden age for Rome. Not only did he construct a palace after the burning of Rome in 64AD which he called the 'Golden House', but even upon his succession he circulated the message throughout Rome that it signified the beginning of such an age. Hence, Seneca at the outset of the reign proclaimed that a new golden age had begun,[322] and other poets like Calpurnius Siculus echoed the sentiment.[323] Of course, Nero had a hand in devising the boundaries of literary license, but the genuine enthusiasm and excitement of writers for the future at the beginning of Nero's principate was unmistakable. In fact, Nero was an artist himself and was on constant display and show to Rome – his audience.[324] The 'golden' day of the crowning of Tiridates was only one such show. The coronation ceremony itself was lavish, as one would expect, and when Tiridates performed obeisance before Nero in the open in Rome the crowds erupted in applause. Nero, fittingly, placed a golden crown upon his head. It must have appeared to many Romans that universal peace was indeed becoming toga-clad.

But the golden age was not to last long. By 69AD Nero had been overthrown and the Roman Empire was gripped by a civil war. Nero's downfall was sealed when he had Corbulo executed for treason. Despite Cassius Dio's assertion that he was killed on Nero's whim, there is reason to believe the general had considered a coup in the past:

117

before he died Corbulo commented that he regretted not seizing the empire beforehand when he could have.[325]

Of course, Nero had acted no different to any his imperial predecessors by punishing disloyalty, but it was precisely the behaviour of his predecessors that the elite Romans hated. To Senators and military staff, Nero's choice of the pursuit of the arts and leisure over giving proper attention to the armies was an inversion of all that was traditionally Roman. Hence, both Tacitus' and Suetonius' narratives are filled with disdain for Nero as an emperor throughout.[326] But despite the total invective of their narratives, the disdain only emerged gradually. While Syme condemned Nero outright, arguing that Tacitus' and Suetonius' comparable portrayal of the emperor must mean that what they wrote had to have been factual,[327] it is worth remembering that the sources which these writers drew upon were by and large Senatorial and courtly, and did not necessarily reflect the opinions of the average Roman. In fact it was from the upper classes that the revolution came, and that only in the last years of Nero's life. Tacitus, Suetonius and Dio were likewise of similar position and wealth: Tacitus and Dio were Senators themselves, and their impressions of Nero were shaped by older Senatorial peers who lived through and remembered those last years with bitterness, when Nero began exhibiting signs of despotism in place of careful attention to the empire and its armies.

The reality is that bitterness towards Nero emerged only slowly and towards the end of his principate. Such a gradual emergence is exhibited in the poetry of Lucan. In the opening of his epic, the *Pharsalia*, more commonly known as 'Civil War', which Lucan began to be write around 62AD, the poet has genuine praise for Nero, waxing lyrical that all the civil wars of Rome's past were worthwhile since they ultimately resulted by means of cause and effect in bringing Nero to the fore as emperor.[328] Lucan himself had even been a friend of Nero's. It is believed that while his uncle Seneca tutored the young Nero, Lucan, who was also a youth, struck up a friendship with him.[329] Hence, when Lucan published his first three books of a total of ten in the Civil War it was peppered with praises for Nero and scorn for Parthia - his one-time enemy.[330] But later the two fell out. As to why they did so is reflected in book seven of the Civil War where Lucan condemned the despotism of Parthia's kings.[331] Of course, Lucan did not specify that this criticism was aimed at Nero, but the conclusion that such invective could also be leveled at the now ongoing despotism of the Julio-Claudian dynasty is inescapable.[332] Nero, detecting animosity being felt towards him by Lucan in his poetry, ordered a ban on all of his books. Lucan was infuriated, and desperate to preserve his living, he entered into a plot to assassinate the emperor. But the plot was discovered by Nero and he ordered Lucan to commit suicide.[333]

However, anti-Nero sentiment was not felt by Lucan alone. Far from it. But it is noteworthy that even Lucan, who deplored civil war and could not envisage Rome without the principate at all[334] came to the realization, along with many other Romans, that something had to be done about Nero's growing megalomania, especially since its victims increasingly included the likes of Corbulo himself. Consequently, within the space of a few years, revolts convulsed the empire.[335] First the Roman governor Julius Vindex raised a rebellion in Gaul; next Servius Galba incited another in Spain and was joined by Otho. Otho would himself raise his own rebellion against Galba upon the latter's seizure of Nero's throne; and later, Aulus Vitellius would make a bid for power with the legions in Rome's German provinces. But finally Vespasian, the commander in the war against the Jews in Palestine, decided the time was right for him to wrestle the empire from Vitellius for himself, and it was eventually he who emerged as Rome's outright emperor and victor of its long civil war. Thus the tirades against Nero were victorious, but so too was the principate itself. Had Lucan lived on to see that day, he would have been well pleased with that outcome.

But Nero's military image had failed not for want of trying towards the end. By the time of his death the emperor had flouted the peace with Parthia and began making extensive preparations for an expedition to the Daryal Gorge in the central Caucasus region, enlisting British, German and Balkan forces for the war.[336] Although he espoused that it was to check any possible inroads by the Albani and Sarmatian nomads from the north of the Caucasus,[337] it was obviously contrived primarily for purpose of imperial conquest throughout Parthian territories that Nero's army would have had to inevitably cross in an effort to reach the gorge itself. In fact Nomad nations from the north, like the Iberians and Hyrcanians, were not considered especially danger-ous to Rome's interests in the East, and had been effectively utilized for war by Rome against Parthia in the past. It was an arrangement that would continue for decades. Hence, when the Alani poured into Par-thia in the mid-70sAD they too found a ready ally for their Parthian war in the Roman governor of Syria, Marcus Ulpius Traianus, father of the future emperor Trajan. (See Chapter Seven) In fact, far from viewing them as enemies, Nero had probably hoped to enlist nomadic support for his eastern adventure against Parthia.

But it was all too little too late. When the emperor learned of Gal-ba's rebellion he committed suicide. Had he still possessed the likes of Corbulo one wonders whether he would have done so, but Nero, never the general, lost all hope and cut short his life. It is said that his last words were commentary on his performance as an actor and artist. But, artistic expression and symbolic power can only extend so far, and as Nero was to discover too late, that applied no less to him-self. At the heart of the empire true power always depended upon the armies, pure and simple, not in artistic license or any boasting about a golden age. Nero had tried to conquer the hearts and minds of the world through symbol and meaning, but real conquest many Romans believed was the armies' domain and purpose, and they resented not being used to their full capacity by an emperor more interested in act-ing in a theatre than giving time and attention to the concerns of his own generals. Thus after Nero's death and a whole year spent in civil war, the pragmatic and brilliant general Vespasian seized the empire for himself and his sons Titus and Domitian, and stability returned to the empire once again, inaugurating a new dynasty: the Flavian dynasty.

CHAPTER SEVEN

FLAVIAN RELATIONS WITH PARTHIA: 70-96AD

Reconstructing Flavian History

U NLIKE THE JULIO-CLAUDIAN period, our knowledge of the Flavian dynasty and its relations with Parthia is based upon scanty evidence. Tacitus' narrative of it in his *Histories* has tragically not survived; Suetonius' biographies of Vespasian, Titus and Domitian are thinly composed; and Cassius Dio's history becomes more fragmentary. Consequently, we must handle the available evidence in these sources with great care, while looking beyond them to other types of ancient evidence for clues about Romano-Parthian relations for this period. Fortunately though, we do not have to look too far to find them. In the literary sphere Josephus' narrative is helpful, even if somewhat brief, and poetry from the time of Domitian's principate is also of some use. But when we turn to archaeology we do find that the general picture can be fleshed out.

As a result of the paucity of evidence, there have been many attempts made by numerous modern historians to reconstruct Flavian imperial and political policy. Some have argued that a 'Grand Strategy' of defense existed and was shared thereafter by all Roman emperors, and others note the striking differences between every emperor thus discounting it completely. In either case though, it cannot be denied that relations throughout the Flavian dynasty were robust.

Of course, almost all attempts at reconstruction depend heavily upon literary evidence that is Roman in origin, but that should not deter the reader. Although some rightly point out that Roman bias ultimately distorts our understanding of Roman and Parthian histories, the argument that Rome mattered little to Parthia[338] ignores the fact that Parthia's response to repeated Roman invasions was often large-scale as we have seen in previous chapters. Looking ahead too, campaigns under Trajan, Verus, Severus and Caracalla resulted in the Parthians' entire military evacuation of Mesopotamia and the regrouping across the Zagros Mountains in order to launch from there new counter-attacks. The logistics and mass-mobilisation required for such operations were vast and consumed the entire Parthian Empire. Thus Rome was important to Parthia, and given that that is the same thematic point inherent within the writings of Romans themselves, that alone shows that Roman sources do, and rightly should, remain indispensable for us in trying to understand Parthian history.

In trying to reconstruct Flavian history, a word must be said about the case for the so-called 'Grand Strategy'. It has been proposed by some that Roman emperors consistently took calculated moves primarily in order to contain Parthia and maintain the peace at all costs. Others have revised this hypothesis, and argue that there was rather a culturally conditioned innate disposition among Rome's emperors to sustain this grand strategy. But it has also been observed by others that such a 'Strategy' can only be detected with hindsight, and is not really based upon the nature of the ancient evidence all which records the erratic, the fluctuating, and the inconsistencies from each Roman emperor to the next.[339] It is this spirit, the spirit of looking for proof to back up one's opinions, that is taken up by the author in this chapter.

Vespasian and Titus

In order to understand the full brevity of Roman and Parthian relations during this period, we must first take into account their underlying political and military contexts. In order to do that, we must turn to Titus' procession through the eastern provinces on his return to Rome following the first Jewish War. In that procession, or rather more correctly that triumphal procession, both Romans and Parthians attempted to project certain public images of themselves. This was in order to both reassure their subjects that friendly relations were in place, and that Roman and Parthian power was being upheld throughout each respective one's empire.

According to Josephus, along his long procession through Syria, Titus took a large detour from his main route soon after he arrived in Antioch proceeding to Zeugma on the Euphrates. It was there that he was publicly crowned with a golden crown by a number of official envoys that had been commissioned for that purpose by Vologases himself. After Titus ceremonially accepted the crown from their hands, the Roman prince then feasted the envoys before returning to Antioch for the resumption of his victory march back to Rome.[340] That Titus' attention was diverted to this public exhibition suggests that it held immense importance to him and to Rome. Its message to the public is quickly discerned: by this display Titus was signaling a reversal of the negative impression created for Rome thanks to Tiridates' own infamous procession and crowning by Nero.

Tiridates' parade through Rome's eastern provinces was a brazen inversion of Roman triumphal custom and must have belittled Rome's power in the east in the eyes of the many who observed it. That is why we find Titus several years later leading his own truly Roman procession from Jerusalem to Rome.[341] The institution of the triumphal procession was of fundamental importance to Roman identity,[342] and Titus's triumphal procession should thus be seen as an effort to rouse Roman nationalist spirit, restore Rome's military pride, and reestablish its image in the East once again. It was a sign that Roman power would be reasserted in the east and that any future threat a Tiridates or any other Parthian might pose along Rome's eastern frontiers would be curbed by a resurgent Roman Empire.[343] But the Flavians were quick to distinguish the nature of that empire from the one their Julio-Claudian predecessors ruled. Coins commemorating their victory over the Jews feature imagery of a supplicating vanquished figure (a personification of Judaea) submitting to an adorned and victorious figure representing Rome. That kind of numismatic symbolism had not been seen since the days of the res-publica. That symbolic revival was a deliberate statement that more such republican-like victories were to come and that those seeking a return to the military glories of Rome's republican history would find satisfaction in the exploits of their new rulers.[344]

However, just as the procession and crowning of Tiridates had a double meaning: it was a success in the eyes of Nero but a mockery in those of Tiridates, so too did the procession and crowning of Titus. Just as it was a public reversal of the bitter taste left in Rome's mouth with Tiridates' crowning, it was also a complete reversal in roles between Rome and Parthia. While Tiridates' coronation ultimately recognized Rome's position as a maker of kings, so too in Titus' own coronation it must have seemed to many Parthians that Vologases was a maker of emperors. Of course, the crowning of Titus was an admission by Parthia of submission in the face of Roman military power in the region,[345] and given Titus' increasing involvement in Adiabene and the election of Titus' uncle Paetus to the governorship in Syria soon afterwards,[346] it was a shrewd move by Vologases. But it also reflected the tentative uncertainty of the new dynasty after several would be dynasts had already failed in the year of the four emperors, and a public display of honour for the new regime by Parthia was certainly as welcome for Titus as it was for Vologases.

But ultimately by accepting this crowning gesture Titus had in effect reassured the Parthian king that peace would be established.[347] Thus, despite the political maneuvers that underlie the coronation, what with Parthia and Rome jostling for the most advantageous public image, peace was the main prize for both. Still, Rome was eager to be seen in total control of the situation, even if that was not entirely the case in reality, and so too was Parthia. Nonetheless, the crowning restored a semblance of public image for Rome among its subjects in the eastern provinces. For Titus for the time being, that was enough. For Vespasian things were more complicated.

Vespasian and Vologases

In 70AD Vespasian emerged from the civil war to become sole ruler of the Roman Empire. Given the fragmentary nature of the literary evidence, many have conjectured and theorized about his relations with the Parthian king Vologases. In the late nineteenth century it was widely believed that Vespasian and Vologases had agreed upon an arrangement of non-aggression that lasted for the duration of their reigns.[348] This was proposed on the grounds that Josephus stated that preceding the Jewish War, Agrippa publicly proclaimed in Jerusalem that Vologases was "anxious to preserve his armistice with the Romans",[349] and that during the chaos of 69AD Vologases actually offered Vespasian the use of forty thousand archers for his bid for the Roman Empire should need arise.[350] This proposal has had longevity.[351]

However, in more recent times most historians have become dissatisfied with that line of argument given the nature of the ancient evidence pointing to the contrary, such as archaeological findings only made through the course of the twentieth century. Such evidence also finds support in Pliny the Younger's *Panegyricus*, an appraisal delivered during the succession of the future princeps Trajan. In it, Pliny recalled that M. Ulpius Traianus, father of the future emperor Trajan, was actually awarded *ornamenta triumphalia* for a military victory over the Parthians while governor of Syria between 73/74-76/77 during Vespasian's principate.[352] Even though the *Panegyricus* was a tribute to the future emperor Trajan, and therefore his father, it still stands that his reference to the award is non-debatable. We know that because other pieces of evidence support Pliny's claims. A lengthy inscription in Greek that was left by Roman soldiers during Vespasian's principate at Harmozica, in Iberia, points to the fact that there were deployments made by the emperor to the East for imperialist purposes. Although it is true that the inscription itself relates that its Roman hands were there ostensibly to repair a fort on behalf of the Iberian king Mithridates, its description of that king as a *philocaesaroi* and *philoromaoi*, the timing of that inscription's composition with the incursions into Parthia by the Alani,

Coin of Vologases I.
Wikipedia.org

and its location by where the Alani marched into Parthia, are most revealing.[353] In light of this inscription the idea of a 'Grand Strategy' established merely defend the empire's eastern provinces is untenable. But it is still tempting to hold onto it. Often in our postcolonial age we think in terms of national borders within which are the extents of its ruler's power. But when approaching the Roman Empire we must discard modern conceptualizations and see the Flavians afresh. The Romans were extremely opportunistic, conquered whatever they

126

could whenever they could, and in general their motives for war rarely included reaching a defensible boundary.[354]

Thus the view that the Flavians simply defended their frontiers is a myth.[355] We may also point out the phenomenon that was Vespasian's bolstering of Roman legions in the eastern provinces, especially in Cappadocia and Syria-Commagene. Along the Euphrates River boundary of Cappadocia, at both Satala and Melitene, were placed the XVI Flavia Firma and the XII Fulminata respectively[356] and another two military bases were established at Samosata and Zeugma in Syria-Commagene. In addition to these deployments is also the fact that Roman military bases were never intended to form a purely defensible military front, but functioned rather to provide bases for invasion.[357] They were also intended as a means of securing local supplies of water and commercial enterprise, thus providing important bases of operation should the need for invasion eventuate.[358] Thus Trajan himself would in time make full use of these military bases in Cappadocia and Commagene to launch his own invasion of Armenia. Granted, after the Jewish War there was no longer any need for Roman forces to be anywhere else in the eastern provinces,[359] but the moving of the legions of the eastern provinces to Cappadocia-Commagene in itself, and indeed why they were still located in the East at all, does seem to suggest that Vespasian maintained imperialist designs for beyond the Euphrates River.

Of course, whatever side one wishes to choose, historical objectivity is key,[360] and it must be remembered that in either case the transformation of Cappadocia and Commagene into military provinces probably served both defensive and offensive purposes.[361] After all, there was the need to defend the empire around the Black Sea against the 'barbarians' from the north, including the Alani, as well as the east against the 'barbarians' of Parthia or Armenia. Indeed, that was Suetonius' take on Vespasian's armament of Cappadocia and the east in general.[362] Thus with the IV Scythia stationed at Zeugma, and the XII Fulminata moved to Melitene in Cappadocia, and the XVI Flavia and other legionary detachments at Satala, Vespasian was clearly shifting the Roman military effort to the north and east.[363] But, the Alani would turn out to be favourable to Rome and Vologases was intent upon keeping the peace. One wonders therefore, whether the ostensible claims for defensive strategy were a calculated front as the military bases along the Euphrates gave the Romans the initiative for campaigning either to the north or to the east despite all the talk of peace.[364]

These massive troop movements under Vespasian were facilitated by extensive road network built throughout Syria under Traianus' supervision as governor.[365] According to Syme these road building projects were closely monitored by Traianus acting as the principal agent of the emperor himself.[366] Consequently Vespasian envisioned troop movement in the eastern provinces to be a lasting legacy. He placed much trust in Traianus. In March 1973 a milestone was discovered near the Judaean town of Afula that was left by Traianus. It shows that he was a staunch and trusted supporter of Vespasian. It reads:

"Imp(erator)/Caesar [Ve]spa/sianus
Aug(ustus) M(arco) [Ul]/pio Tr[ai]an[o]
Leg(ato)/ leg(ionis) X Fret(ensis)/XXXIV"[367]

Given that this inscription includes none of the honors voted to Vespasian by the Roman Senate, it must have been erected by Traianus beforehand. Josephus too had recorded that he had supported Vespasian's bid for the principate right from its outset.[368] Thus, Traianus was a reliable representative for Vespasian's policy from very early on. As a reward Traianus was given the consulship in 70AD, and with that, a place in the senatorial patriciate in 73AD. As with the awarding of the *triumphalia ornamenta*, Vespasian was keen to promote those like Traianus who remained loyal to Vespasian's cause during the early years of his principate.

Of course, others have seen Vespasian's policy in the east differently. Some have argued that Traianus was sent to Syria in 73/74 merely to oversee the mass urbanization of the province for economic advantage. There, it is hypothesized, Vespasian was providing essential infrastructure for the sake of local entrepreneurs like those in Palmyra to use voluntarily and exploit for their vocations, livelihoods and wealth. It was this some hold that which was Vespasian's true 'Grand

Strategy'.[369] The argument has some merit. In the early 1st century AD, Strabo noted that security around the Euphrates was low, and that bandits often attacked passing merchant caravans passing by.[370] By militarising the Euphrates and developing the whole region with roads as Vespasian did, the emperor was ensuring safe passage for caravans trading throughout Anatolia and Syria and along the Euphrates. Given that Syria was one of the most lucrative centers of commerce in the whole Roman Empire,[371] with its tax posts reaped a handsome 25 percent duty on all foreign goods passing through,[372] such a theory certainly seems attractive. But although it is still debated whether the high duty on goods from the East reflects demand on the one hand,[373] or Rome's acute desire for funds after the ravages of civil war on the other, the answer probably lies with both sides. That is because the Euphrates River was never a true frontier, but was rather a hub of maritime trade linking Mesopotamia with Armenia to the north, Syria and Anatolia to the west and the Persian Gulf to the south. Thus by linking Syria with the Euphrates Traianus was opening up this lucrative trade to Syrians and Anatolians eager to make a profit from it, and taking necessary steps to reestablish Rome's economy and market demand as only Rome deserved as best he knew how to under Vespasian's orders.

It must be remembered, however, that Vespasian's motives in the eastern provinces were not exclusively economic. Other evidence shows that Vespasian, a shrewd and intelligent emperor, had any number reasons for his deployments to the east: and one was clearly being to prepare it for future campaigns in the region. As is almost proverbial, roads were an important means of operation of troop movement in the eastern provinces. Hence, in 66AD Cestius Gallus used the Antioch to Ptolemais road built eleven years earlier to move troops against Judaea, while Vespasian himself saw the need for good road-building when he used that same road for precisely the same purpose one year later.[374] Furthermore, Trajan used the roads built under Vespasian for his invasion into Armenia. Of course, Trajan may have simply made best use of the conditions presented to him at the time, but those conditions, established under Vespasian, had certainly been intended to prepare for military campaigns like Trajan's own. That Vespasian's road network was used to transport Trajan's massive army with success at all suggests that it was no ordinary road network – it was certainly designed for multiple purposes, but one of them was surely the one that Trajan used it for.

Meanwhile, Vologases was also expanding Parthia's imperialist claims. He had already successfully installed his brother Tiridates on the Armenian throne during Nero's reign despite Corbulo's best efforts to stop him, and was consolidating Parthia's position throughout other areas of his empire too. By 73AD Parthian armies had penetrated west of the southern region of the Euphrates River, and recovered Babylonia and Spasinou Charax for Parthia which had been lost to them in the early first century. The new city of Vologasias near Seleucia and Ctesiphon was also built, and its importance to Vologases' reign was immense. At the outset of his reign, Vologases was faced with a contest for the Parthian throne by Vardanes II who issued his own coinage throughout 56-58AD.[375] Notably, from that point Vologases began featuring Aramaic as well as Greek on his coinage and began issuing coins markedly more Parthian in style, and continued this practice until he died in 79AD.[376] This imagery tells us that Vologases had secured the support of his empire's Iranian power-base and decided it was useful for stable government in the long-term.[377] Also, it is no coincidence that Vologasias, which served as the new Parthian capital to rival Seleucia, was built during this time, and nor is it an accident that when Vologases was faced by a challenge for the throne from Pacorus II, the usurper was forced to revert to the use of Greek on his coinage minted at Seleucia.[378] These and the other public works carried out under Vologases across Mesopotamia, including the rebuilding of Ziggurats at Enlil and Nippur, show an unmistakable policy on the Parthian king's part to extend his and Parthian claims throughout and beyond his empire.[379] Therefore, as both Romans and Parthians stimulated trade and securing the trade with capital and infrastructure, they were also extending their imperialist aspirations with manpower.

Such imperialist aspiration is certainly more than conjecture. According to Josephus, in 73/74AD reports were made by Titus' uncle, Caesennius Paetus, who had preceded Traianus as governor of Syria, that Antiochus king of Commagene was planning to defect with his kingdom to the Parthians. Vespasian was furius and Paetus soon appeared in Commagene at the head of an army. Although Josephus did not place any trust in Paetus' report, and he personally believed that Paetus' report was made to spite Antiochus, Josephus did state, nonetheless, that upon Paetus' appearance in Commagene, Antiochus' sons fled to Vologases' court where they were welcomed and kept with royal honours.[380]

This was no spontaneous crisis. It is precisely the response by the King of kings we should expect if his dealings with Commagene were longstanding and conducive to defection generally. It is a clear sign that beneath the amicable Roman and Parthian exterior there lurked mistrust and underhand maneuvers. Notwithstanding diplomatic niceties to the sons, if Vologases had retained Antiochus' sons that could have destroyed Roman and Parthian relations altogether: Caracalla was later to use the Parthian retainment of certain persons as pretext for war.[381] As for Josephus as a source for the crisis, it is noteworthy that his main audience was primarily Greek-speaking Roman and that he therefore had every reason to maintain Vespasian's peaceful venire when he wrote the Jewish War in the mid-70s.[382] It is also worth pointing out that the original purpose of the *Jewish War* was to warn Parthia's Jews of Roman encroachment. Initially written in Aramaic by Josephus before he translated it into Greek, the *Jewish Wat* was composed for a Parthian-Jewish audience. The reason was clear: after narrating in full the Jews' defeat at the hands of Rome, Josephus leaves the reader hanging with Roman encroachments in Commagene and elsewhere in the East – Josephus believed that Parthia was Rome's next victim and wanted to warn it ahead of time. Therefore, it is only natural to suspect, and perhaps rightfully so too, that as Josephus saw it beneath Vespasian's aloofness in the whole of the affair existed a more aggressive tone in the mind of the emperor.

Antiochus himself was captured by Paetus and sent in fetters to the emperor who kept him as a hostage in confinement in Sparta. Previous chapters tell us that the use of hostages had always been an important part of Roman diplomacy. They served two main purposes. The first was to keep Rome's glory maintained and other nations in check - for defying Rome's wishes could mean the death of that hostage. Thus, Augustus boasted that the Parthian king Phraates' entrustment of his sons to him served the interests of the Roman people,[383] and Velleius Paterculus later saw the giving over of the Parthian king's sons to Germanicus was an indication of the greatness of Tiberius and Roman power.[384] The second purpose of hostage-taking was that while hostages were within Rome they could become Romanised and thus when they returned to their country of origin they could maintain Rome's interests there.[385] However, that was never a solid guarantee that unfolding events would unfold as any emperor desired. Parthian kings sent their children to Rome did so to maintain their own position by removing them from power in the Parthian court, and they also knew that once any hostage returned to their own countries they were often rejected by their countrymen who saw them as foreigners and outsiders.[386] Therefore, with both Rome and Parthia possessing hostages from Commagene, the stage was set for a complete breakdown in relations.

But war was averted. An inscription found at Baalbek in Syria indicates that the Romans eventually secured the handover of Antiochus' sons. It reads:

> "To Gaius Velius Rufus son of Salvius... He was sent into Parthia and brought back to the Emperor Vespasian Epiphanes and Callinias, the sons of king Antiochus [of Commagene], together with a large number of tribute-paying persons."[387]

That it was a peaceful and staged handover as opposed to a covert operation is demonstrated by the fact that peace was once again quickly reestablished. But such behind-the-scene goings-on underpin the fact that relations between the two empires were not as amicable as once maintained. In fact, there was a freezing in relations. It is no coincidence that, according to Cassius Dio, around this time Vologases began dropping Vespasian's titles in private correspondence, addressing his letters 'Arsaces, King of kings, to Flavius Vespasian, Greetings'.[388] Such freezing is also reflected in the three so-called 'False Neros', the first of which appeared in 69AD, the second later in Vespasian's principate, and the third during Domitian's. These Neros were Parthia's reply to the nominees which Rome had tried to force upon the Parthian imperial throne in order to destabilise the Roman regime.[389] But they proved just as useless: the false Neros were in every case recognized as being false. However, it is made clear by these Neros that Parthia was prepared to repeatedly destabilize Roman politics in an aggressive, albeit subtle, manner.

In time relations were bound to falter completely, and from what we know from Pliny the Younger, Traianus soon won *ornamenta triumphalia* for a military victory over the Parthians. Traianus had replaced Paetus as governor of Syria and his victory was no doubt the result of cooling relations stretching further back into Paetus' own tenure. That breakdown may even have been the direct result, if not a progression, of the events in Commagene which took place under Paetus. But it is important that we know exactly what we are describing in regard to Traianus' *ornamenta triumphalia*. It is most likely the case that it was won in concert with the Alani invasion of Parthia in c.73AD. According to Josephus, the Alani, in concert with the Hyrcani, overran the Parthian territories of Armenia and Media several years after Rome's victory in Judaea.[390] The existence of the inscription left by Roman soldiers at Harmozica, precisely where the Alani entered the Parthian Empire at the same time cannot be ignored. The reference in that inscription that Mithridates was a 'friend of Caesar' and a 'friend of Rome' tells us that the king was serving Rome's imperial interests in his kingdom, because such terms of friendship were adopted by Rome's allies to advertise Rome's over-riding power over themselves. The timing of the Alani invasion and the timing of the inscription which was found near where the invasion progressed, therefore, cannot have been mere coincidence. The Roman troops had been acting on Traianus' orders in concert with Mithridates and the Alani, and their mutual attacks and victories over Parthia is no doubt what earnt Traianus his *ornamenta*. It was an astute move on the emperor's part to honour Traianus in this way. Nero had been overthrown partly because of his unappreciative treatment of his generals, in particular Corbulo. Vespasian would not make that same mistake. Instead, by making a display in honouring his general, Vespasian was sending out a clear message to his armies and their commanders that he did appreciate their efforts and that they would be rewarded for such. It was a message that his generals and their men heeded well.

However, for all of Vespasian's bravado and Josephus' dire warnings of a coming war Vespasian could not escape the awkward truth that he simply could not afford a war with Parthia. Suetonius states that upon securing the imperial throne, Vespasian found that the imperial treasury was in arrears by 40 billion sesterces.[391] Although that figure has been amended by modern historians to 4 billion sesterces, it was still a huge debt to incur. Rome received 800 million sesterces into its treasury annually, so by taking into account Roman expenses a small surplus could only be attained after perhaps five years.[392] During Traianus' governorship therefore, Rome's treasury was still empty. But at the same time Parthia's own economy was expanding under the leadership of Vologases, who had united the empire, and large-scale trade was booming throughout all of Parthia. (See Chapter Seven) Therefore, a full-scale war against Parthia at this time was simply unaffordable for Rome, and without the necessary funds such a war would have been doomed to fail, especially against so rich an opponent as Parthia, and Vespasian knew it. Vast numbers of legionnaires were required not just for fighting but also for sieges, and garrison duty, and the bleak terrain of the Parthian Empire meant that any potential for foraging was virtually non-existent.[393] So after the wastefulness of Nero and the civil wars of 69AD Vespasian could not afford any major war.

Nor could he afford any threat to his own position that such a war might throw up around the other areas of his empire. He had wrestled the empire from Nero: what was stopping another taking it from him? But Vespasian could afford the costless victories of the Alani and make valuable political capital from Traianus' service with them, and by doing so made himself and his armies look strong to Rome's neighbours, as well as to any other Roman general who might happen to harbour their own aspirations for the imperial throne. However Vespasian could afford to play Parthia's other neighbours off against it, and his collaboration with the Alani was in keeping with Rome's alliances with the Iberians and the like in the past. Such power-play would serve as a precursor to similar policies under later emperors: Domitian and Hadrian were later to cement ties of friendship with the Alani, the Hyrcanians, and other neighbors of Parthia to contain it.[394] Vespasian had clearly learnt well from his predecessors Augustus and Tiberius.[395] Their legacy would be passed on to others as well.

Perhaps the most glaring objection to the above reconstruction is Dio's unavoidable statement that Vespasian once said he never desired to interfere in other's affairs.[396] But if in fact Vespasian did actually make such a comment it was certainly not intended to be a true reflection of his whole eastern policy at all times. Furthermore, the importance Dio placed in it originated with Dio himself. By reporting Vespasian's comment, Dio was in fact drawing comparison with the emperor of his own day, Septimius Severus, who he believed was juxtaposed as unwise. Dio expressed his deep dissatisfaction with Severus' principate precisely because, unlike Vespasian as Dio would have us believe, Severus did interfere in others' affairs in the east.[397] In short, Dio projected his own judgment on Severus' eastern policy, which he believed to have been a source of constant wars and great expense,[398] onto Vespasian. In doing so he portrayed the latter favourably compared to Severus, and his Severan audience would no doubt have recognized that. In fact, Dio's grievance against Severus was held by many of his peers[399] on the following grounds: firstly, there was Severus' handling of the Senate. From the outset of his reign Severus openly praised the cruelty of Marius, Sulla and Augustus in their harsh dealings with senators, and that shocked the fearful and outraged Roman Senate of which Dio was one.[400] Secondly, unlike other Roman historians, Dio generally frowned upon imperialist expansion,[401] and as a result, the absence of foreign war during Vespasian's principate served his thematic purposes. Thus, Dio's comment must be recognized as not being entirely faithful to the original context Vespasian's words were spoken in, and that means the overall case for warm relations existing between Vespasian and Vologases is overstated. Dio's narrative was commentary for his own Severan audience, not a Flavian one. Vespasian was the opposite to Severus and was thus a model emperor. Or so Dio would have had his audience believe.

Domitian

After the deaths of Vespasian in 79 and Titus in 81 Domitian in turn became emperor. At heart Domitian was a general and tactician. But although the view that Vespasian's policy was so that an invasion of Mesopotamia would be left to Domitian himself[402] is unsubstantiated, at least for the early stages of his principate, Domitian's eastern policy differed little from his father's.[403] Through alliances with Parthia's neighbors the Iberians, Hyrcanians and Albanians, together with roadbuilding and increased militarization throughout Cappadocia, Domitian kept Parthian imperialist aspirations in check.[404] But he did not have to try too hard. After the death of Vologases I in 79AD the Parthian Empire reverted once again to civil conflict. The contenders for the throne, Pacorus II and Artabanus IV, issued their own separate coinage until 83AD when it appears Pacorus finally prevailed. It is only his coinage that was minted from that point on.[405]

It is often argued that this was the extent of Domitian's plans for the East. Some look upon his extensive wars around the northwestern frontiers of the empire as a sign that he had forgotten all about the east once he became emperor. Others discard the possibility that he had any designs on Parthia on the grounds that the only Roman literary evidence for a possible war with Parthia is the sycophantic poetry of Statius designed more to enhance Domitian's self-image than an accurate historical source.[406] But that ignores all evidence to the contrary. For one thing Statius' *Silvae* is indeed replete with references to future conquests for Domitian over the East,[407] and since Domitian was harsh on poets during his principate,[408] Statius' task to faithfully represent the emperor's firm policy was thus all the more present. Although it is often Statius' literary style and poetic allusion that is often remarked on and the comment is often made that in such conquering imagery over the East the poet was simply evoking the style of Virgil or Homer,[409] the fact remains that they are still there and archaeology indicates that Statius' poetry holds some truth in this matter. An inscription left by Roman soldiers during Domitian's time as emperor on the Apsheronsky peninsula on the Caspian coast near Baku, indicates that he definitely had designs on Armenia and Parthia. The inscription reads:

"Imp(eratore) Domitiano Caesare Aug(usto) Germanic(o) L. Ilius Maximus (centurion) leg(ionis) XII Ful(minatae)".[410]

It is in fact well-known that Domitian had for a long time held dreams of an Eastern campaign – during Vespasian's principate he had even tried to secure an auxiliary force to help the Parthians against the Alani. He even began issuing coins during his father's reign depicting the surrender of the lost standards of Crassus that seem to canvas himself as a potential Tiberius of sorts to be used at the Augustus-like emperor in Vespasian.[411] Vespasian, Suetonius states, flatly refused.[412] Obviously, Vespasian had already decided to use the Alani against Parthia.

The detachment from the XII Fulminatae that Domitian had sent ahead to the Caspian coast probably had orders to gather sorely needed intelligence for a future campaign there as Nero had done only a few decades earlier in preparation for his Parthian war – a war that never eventuated.[413] However, Domitian never got to campaign in the East, and therefore we will never know the full extent of Domitian's ultimate plans were for the East, because Domitian was assassinated in 96AD, and thus the Flavian dynasty came to an abrupt end. It murder happened as the result of a plot hatched by his chamberlain named Parthenius.[414] As for the Parthians from whom he got his namesake, their relief over the postponement of war would soon turn into uncertainty: they too had lost their own ruler themselves, as the minting of Pacorus' coins ending that same year tells us. Thus it would be left to the successors of Pacorus and Domitian to lead the two empires into both their futures and into history. After the death of the elderly Nerva, Trajan succeeded to the principate, and it would be he who would shake both the Roman and Parthian Empires like never before.

Summing Up

As can be seen by the above discussion, Roman policy could, and often did, alter from emperor to emperor. Titus was happy to restore the status quo, while Vespasian repeatedly sought to undermine Parthian power. However he could only do so largely by indirect means as his purse was far from full after the civil war of 69AD. Domitian, by contrast, did have the funds, and he did lay plans to invade Parthian territory as Nero had also hoped to do, but his hopes were dashed upon his premature death. Thus, there was no grand strategy to speak of, only the imperial agendas of each individual ruler, and their abilities to wage war. Of course, that does not mean there were no similarities between the Flavian emperors' methods. All three did try to undermine the growth of Parthian power in the Near East. Through the use of Parthia's neighbours, Vespasian and Domitian successfully checked Parthian power and imperial expansion. However, such methods simply made use of the conditions that each emperor was faced with. Domitian may have copied his father in this respect, but there was no established strategy understood and handed on from emperor to emperor, only the examples of successes left behind by the rulers of the past worth attempting to replicate. But such replications were not put into practice by every emperor. Titus did not invite Parthia's neighbours to attack Parthia. Rather, he was content to remain at peace with it and consistently welcomed its gestures of goodwill as was the case at Zeugma.

But of course, such facts are largely reconstructed facts, and given the gaps in our knowledge of the Flavian dynasty it is sometimes difficult to understand them. However, as has been shown here, with a return to the ancient evidence such reconstruction is nonetheless still possible. But in doing so one must appreciate the nature of each piece of evidence, from inscriptions to the Flavian writings available to us today like Josephus' histories and Statius' poetry, to the remarks made by other historians of the past such as Suetonius and of course Cassius Dio. Needless to say there will be discoveries in the future which might alter our picture of Flavian relations with Parthia, like the discovery of new inscriptions, but any new discovery needs to be set within the overall historical context. Likewise, any modern theory on the Flavian's eastern policy must take into account all of the available evidence on the subject. Sweeping generalizations can ignore anomalies that discredit them. That should be kept in mind when we turn to Trajan and the reasons for, and conduct of, his Parthian War.

CHAPTER EIGHT

TRAJAN'S PARTHIAN WAR

Searching for Trajan's Motives

THE NATURE OF Trajan's Parthian war is debated among modern scholars to this day. That is because the ancient evidence at hand is far from complete, and some of it, particularly the relevant written records of the fourth century, are sometimes grossly misleading. But the subject can be recaptured from the mists of time, I believe, if we look at all the evidence at hand and try and understand what it is all pointing to. By tracing this evidence it will become clear that although there had been extensive planning for a Parthian war years before one was launched, it was not decided by Trajan to apply it until he had conquered Armenia. I will also show that economic motivation underpinned the emperor's eventual decision for war.

According to our main and most reliable sources, Dio and Fronto, Trajan invaded Parthia simply for the sake of attaining more military glory,[415] and that is a view which still carries much weight today. Few imagine that whatever Trajan's actual motivations were, concern for the stability of the Roman Empire was certainly not one of them.[416] But while most historians agree that Trajan had self-serving plans in mind, they often disagree as to what form those plans took. Some imagine that Trajan's real reason for war was a wish to recapture the vigour of his youth,[417] while others hold that Trajan had hoped to re-enact Alexander's conquest of Iran for decades.[418] Most, however, believe that Trajan's war had been planned for years, stemming from his consistent policy to conquer wherever possible. So their argument goes, by the time of Trajan began his Parthian war he had conquered Dacia and annexed Arabia, and now, being swept up by his endless desire for glory he had no option but to embark on yet another foreign campaign.[419]

However, I believe that Trajan, although he had laid out tentative plans to invade Parthia while he planned the last stages of his Armenian invasion, he only finally decided upon invading Parthian territory once he had conquered Armenia.[420] Now, some might disagree, but today many historians think that Trajan's campaigns in Dacia and Mesopotamia stemmed from more immediate concerns rather than any warmongering premeditation on the emperor's part,[421] and many are also of the opinion that for the immediate sake of securing Rome's interests in Armenia, which Trajan had made into a province, the emperor actually had no option but to invade Parthia.[422] Now, I believe these lines of thinking perhaps a little naive, but their basic points must be borne in mind, because as we have seen, the susceptibility of Armenia to Parthia had been an obvious reality in Rome for decades by the time Trajan became emperor. But it is also true that by then the Romans knew that Parthia as a great military power,[423] and Trajan, who exploited intelligence gathering himself,[424] must have had prior knowledge of the fighting conditions in Parthia for quite some time. Put simply, Trajan knew what he was up against in Parthia, and war with it could never have been the result of a whim or mere follow-up after conquering Armenia. However, that does not necessarily mean that Trajan had been planning his war with Parthia for a very long time. My view is that given Trajan invaded Parthia from Armenia, he must have laid plans to do so at about the time he was laying out his plans for the last stages of his Armenian war.

But as regards those popular theories that Trajan had been planning a Parthian war for decades, they can all be accounted for. Some have noticed Pliny the Younger's atypical appointment by Trajan as procurator of Bithynia in 110AD and believe that that must have been made to facilitate troop movement to the east as part of a long process of an imperial shift towards the north-east leading to the foundation of Constantinople as capital of the eastern empire.[425] It is an old argument indeed[426] but as others have observed,[427] there is no evidence in Pliny's many letters written before, during, or after his procuratorship, that indicates any of the kind of troop movement some have read into them. In fact Pliny's letters tell us that his appointment to Bithynia was only for atypical accountancy and policing purposes: cities' accounts and local disturbances and inefficiencies were his prime concerns.[428] In any event, neither Trajan nor Pliny could have foreseen the rise of Sasanid Persia in the third century AD which was in itself the most important reason for increasing Roman attention in the east from that point on, and nor could they foresee the foundation of Constantinople as an imperial capital.

Some have also pointed to the militarization of Cappadocia-Commagene under Trajan's father in the 70s and surmise that Trajan, whilst serving as legate under his father there, could not escape being inspired to win glory in the East. But it must be pointed out that while Trajan did indeed use these provinces as staging points for his invasion of Armenia; it was not from there that he launched his invasion of Parthia. He launched it from Armenia. This tells us that the militarization of these provinces under Trajan's father during the Flavian period was indeed intended for a future war, but one in Armenia, not Parthia.

But some historians have traced Trajan's desire for a Parthian War even further back than that. In 100AD, only two years after Trajan became emperor, the rhetorician Dio Chrysostom began publicly comparing Trajan with Alexander the Great, who conquered Parthia's forerunners, the Persians. Therefore they believe this as a sign that Trajan was planning to emulate his conquests as early as then.[429] This of all the arguments for a longstanding plan for a Parthian war has the most going for it: Cassius Dio believed strongly that Trajan admired his hero Alexander the Great,[430] and indeed his account of Trajan's campaign in the East does read a bit like a sightseeing tour, with Trajan visiting Gaugamela, the site of Alexander's most famous victory and burning incense to the spirit of Alexander at Babylon. But that said, many Romans liked to be compared with Alexander, like Pompey, who adopted the cognomen 'The Great'. However, Pompey himself never intended to conquer all of Alexander's empire. In fact his total conquests were only a fraction of that Macedonian king's.

At the core of the whole issue is whether or not Trajan had a longstanding dream to conquer the Parthian Empire. Of course Trajan admired Alexander: that much was made clear by the princeps himself when setting eyes upon a ship sailing for India on the Persian Gulf. However, Trajan never seriously considered replicating all of Alexander's achievements. He had made that clear himself, for when he arrived by the Persian Gulf and saw that ship sailing away for India, he admitted to all those present that he was totally incapable due to his age, of equaling Alexander. He said: "I should certainly have crossed over to the Indi, too, *if I were still young*".[431] In this one remark Trajan openly differentiated himself from Alexander.

Of course, that is not to say that Trajan had not planned a Parthian war for some time. In fact I believe he had. But it is just that the evidence often cited as support for this case so often falls back upon itself. Take the most widely accepted case for a longstanding Trajanic dream of a Parthian war.[432] It is discounted by the very nature of exactly the same evidence it is claimed that support it. The main points of the case are five in number: 1) Hadrian's appointment to a command in the east in 112, 2) the numismatic evidence from 111/12-13 bearing the words FORT[una] RED[ux] (Fortune who guides back), 3) coins in 111 commemorating the deification of M. Ulpius Traianus, 4) the restoration of the Via Egnatia in 112, and finally 5) the annexation of Arabia. On the first count,[433] that Hadrian's appointment must have been made in order to mobilize the eastern provinces for a Parthian War, evidence is simply missing. That is because there was actually a break between Hadrian's first legateship in 112 and his later governorship of Syria in 117,[434] and the chronology in Dio makes it clear that Hadrian's later command began only in the final stages of Trajan's life after the Parthian war had already run its course.[435] Although Hadrian was indeed sent by Trajan to Athens in the interval years between his two commands in anticipation of a war in the East, there is nothing to suggest where, besides Armenia, that theatre of war could have actually been.

The second and third points about the numismatic evidence, which have been proposed as evidence for a very long time,[436] are also shaky.

For the coins seeking Fortuna to return Trajan safely from abroad anticipated Trajan's return from his Armenian campaign, which they immediately predate. Also, the coins commemorating Trajan's biological father's deification have to be seen in the light of Trajan's general approach to the memory of his father. About that same time Trajan formed two new legions, the II Traiana and the XXX Ulpia *Victrix*.[437] These two new legions, named in honour of his father, were actually created for service in Dacia and Arabia.[438] So, Trajan's commemoration of the memory of his father took various forms and never had anything to do with a Parthian war.

Even the restoration of the Via Egnatia and the annexation of Arabia can be explained. Trajan restored many roads throughout the empire including the Via Traiana from Beneventum to Brundisium, and the Via Egnatia extended east so far as Byzantium. Furthermore, milestones along it indicate that the coins which commemorated the restoration of the road in 112 were struck three to four years after the road was actually restored, well before the Parthian war.[439] In fact the Via Egnatia was restored to serve Roman movements to and around Dacia, which was still only newly added to the empire. There is also no evidence that the annexation of Arabia was a precursor to war with Parthia. If it was, the later movement of troops would certainly have been different: during the Parthian War, the II Traiana and the XXX Ulpia Victrix were both engaged in Mesopotamia[440] thereby depleting Arabia of Roman garrisons. If keeping Arabia in check during a war with Parthia was indeed the point, then troop movements away from Arabia had seriously undermined it.

More could be said on this whole matter. For instance, we could look deeper into the famous meeting that Trajan had with a Parthian envoy in Athens while on his way to the East. According to Dio the envoy lobbied Trajan there for the renewal of alliance. Trajan's reply is revealing: he said that friendship is determined by deeds and that "when he [Trajan] should reach Syria he would do all that was proper."[441] Although Dio considered such words in effect a declaration of war, they appear to have been taken out of their original context. Despite his shrouded usage of words, Trajan made clear enough that by 'proper' arrangement peace could still be affirmed. What that 'proper' result was Dio's fragmentary narrative does not make clear, but Trajan was clearly hinting that a Parthian war was only one option among several at that early stage.

Trajan's hesitation resulted from two main concerns. Firstly, as his contemporary Plutarch took for granted, the Parthians were far more adept at warfare than the Armenians.[442] A hasty invasion was therefore unwise. Secondly, Trajan was increasingly aware of his old age and failing health. As we have seen, when he came to the Persian Gulf he admitted that age was a hindrance to future conquest. Some have argued that was the first time Trajan had ever given this concern any due recognition,[443] but it is actually traceable further back: hence his reply to the Parthian envoy in Athens well beforehand which in itself shows a keen awareness that future use of the military was only one option among others being considered by Trajan. It was an admission that the extent of his leadership was now limited in his old age. In any case, Trajan's acceptance of triumphs and the title *Parthicus* prior to the Gulf excursion[444] is certain proof that in this the princeps knew he had at last reached his limits.

Perhaps the most sensible scenario presented by historians is that after his resounding success in Armenia and upon observing the civil chaos that was engulfing Parthia at that time, Trajan only then made his final decision to put his tentative plans into action and embark on a Parthian war.[445] Trajan clearly planned and executed an invasion of Armenia – of that there is no doubt. But again, given that he invaded Parthia from Armenia itself, this points to the inevitable conclusion that he had indeed made tentative plans to do so while marking out his final plans for Armenia. But it was only after he was buoyed with his success in Armenia that Trajan came to his final decision to invade Parthia's western regions. He knew that Parthia's armies were preoccupied waging civil war in its empire's eastern realms.[446] There Osroes and Vologases III were waging a bitter civil war against each other. Trajan certainly knew about it, because that civil war did from time to time spill over to the west: between 109 and 129AD the mint at Seleucia produced coinage for both contenders in turn one after the other.[447] With that knowledge at hand, Trajan prepared to make his move, but given that the Parthian armies were active in the east, he would make that move only upon the Parthian Empire's west.

On the basis of this literary evidence alone, it is clear that Trajan, who knew that the Parthians would prove themselves to be a very different kind of enemy than the Armenians, was quick to take advantage of their moment of weakness and stake his claim to Mesopotamia, and in doing so would also serve to secure Armenia. He had observed the civil unrest there and so, as he drew up his plans to take over Armenia, he also made contingency plans to attack Parthia if that unrest was to continue and present an opportunity for him to intervene there. It was a bold move, but Trajan was willing to take his chances. But there is more to the story because literary sources are not our only evidence. Archaeological evidence is copious, and adds to our knowledge in interesting ways, and shows us that in Trajan's Parthian War lied not just strategic concerns, but also a profound monetary-driven motive in Trajan's own mind.

Trajan and Trans-Euphrates Trade

Throughout the Julio-Claudian and Flavian periods, both the Parthians and Romans had an important stake in the trade that flourished between Syria and the Persian Gulf and beyond.[448] Much of the taxed profits of wealthier provinces in the East like Syria were spent by Rome on its huge standing Roman army as well as to boost agricultural production within the less wealthy provinces in the western Empire like Britain.[449] But it was the rich who mainly benefited: the high duty of 25% placed on all eastern goods must have served as a financial discouragement for many prospective lower-class buyers.[450] However, that there was sufficient profit left within local treasuries in Syria to build extensively is demonstrative of expansion in both the monetization of the province, and the purchasing power of the richer elites throughout it.[451] As for the high duty on goods from the East passing through Syria, that also increased production and commerce among its inhabitants as they had to then accrue higher takings to account for any taxable loss.[452]

The main overland trade route that saw the most thoroughfare between East and West was the Silk Route.[453] According to Isidore of Charax, the route crossed from China in the east across the steppes to

Bactria, from where it forked south to the Indus River, and west through Parthia, along the Euphrates and finally into Syria,[454] from where eastern goods were traded around Roman markets. Along with his testimony, the Chinese source the *Hou Hanshu*, also provides further information about the route. The *Hou Hanshu* was a collection of documents compiled in the fifth century AD, drawing upon a multiplicity of earlier sources, and treated various historical topics going back to the Han dynasty in the first to third centuries.[455] The section of the *Hou Hanshu* which concerns us here is the chapter 'Records About the Western Regions', or the *Xiyuzhuan*.[456] It states that the main purpose of the stations, besides sustenance, was to protect travelers from natural hazards including packs of wild animals and geographical obstacles.[457] Given there was in this comment no mention made of any threat from bandits, the trade that passed through trading stations of the Parthian Empire leg of the Silk Route was mainly healthy and secure.[458]

Parthian traders carried on extensive contact with Roman traders as well as with the Chinese, particularly north along the Euphrates from the Persian Gulf. Pliny the Elder stated that various Persian goods such as steel, leather, rhubarb (which was used in antiquity for medicinal purposes), and the peach, were popular in Roman markets.[459] Other foodstuffs like the pistachio nut and the condiment asafetida were introduced into the Roman Empire via the trans-Euphrates artery.[460] Parthian food even became popular in Rome: the Roman cookery book of Apicius even featured both lamb and chicken "in the Parthian manner".[461]

But in Trajan's time it was the Parthians who controlled trade from the Gulf to Roman markets and reaped the most handsome profits from it. According to the ancient Chinese source the *Hanshu*, a first century AD Chinese history not to be confused with the later *Hou Hanshu*, the Parthians utilized the Euphrates for trade to the exclusion of all others. In fact it was not until 166AD that the Romans opened trade with China directly:

> "Their [the Romans] kings always desired to send embassies to China, but the An-his [the Parthians] wished to carry on trade with them in Chinese silks, and it is for this reason that they were cut off from communication This lasted till the ninth

year of the Yen-his period during the Emperor Huan-ti's reign [=166AD]."[462]

Although some have entertained that the Parthians alone used the Silk Route throughout Parthian lands, and that they actually stopped most of the Silk Route goods from crossing the Euphrates and heading to Rome out of "active rivalry", and indeed even that the Silk Route's later passing out from Western literature is certain proof of this,[463] such claims have been proved illusory. The *Han* annals only state that Parthia cut *communication* alone off between China and Rome, and that the Parthians rather acted as middlemen to reap retail profits. The Parthians, who were only too keenly aware of their own monetary interests, knew that if they destroyed the east-west trade they would in turn destroy the vast revenues they accrued from it. Rather, they simply kept their two greatest foreign markets firmly apart, and thus avoided any embarrassing comparison of prices, meaning they could continue to reap their higher profits.[464] Hence, the Chinese might indeed have known about Parthia and Rome, but they had no real understanding of the regions west of Parthia itself.[465] That indicates they did not utilise the leg of the Silk Route between Parthia and Syria and that the Parthian policy to debar foreigners from using the overland Route really was an effective one. As for the passing of the Silk Route out of western literature, the fact that there is a paucity of Roman pottery around the Persian Gulf in late antiquity is due to the overall decrease in trade because of increasing warfare between Rome and Sassanid Persia.[466] In short, it was this later political climate that resulted in the decline in Roman knowledge of the markets of the East.

However it is necessary to clarify who these 'Parthians' were. The evidence suggests that it was not just the pure Parthians alone (i.e. the Parni from Parthia itself) who conducted trade, but their subjects as well. Local knowledge was crucial to the success of trade and each region's population clearly supported and facilitated the trade that ran through it. Hence even during times of civil unrest trade was still conducted by local kingdoms,[467] after all they had a stake in the trade too. Once the Parthian kingdoms became familiar with surplus from trade, taking part in trading ventures became all the more appealing. In the case of Hatra, a Parthian city founded to the east of the northern arm of the Euphrates around 50AD, its population benefited heavily from trade: imported luxury goods from Palmyra and sculptures have been found by archaeologists working there.[468] Archaeologists have found at Zeugma too, also by the Euphrates, many luxurious houses built there during the first century AD.[469]

But just as goods were traded along the Euphrates, so too were ideas. The 5,000 inhabitants of Dura-Europos, situated in the middle Euphrates region, benefited exponentially from the exchange of ideas between Rome and Parthia. There, archaeologists have discovered that religion in Dura was heavily influenced by Greek, Roman and Parthian religious symbolism. They also found that its citizens took their gods and religious symbols and ceremonies west to Palmyra in Syria. But it appears that the town's inhabitants' nods to the prevailing cultures of the day were largely nominal. The use of Greek and Parthian titles within its civic administration was simply following convention. That suited their Parthian masters, who, as we have seen with their handling of trade generally, were happy to rule through and profit from existing hierarchies throughout their empire.[470]

Meanwhile, at Palmyra, reliefs dated to this period show both Roman and Parthian influences, and depict Palmyrene gods wearing Roman cuirasses and Parthian trousers and shoes.[471] Such influence was apparently freely adopted by the locals rather than forced onto them.[472] Thus the Euphrates, although a marker of the boundary of empire, was never considered a barrier to human movement. It served the purposes of trade.[473] It was a highway of large scale commerce between East and West for the advantage of those who lived on both sides of the river and all along it.[474] But, as Isidore put it, along the Euphrates and to the east all trade was under the Parthians' control.[475] Meanwhile, Trajan looked on with an envious eye.

By all accounts the Parthians took this trade very seriously. But the Parthians' largest markets were to the east along the shores of the Indian Ocean: archaeologists have found remains of port cities all around the Persian Gulf.[476] It also attracted Roman interest. Silks from China also arrived in Roman markets via the Gulf trade. When such silks arrived in Roman territories the raw silk would be transported to manufacturers in Phoenicia and Egypt where it was then dyed and the fabric turned into fashionable garments for Roman markets.[477] In several tower tombs in Palmyra in Syria archaeologists have even discovered silks stamped with the Chinese Hunan province symbol, along with cashmere from Afghanistan.[478] In fact Roman merchants were taking such an interest Indian Ocean trade that hoards of coins from the Julio-Claudian period have been found in great number around Indian ports such as Coimbatore and Karur.[479] Thousands of amphorae fragments have also been found around India's coastlines.[480] In 2010 archaeologists working in Pattanam in southern India even discovered one amphora that had been manufactured in Catalan in far-off southern Spain during the 1st century A D.[481] Needless to say, this kind of discovery is extremely rare, but nonetheless, this demand in India for Roman goods reflects a growing desire there for objects like them, a familiarity that Roman traders were ready to take advantage of. Trajan knew that if he proved successful in his Parthian war, Rome be able to do likewise.

Trajan was keen to lay claim to a piece of this pie. Sure, Roman merchants already had access to the Indian Ocean via the Red Sea, and Trajan had made sure by annexing Arabia along its north-eastern shore, that Rome would have more control over the Red Sea routes; and it would continue to facilitate the importing of foodstuffs, gems, and textiles among many other things from the East by way of that Sea.[482] But those routes simply did not measure up when compared with the advantages of the Persian Gulf. But comparison it had far fewer markets and many pirates, and the Romans were keen to access the Indian Ocean by a more lucrative detour.[483] The Persian Gulf fitted the bill.

The exchange of goods between the Roman and Parthian Empires increased to such an extent that by the early 2nd century Juvenal complained that for too long there had been excessive amounts of cargoes of Eastern goods arriving in Rome from the Silk Route via Antioch.[484] Although Juvenal was prone to exaggeration and license,[485] his satires remain an enlightening mirror for viewing Roman society generally.[486] Juvenal's remark therefore captures a combination in the lines of thinking in Rome between some Romans like Juvenal himself on the one hand, who felt a bitterness for the *otherness* in Orientals, and certain others, more entrepreneurial, who profited handsomely from trading with Orientals who to them were *familiar*. This social development has indeed been noted by others who observe both the colonial stereotypes of barbarians propagated by the Roman elite in order to dehumanize and make conquest more palatable, and the struggles of those of lower positions to resist.[487] Trajan, sensing opportunity to please both, believed he could merge the two. He would go on and conquer in the East, which appealed to the Roman elite, and he would also please the lower classes by adding to their finances. It is my view that main reason for Trajan's Parthian war was not just glory, and nor was it solely about protecting Armenia. Rather, it was a means of accruing vast resources, funds, and fund generating infrastructure – the most glaring being the trade arteries that operated down those rivers and around the Persian Gulf. Trajan must have been well informed about the lucrative trade networks down the Euphrates to the Persian Gulf and beyond, and that financial profit was still a huge driving force for conquest in Rome during Trajan's principate.

Trajan might have been a soldier-emperor, but he was also a leader in other respects including in the realm of Roman finances. For such reason he delighted in his official title 'Optimus', Most Excellent, above all others, for it described him not only as a great general, but also a leader in every respect, including that of the Roman economy. His reasons for his Parthian war therefore, had more to them than just dreams of Alexander and protecting a frontier. They were motivated by a desire to obtain massive gain for Rome's coffers, as well as the purses of many a subject: a necessary means of insuring support at home while abroad in itself. Only time would tell if he could actually rely upon that kind of insurance to bring victory. After all, not everyone in the Roman Empire was solely motivated by greed.

Trajan's Parthian War

Trajan's army was well prepared for the coming fight. Together with his manpower he had at his disposal artillery weapons and siege equipment that could be carried long distances by horse and chariot, the kinds of which are shown on Trajan's column.[488] This contributed to his initial successes. In 114AD the emperor marched north from Syria into Cappadocia and then onto Armenia which he took and made into a Roman province, ejecting Parthamasiris, the Parthian nominee, from its throne. Parthamasiris was an Arsacid and had been produced by the Parthian king Osroes partly to appease Trajan. Previously, Exedares had been crowned Armenia's king by Osroes and this caused serious offense to Trajan who recalled the precedence of the crowning of Tiridates by Nero. Trajan demanded satisfaction for this breach of protocol. Consequently, Osroes deposed him and put Parthamasiris in his place. Of course, such a move was very convenient for the Parthian king who saw a perfect opportunity to advance his family's power in the region. The price he had to pay was nominal: Osroes sent to Trajan and told him that he could crown the new king if he so wished just as Nero had done. But the offer was refused. When the new Armenian king placed his crown at the feet of the son of Marcus Junius, governor of Syria, expecting in return to receive it back the Roman, he did not return the gesture by crowning him. Meanwhile, Trajan marched into Armenia and took it over.[489]

Trajan then marched south, and captured Nisibis and Batnae. At this point, Dio states, Trajan was voted the name of *Parthicus* by the Roman Senate.[490] But the princeps would not accept this title until he believed he had achieved enough to warrant it: he only adopted it after he had captured Ctesiphon. After garrisoning Nisibis and Batnae, Trajan then marched to Edessa where he spent the winter.

The next spring, the emperor advanced across the Tigris River and marched through Adiabene taking Singara without a battle. With winter approaching again, Trajan returned to Antioch. In 116AD, in the following spring, Trajan once again marched east to the Tigris River. While trying to bridge it he was met by a detachment of the Parthian army who tried to disrupt his crossing, but in the face of Trajan's army's numbers they had withdrew and Trajan's army pressed on. Trajan had some eighty thousand soldiers at hand including eight whole legions drawn from the provinces Syria, Cappadocia, Judaea and Arabia, together with many Danubian auxiliaries. It was a vast force, and although it was not as great as Antony's, it was twice as large as

Marcus Crassus,' and not surprisingly it struck fear into the kings of the Near East. Terrified, king Abgarus of Edessa, Mannus the ruler of Arabia, and Anthemusia ruler of Sporaces quickly submitted. But such niceties did not restore the region's fortunes. Armenia was in a state of turmoil and when Manisarus ruler of Gordyene invaded it the gaping power vacuum was made clear to all.

The lackluster performance of Parthian armies up to this point, Dio stated, was due to the civil war to the east that still embroiled all their military forces pitted against each other.[491] At this point Osroes had marched from his power-base in Babylonia to fight Vologases III in Iran.[492] That suited Trajan perfectly and because his march through Adiabene was virtually unopposed he promptly took control of it. According to Dio this was the area of Assyria called 'Atyria' by the locals who pronounced the S as a T.[493] If Dio is correct, then this must have been the province of 'Assyria' that Trajan later established. This resolves the confusion felt by some over the question of the exact location of Trajan's province of Assyria. This confusion has even led many fine historians into thinking that Cassius Dio's statement about Trajan's crossing of the Tigris is erroneous, and that Dio had wrongly assumed that Assyria was east of the Tigris. It is presumed that Trajan's triumphal arch built at Dura-Europos on the Euphrates shows that the emperor was active there rather than east of the Tigris in 116AD.[494] Proponents of this view also point to Ammianus Marcellinus' statement that there existed a tribunal throne of Trajan's at Ozogardana, southeast of Dura on the Euphrates bank.[495] However, Ammianus' remark was actually based on the testimony of locals during Julian's Persian campaign,[496] and upon closer inspection into these testimonies the nature of the evidence makes them appear dubious at best. For one thing, those locals' testimony was no doubt made in order to curry favour with Julian and his invading army, because Zosimus recorded later that those same locals had completely ceased identifying the stone 'throne' as Trajan's.[497]

But the claims of the sources from late antiquity still loom large,[498] and some historians point out the statements of fourth century Sassanid and Roman writers to back them up. They point out that the Sassanids later called the lower Mesopotamian region 'Asuristan', and that Festus and Ammianus Marcellinus wholeheartedly believed that Trajan's campaigns proceeded only as far as the Tigris, and that, therefore, Assyria was located within this 'Asuristan' in Mesopotamia rather than to the east of the Tigris.[499] However, closer inspection into the sources challenges these views. For one thing, Dio's designation of Assyria was not obsolete in Trajan's day at all, for the locals beyond the Tigris themselves called their homeland 'Assyria' in Dio's time. Furthermore, regarding the triumphal arch at Dura-Europos: some have argued that Trajan erected the arch to celebrate his capture of that town, meaning that Dio was wrong and that Trajan advanced south down the Euphrates and not the Tigris River.[500] But that view is on very shaky ground too. Rather, it was probably built soon after Trajan's capture of Ctesiphon when the Senate voted him a triumph[501] and a corresponding triumphal arch in Rome itself.[502] It is also unclear how Trajan could have later appeared so quickly in Babylonia if he had been detained all the while at Dura-Europos. However, if Trajan had indeed marched down the Tigris and entered Babylonia from there as Dio maintained,[503] then that would account for his speedy arrival there. Numismatic evidence also lends support to this scenario. Parthian bronze coins clearly circulated freely throughout western Babylonia during Trajan's march south, and the consistent distribution of coinage indicates that the economy of the population there was totally unaffected by war, as it would have been if it was indeed missed by Trajan's army to the east.[504] Of course, coin distribution data can not emphatically prove broader social conditions, but taken with Dio, a march down the east of the Tigris is the most solid conclusion to draw.

But we need not rely on them alone. Dio's claim that Trajan marched down the eastern bank of the Tigris whereupon he later crossed into Babylonia and Characene[505] is also corroborated by archaeological evidence. An inscription on the base of a statue of Herakles etched by Vologases V, discovered by archaeologists at Seleucia in 1984, commemorates the Parthian king's recapture of Characene for Parthia, which shows that after Trajan's death Characene remained a staunch client-kingdom under Rome's influence from Trajan's Parthian war onwards until then.[506] Efforts by Vologases IV in 161AD to retake Elymais, a territory located to the east of the Tigris precisely through where Dio stated Trajan marched, proved unsuccessful.[507]

The Fourth Century Evidence

Centuries had passed since Trajan's war when in late antiquity writers began making their own claims about that emperor's Parthian war. But despite the fading of memory through the mists of time one can still detect in the fourth century sources a tradition that Trajan had campaigned well beyond the Euphrates.

Festus, for one, believed that Trajan annexed only the area between the two rivers, but he believed this because he assumed it contained Persia which as we know was located to the Tigris' east:

> "[Trajan] received and maintained Anthemusia – Persia's finest region – Seleucia, Ctesiphon and Babylon; and, after Alexander, even reached the ends of India. He established a fleet in the Red Sea. He made provinces Armenia, Assyria, and Mesopotamia, which, situated between the Tigris and Euphrates, is made equal to Egypt in fecundity by the flooding rivers."[508]

In this garbled account it does appear that Festus had preserved an older tradition which passed on that Trajan had crossed the Tigris into Persia just as Dio stated. He simply misconstrued the exact locations of the territories that Trajan had annexed.

Ammianus Marcellinus was another writer and since that he traveled throughout Mesopotamia while serving under the emperor Julian in 363AD, he had first hand knowledge of the region, making his writings appear trustworthy at first glance. However, he too was clearly totally confused as well. In fact he had real difficulty locating where Assyria was located due to the fact that its borders had shifted over time. He wrote:

> "Nearest to us of all the provinces is Assyria, famous for its large population, its size, and the abundance and great variety of its products. This province once spread over great and

prosperous peoples and districts, then it was combined under a single name, and today the whole region is called Assyria."[509]

But in added confusion, Ammianus goes on to say that:

"...within this area is Adiabene, called Assyria in ancient times."[510]

Ammianus' confusion as to whether Assyria was near to the Roman Empire, or across the Tigris, or perhaps both, is clear. But it is very apparent that he corresponded Adiabene with Assyria, both of which Dio maintained were indeed east of the Tigris.

But perhaps our clearest fourth century source on the issue, Eutropius, at last did acknowledge that Trajan really did campaign well beyond the Tigris just as Dio had sated all along. However, regarding the details of Trajan's war he clearly knew very little. He wrote,

"He [Trajan] advanced as far as the boundaries of India, and the Red Sea, where he formed three provinces, Armenia, Assyria and Mesopotamia, including the tribes which border on Madena [Media]."[511]

Although this was clearly an exaggerated account, it does preserve the tradition in Dio that Trajan passed through and annexed regions east of the Tigris.

Therefore, the testimonies of the fourth century sources are not at all certain, and in the words of one modern historian, the fourth century historians really needed a good history lesson.[512] However, their testimonies do pass on a tradition, albeit confused, that echoes Dio's own. Therefore, by taking all the evidence at hand we can determine that: Armenia was annexed as a province, the territory between the Tigris and Euphrates River became the Roman province of Mesopotamia under Trajan, and that the areas east of the Tigris which had submitted to Trajan, including Adiabene, became the province of Assyria under Trajan. Fourth century sources or not, modern confusion or not, that much is clear.

Trajan's Advance and Retreat

Advancing from Babylonia, Trajan entered the Parthian capital Ctesiphon unopposed. There he captured the royal Parthian throne, and a number of royal family members including Osroes' own daughter, was hailed *imperator*, and at last he finally felt that enough had been achieved to warrant the title *Parthicus* voted to him by the Senate: Roman coins now began to feature 'Parthico' to commemorate Trajan's adoption of the title.[513] From there Trajan entered Mesene, otherwise called Characene, roughly modern-day Kuwait, and established there an alliance with Athambelus, its ruler, who welcomed him warmly.[514] With Trajan's declaration of his three new provinces of Armenia, Mesopotamia and Assyria the emperor had signaled his wishful hopes of permanent conquests. Next he began to link his military bases at Nisibis in southern Armenia with Singara in Mesopotamia together with roads as milestones discovered in the 1920s near Singara, from this time show.[515] The Senate also prepared for a homecoming triumph and at that point began construction of a number of triumphal arches for their triumphant emperor.[516] No doubt it was at that point that the triumphal arch erected at Dura-Europos was likewise built to celebrate Trajan's army's long march to Rome north along the Euphrates bank.

But all such was very wishful thinking. Trajan had not even met a Parthian army in battle yet and this whole last, greatest conquest turned out to be his most foolish. During his expedition to Characene signs started to emerge that all was not well for Rome's new eastern provinces. There he received news that almost every one of the nations that he had taken control of had rebelled. Promptly, the emperor dispatched his generals Lusius and Maximus to put down the rebellion. But they had mixed results: while Lusius was able to recapture Nisibis and sack Edessa, Maximus was killed in battle. Meanwhile, in the south Seleucia was sacked by the emperor's generals Erucius Clarus and Julius Alexander. But Trajan had now to recognize that his cause was a despised one and so in order to pacify the locals Trajan decided the best move to make was to remove his person from the scene altogether. After he had symbolically crowned Parthamaspartes as Parthian king he then cautiously withdrew. But things got worse. During his march north he besieged Hatra to the north which still held out against him. The siege failed. Trajan, giving up for the time being, decided to return to Antioch. But it was then that the Parthian armies finally made their own presence felt, and they harassed and repeatedly attacked Trajan's army right along its slow return to Syria.[517]

Morale in Trajan's army was now at a low, and Trajan's abilities as a commander-in-chief came into question within its ranks. One detects from Trajan's soldiers an ongoing grievance. Giving expression to it they complained about the heat and insects around Hatra as well as its impregnable walls during the siege.[518] Indeed the very capture of a town or city often served to raise morale among troops and secure an army's goodwill,[519] so Trajan was probably trying to placate the army's displeasure with his leadership. But now Trajan's siege proved a failure. Understandably Trajan knew he had to return to Antioch quickly, and plan how he could recapture his eastern conquests from the now-present and battle-hardened Parthian army. His idea was to recover his conquests the following spring. But, before he could make plans in full, he fell ill which was probably exasperated by the failure of his campaign, and in Selinus in Cilicia, while on his way to Italy for medical treatment, he assigned control of the eastern armies to Hadrian and died.[520]

This campaign and the rebellions that erupted during it pose glaring questions, not the least of all being: were those rebellions orchestrated to be simultaneous? And if so, who orchestrated them? What is certain is that at the same time Trajan's newly conquered kingdoms in Mesopotamia rebelled so too did the Jews in Cyrene, Egypt and Cyprus rebel exposing Trajan's drastic weakness in his rear. Although conclusive evidence is lacking, their synchronisation does make them appear planned for execution at the same moment. Certainly the Parthians employed espionage during this period, and there was an extensive degree of Jewish political cohesion right throughout the east.[521]

Also, the Parthians had seen within their own empire that Jewish and Grecian populations could be a volatile mix. Thus, the Parthians might even have deliberately fermented such volatility throughout the Roman Empire and the violence there that was to follow. If so, such incitement did not go without welcome by the Jews of Egypt, Cyrene and Cyprus in the least. There had always been a residual disdain for Roman rule both east and west of the Euphrates River following the first Jewish war (66-70AD),[522] and that is why the idea is one that I can not escape entertaining.

Faced with this rebellion Trajan had no choice but to withdraw and regroup in Syria. But his death cut short his intensions. His Parthian war was a complete and utter disaster, even if pockets of allegiance in Characene and Elymais did still remain. But Trajan had changed the status quo of the whole of the economic geography of the area between the two Rivers. Where Trajan had failed to control and hang onto his three new provinces by use of force, in the principate of his successor Publius Aelius Hadrian, trade advanced Rome's economic interests there. It was a phenomenon that Trajan himself could have used, but he was a military leader seeking military glory and only the finest army could secure the riches of the East. Or so he liked to think. In reality, commerce would facilitate with the weapons of peace where those of war had failed, and during the principate of Hadrian trade along the Euphrates would boom like never before.

CHAPTER NINE

HADRIAN AND CONSOLIDATION

Hadrian and the Eastern 'Frontier'

WHEN HISTORIANS TURN to the subject of Hadrian's eastern policy, and particularly in regard to Parthia, they invariably always find that scholarship is severely lacking. That makes it very difficult to ascertain the history of Roman and Parthian relations from Trajan's reign onwards. The main reason for this dilemma is the paucity of ancient evidence for the period following Trajan's death. That means that some find it difficult to describe Roman and Parthian diplomacy in that period, despite their very best efforts,[523] while others' descriptions are all too brief. So, because there is such a gap in our knowledge, often historians are content simply to accept the current generalisations of Roman imperialism[524] that are so often based upon the purposes of Hadrian's Wall, and project them upon Hadrian's entire foreign policy, including in the east. But I believe, and I am sure I am not alone in saying this, that crucial details are lost by this method - details which in themselves show that Hadrian's Parthian policy was far more complex than what is so often taken for granted. In those details we actually find that Hadrian's so-called intended benign eastern policy was not as benign as is usually thought, and that it was largely forced upon him to undertake; and we also find that during the principate of Hadrian, Rome's political, economical and imperial interests in the East did not cease to be pursued at all. If anything, the Euphrates frontier served as much a thriving artery for human movement and trade as any other trade artery did.

By looking afresh at the evidence at hand, as will be done here, we are able still to see something of Hadrian's policy in the east, and what emerges is a very different picture to what many history books might portray. In it we detect a certain level of continuum with Roman policy that had gone before him, especially in the pursuit of containing Parthia which was already well established in Roman politics. Thus we can see the use of precedent and expediency by an emperor in touch with the past. But on the other hand it is also clear that Hadrian established a new status quo which had a lasting legacy. With the compliance of the Syrian trading-city Palmyra secured, Hadrian ensured that Roman interests could be pursued beyond frontiers in a way that Trajan could not have imagined.

The Succession

Upon Hadrian's succession to the imperial throne, Rome's armies were still in the process of being withdrawn back across to the western banks of the Euphrates River as they were under Trajan's command. Historians often pinpoint this as the precise moment Roman conquest was brought to a close and a new defensive policy, whereby Rome chose to secure its conquests rather than undertake new ones, was effectively begun.[525] To back this claim up many look to the famous statement made by Aelius Aristides, who said that during his lifetime it was "perfect policing", rather than conquest, that characterized the empire and made Rome truly great.[526] But there is a real danger in taking this remark too far out of its original context and foisting it upon the far more complex phenomenon that was Hadrian's eastern policy. International politics were, and are, to put it simply, never so simple. In fact, the transition was far less clear-cut as many have presumed: and just as Hadrian's imperial predecessors varied from one to the next when it came to imperial policy, so too there were imperial successors who took part in campaigns against Parthia. Indeed even Aelius Aristides himself was not unaware of this fact, and even he had to concede upon his own observation that the empire was not an isolated static organism in his day. Rather, he acknowledged that Rome's population depended heavily upon dealings and trade with nations beyond itself in order to thrive, and that such dealings could change from time to time, As he put it:

> "...anyone who wants to behold all these products must either journey through the whole world to see them or else come to this city [Rome]... Clothing from Babylonia and the luxuries from the barbarian lands beyond arrive in much greater volume and more easily than if one had to sail from Naxos or Cynthos to Athens, transporting any of their products."[527]

It almost goes without saying that interstate trade depends heavily upon economic relations and robust diplomacy. That is why Aelius' idealised comments regarding policing over conquest should be treated with some weariness. They were never intended to be an absolute expression of imperial policy, rather one layperson's impressions of his times. The truth is that Rome continued to exploit the Middle East exponentially. Rome's hunger for luxury goods from the east had not waned in the aftermath of Trajan's Parthian failure and death. But the method of exploitation had certainly changed. Whereas under Trajan the army had been used en masse to conquer and exploit, during Hadrian's principate trade and political pressure were the tools used to bring that exploitation about.

As for the military withdrawal, which is so often pinpointed as a momentous event in history, it was actually forced upon Hadrian and was not of his initial choosing. Upon his succession the Empire was in complete turmoil. That turmoil had resulted directly from Trajan's military and political failures, since he was absent from the empire in the last two whole years of his life.[528] Then when he died he left that unrest neglected and unchecked. Not only were the Moors, Britons and Sarmatians mobilizing for war with Rome, but there was also civil unrest in Egypt, Libya and Palestine, and even Parthamaspates - Trajan's nominee for the Parthian throne - was rejected by the Parthians.[529] But that was not all. Ancient sources also relate that Hadrian was faced with competition for the imperial throne itself. Rome's City Prefect, Baebius Macer, was vehemently opposed to Hadrian's succession, while the exiles Laberius Maximus and Crassus Frugi had their own designs upon the empire. Furthermore, Lusius Quietus, the governor of Judaea, also had his own imperial ambitions.[530] Of course, our main source for all of this, the *Historia Augusta*, is notoriously invaluable on certain points in its chapters and is even totally unreliable on others. The *Historia Augusta* is actually a collection of biographies of Roman emperors starting with Hadrian that was written by an unknown hand in the fourth century, although it claims to have been written by several. Unquestionably, its 'secondary lives' of imperial usurpers are largely spurious, and follow the infamous popular literary trend in the fourth century to 'bend the truth'.[531] But that granted, its biography of Hadrian is of great value to the historian and ranks as one of the *Historia Augusta*'s most reliable biographies. So when it comes to the basic historical facts for his reign as emperor, as a source of information it is trustworthy enough, even if it does appear at times to have been somewhat hastily composed.[532]

Aware of the poor state of the empire and his own position too, Hadrian had to act quickly and decisively. In so doing, Macer and Quietus were deposed and replaced, Crassus was executed, and Maximus was kept in check by Hadrian's extortionate control over his son in law, Bruttius Praesens, at that time governor of Cilicia.[533] Hadrian also set about the withdrawal of Rome's troops from Parthian territory in order to use those forces to properly address, and confront, the issues of civil unrest and political instability that threatened the empire. The Parthian war, which had turned out so badly for Trajan, must have seemed like military foolishness to press on with to Hadrian, especially when he considered the desperate state around the Roman world. Conquering another's empire was no doubt still a glamorous Roman pastime to undertake, but when one's own empire was on the brink of civil war, such a pastime seemed less of a priority.

Looking for Hadrian in Fronto, Tacitus, Suetonius and Plutarch:

Hadrian's withdrawal was not without its critics though. Fronto, for one, openly condemned it. Fronto was a distinguished counselor, tutor and friend to the imperial family for over thirty years during the Antonine period, and his written communications with the family remain as priceless insights into their affairs. In certain respects they are key to understanding many political and cultural issues of the day and to some degree reflect a typical Roman aristocrat's feelings of the time.[534] Fronto's comments on Hadrian, therefore, can not be ignored. According to Fronto, Hadrian really just gave up Trajan's conquests due to his own poor leadership skills. Rome, Fronto added, could have recovered and held its Parthian conquests, regardless of political uncertainty throughout the Roman Empire, if only Hadrian had possessed the ability to do so – but, Fronto remarked, he apparently did not.[535] It is a damning judgment, and one made by a source contemporary with Hadrian himself. However, despite Fronto's eminent position, we should not invest too much importance to this particular judgment as a reflection on the truth, for it was written by Fronto in a preamble to a history of a later Parthian War in 163-165 AD led by Lucius Verus, brother of Marcus Aurelius. Since that war stood in direct opposition to Hadrian's earlier policies, it was expedient for Fronto to praise Verus' aggression over Hadrian's lack thereof. So it should be treated as a later rhetorical device made under a later emperor who had very different designs on Parthia than what Hadrian did, in order to achieve a deliberate response by its Antonine readers.

But aside from Fronto, identifying Roman views on Hadrian's foreign policy within other contemporaneous literary sources is even more problematic. Some modern historians have argued that hostility towards Hadrian's foreign policy is reflected in the writings of Tacitus, Suetonius and Plutarch. For that reason, both Syme and Birley have entertained the idea that the statement made by Tacitus in the *Annals*, to the effect that Tiberius had no interest in extending the empire, was a criticism of Hadrian's own foreign policy.[536] Syme argued that in Tacitus' comment in the *Annals* that the Roman Empire in his day reached the Red Sea is a reference not to what we know today as the Red Sea at all, but to the Persian Gulf. That means, so it is thought, that it must have been composed sometime *after* Trajan's principate. Thus, Syme famously concluded, Tacitus' criticisms of Julio-Claudian emperors in the *Annals* were really shrouded negative remarks aimed

at none other than Hadrian himself.[537] Granted, there is some logic in
this argument, for it has been shown by Gawlikowski that Characene,
situated by the Persian Gulf, acted as a client kingdom under Rome's
influence from Hadrian's principate to that of Septimius Severus', at
which time Vologases V (reigned 191-207/8AD) recovered it for Parthia.[538] Since Characene offered its allegiance to Rome only in the last
year of Trajan's life, and remained under Rome's influence for almost
a century thereafter, it therefore follows that if Tacitus had indeed
referred to the Persian Gulf as an extremity of the Empire, then logi-
cally Tacitus must have written the *Annals* after Trajan's death.

However, other historians contest this whole argument, as do I,[539]
and even Syme himself undermined his own main point by conceding
that since the overall picture of Tiberius in the *Annals* appeared the
same to him as those in Suetonius' biography and Cassius Dio's narrative it must therefore have actually been an unbiased account.[540] There
are also other serious problems with Syme's hypothesis. Epigraphic
evidence discovered in the Roman province of Arabia shows that since
its annexation in 106AD the province extended considerably along
the Saudi Arabian side of the Red Sea.[541] Consequently, it has been
observed that the *Annals* could have been written not long after 106.[542]

However, it is in Tacitus' own words that one detects most clearly
that he was referring to Rome's control over the Red Sea as we know it
today rather than the Persian Gulf itself. To quote Tacitus:

> "He [Germanicus] came to Elephantine and Syene, once the
> frontier posts of the Roman Empire, which now, however,
> extends to the Red Sea."[543]

One must consider why Tacitus would compare Elephantine and
Syene with the extent of the empire in his own day if they are not
related. Certainly, if Tacitus intended to indicate the Persian Gulf as
the empire's extent in his own day then his references to Elephantine
and Syene would seem to his immediate Roman audience entirely out
of place. Rather, a reference to the Roman Empire's frontiers in the
upper extremities of the Euphrates during Germanicus' visit to either
Syria or Armenia would have been more in keeping with a comparison

of the Persian Gulf where that river discharges into the sea. However, if Tacitus actually intended his reference to indicate the Red Sea as we know it then this confusion vanishes altogether. In fact, Tacitus was pointing out to his readers that where once the empire extended to Egypt's Nile, in his day it extended to the Red Sea which straddled Egypt's east coast. On the basis of this discussion alone I, for one, cannot accept that Tacitus' *Annals* was a lengthy commentary on Hadrian's perceived political failings.

But even that is not all. Other factors cast doubt upon Syme's well known hypothesis too. For one thing there is no explicit reference made by Tacitus about Hadrian at all. That has led some historians to jump to the conclusion that when Tacitus criticized his subjects he was in fact criticizing Trajan, not Hadrian, and the institution of emperor in general.544

But I disagree with that hypothesis too. It is my tendency to conclude that in Tacitus' criticisms of Tiberius' disinterest in expanding the Roman Empire545 there was actually a deliberate rhetorical ruse to contrast that principate with the military glories of Trajan's own. It was never intended to be a reflection upon Hadrian, who was not yet emperor, but as a tribute to Trajan. At the beginning of his *Histories* Tacitus informs the reader that he intended to write a history of Nerva and Trajan after the composition of the *Histories* saw completion. But notably, after it was completed Tacitus did not write about those emperors at all, but instead wrote the *Annals*. This has led some to suppose that the author was projecting upon the Julio-Claudians his own shrouded political invective toward his own contemporary imperial rulers who he had initially intended to write openly about. But it was nothing of the sort. Tacitus himself declared that his times were happy under Trajan, and that he enjoyed freedom to write what he thought and felt without any interference by an emperor.546

The key to understanding Tacitus' treatment of the Julio-Claudians lies in Tacitus' own comments and the comments made by Suetonius in his closing remarks at the end of his *Twelve Caesars*. Suetonius served as secretary to Hadrian until his sacking in 122AD. Some have wondered whether the dismissal inspired him to write negatively about various emperors, as Tacitus did, after his sacking in criticism toward Hadrian.[547] However, this does not account for Suetonius' positive accounts of the lives of Vespasian and Titus, nor the fact that nowhere does Suetonius ever openly criticize Hadrian in his *Lives*. In fact, the glaring similarity in mood between Suetonius' Tiberius to Tacitus', simply demonstrates that like Tacitus, Suetonius' criticisms of Tiberius were aimed at that particular emperor, Tiberius, not Hadrian. Now compare Tacitus' comment about the freedom under which he was writing with Suetonius' closing comments. At the end of his *Twelve Caesars*, his brilliant work of biographies of Rome's emperors from Julius Caesar to Domitian, Suetonius expresses that he wrote about those Caesars in order to compare it with the much happier times he enjoyed under their successors. He wrote:

> "The Empire would be richer and happier when he [Domitian] had gone, and soon the wisdom and restraint of his successors proved him right."[548]

In short, Tacitus and Suetonius wanted to write about subjects that would compare dismally with their own times, and show to their immediate audience that they lived in a golden age in contrast to those that had gone before them. That theme was not confined to their works alone. In fact the idea that under Nerva and Trajan all Romans were living in a golden age unlike those who had gone before was a common one. Even the racy and lude poet Martial believed that under those emperors Rome had been "reborn from fire, to live a thousand years or higher" like a phoenix from the ashes of the chaos of the past.[549] In fact times were so good that the great historian Edward Gibbon, writing in the eighteenth century, believed they were the happiest in all of human history.[550] We can confidently conclude, therefore, that Tacitus and Suetonius were not criticizing Hadrian at all. Rather, they were criticizing Tiberius and his Julio-Claudian heirs, their works' lackluster subjects, because they wished to highlight and savour the blessings under which they and their reader-peers lived.

There is also a lack of criticism of Hadrian's foreign policy in Plutarch's *Parallel Lives*, his Greek and Roman biographies written between the mid-90s and the author's death in c.120. Of course, the following points must be duly considered: there is dramatic Parthian despondency over Sulla's prestige in diplomatic meetings with Parthian ambassadors,[551] an assertion that Pompey and Rome can fit their border in the East wherever they please,[552] there is Caesar's unfinished business of conquering Parthia at hand,[553] and of course there are Antony's glorious victories despite huge losses in manpower against the Parthians in battle after battle.[554] It is also noted that Plutarch, a native of Chaeronea and a Roman citizen, sought to affect his readership profoundly,[555] and that Plutarch wrote his *Parallel Lives* in order to condition his audience.[556] Consequently, a case could be made that his writings provided some fodder to inspire some spite towards Parthia. However, before we pass judgment that Plutarch's writings were intended to stir up war again, we must remember what Plutarch's professed intentions were as he himself saw and described them. Plutarch was open with his audience that his sole aim in writing biography was to present examples of virtue in order to develop that quality among his readers.[557] In his *Life of Alexander*, Plutarch stated that he wished to achieve that above all else, even at the cost of military, political, and historical, considerations.[558] So, a more solid argument could follow that Plutarch's references to Parthia in his lives of Sulla, Pompey, Crassus, Caesar and Antony, were not so much designed to instill a spirit for war with Parthia, but were rather intended to make points about his subjects' personalities and encourage the imitation of those points in the lives of his readers. In other words, if there was conditioning, it was for the sake of encouraging virtue, not the hubris of a Crassus or Antony in the East. Or for that matter, another Trajan.

Hadrian and the Roman Army

However, whilst it is indeed difficult to ascertain whether or not Hadrian's withdrawal across the Euphrates River was popular among his literary peers, there are indications that it was popular within one element: the army. Even Fronto, grudgingly, concurred that the Roman soldiers loved Hadrian, and held him in high honour as a ruler.[559] This popularity is also reflected in the *Historia Augusta* where it records that since Hadrian showed careful attention to the interests of the army he was highly regarded by it.[560]

Hadrian's popularity with the armies developed as a direct result from his withdrawal of Roman forces from the Euphrates. They were aware of the chaos at home and were keen to return there to settle the unrest around the empire. He also continued to maintain this goodwill by making an official statement, preserved throughout the narrative of Dio, that Trajan acted solely on selfish ambition when he invaded Parthia, and that it ultimately failed not because of any lack of bravery among the soldiers, but because of his predecessor's misman-agement of the campaign.[561] In short, he was apologizing to the troops for Trajan's short-sightedness, not reprimanding the troops for their defeat. That sealed their goodwill. It also signaled that Hadrian unlike Trajan, or rather his official image of Trajan, he would not be leading armies abroad through any similar recklessness such as that he had accused Trajan of possessing.

Thus, by condemning Trajan's failure at the outset of his principate, Hadrian was promising hope to the public and future successes under his rule, and that was a promise all Roman soldiers respected. With their support, Hadrian's legitimacy was quickly and firmly established, and he was able to stabilize the empire. The empire strengthened, and the continued goodwill of the armies secured, Hadrian was then able to strive to become even more palatable to his subjects, who sorely needed such consideration after the civil disorders in the wake of Trajan's death. Although Hadrian's right to rule would depend for its ultimate survival upon his popularity, thankfully for the stability of the empire and the interests of armies weary from the military failures of Trajan's final years, Hadrian proved successful in sticking to his promises and to his army.

Hadrian's Containment of Parthia

By appealing to the Roman armies Hadrian had demonstrated con-summate skill as a politician, and that skill was to be repeated for the duration of his principate, and especially in relation to his dealings with Parthia. Almost immediately he contained any possibility of a

Parthian military threat in the aftermath of Trajan's death. To achieve this he quickly forged ties of friendship with Parthia,[562] thus saving the Roman Empire's east from invasion, and thus giving him time to take the political initiative With peace secured Hadrian next forged ties of friendship and alliances with Parthia's peripheral neighbours: the Armenians, Edessa and Oshroene in Parthia's west, the Alani, Iberians, and Hyrcanians in its north, and Bactria in its east.[563] Although the *Historia Augusta* dismisses these alliances as hollow tokens,[564] Hadrian was in fact exercising his diplomatic strength with considerable skill, keeping allies in reserve all around Parthia should the need arise to make use of them tactically against it in case of war.[565]

We have already seen that the use of enlisting the help of Parthia's neighbours had a long history. As we have seen, Domitian had employed the same model, but on a smaller scale. (See Chapter Seven) He had secured alliances with the Iberians, Hyrcanians and Albanians.[566] Going further back we can also recall how Tiberius (See Chapter Six) and Vespasian (See Chapter Seven) had used to it too: in 35AD Tiberius persuaded Iberian and Sarmatian allies to eject the Parthians from Armenian and then turn against Parthia,[567] and in the mid-70sAD Vespasian had allowed the Alani and Hyrcanians to overrun Parthia.[568] Consequently, Hadrian's policy of containment was well established by precedent that ensured that Parthia's rear was constantly threatened on every side in case its relations with Rome broke down.

We know that those neighbours often had great success in war against Parthia. Around the year 136 the Alani once again poured into Media Atropatene, Armenia and Cappadocia, with help from Pharasmanes, king of the Iberians, and the destruction they wrought was so extensive that Vologases tried to bribe them to withdraw. But they refused. Fortunately for Parthia though, when the Alani's homeland was in its turn threatened with invasion from nomad tribes to its north they were finally forced to withdraw. Intriguingly, Vologases then complained to Hadrian about Pharasmanes.[569] Pharasmanes and Hadrian had something of a fluctuating relationship, but we do know from the *Historia Augusta* that the Iberian king was of fundamental military importance to Hadrian, who showered him with an elephant, a 500-strong military quingenary cohort, as well as many other gifts.[570] The cohort in particular was a symbol that Hadrian was counting on Pharasmanes to embark upon military ventures against their mutual enemies at some point in the near future. If Hadrian had indeed encouraged the Iberian king to stir up between the Alani and Parthia that would indeed be in keeping with what is known about Roman imperial policy of containment in general. Pharasmanes would go on to be of similar use to Hadrian's successor Antoninus Pius as well.

But of course, such a policy had its limitations and Hadrian could never conquer Parthia using it alone. Nevertheless that should not be taken as a sign of any cessation of Rome's expansionist interests. After all Verus, Severus and Caracalla were all still to follow. But Hadrian was still able to assert some influence over the Parthian imperial court. In 128/9 Hadrian made overtures of friendship towards Osroes by restoring to him his daughter that Trajan had previously captured. He also gave a promise that he would return the Parthian throne that Trajan had confiscated in Ctesiphon.[571] These overtures were welcome ones for Osroes, for there was a renewal of acute internal division in Parthia during this period: coinage minted separately by Osroes, Vologases, as well as several contenders for the throne throughout this period make that much abundantly clear.[572] Parthia therefore, could not resist Roman interferences in its affairs altogether. But although Mesopotamia was still weak thanks to Trajan's efforts, Iran was largely intact. Hence, Drachms of Vologases III from 105-147AD are so common they point to a healthy and robust economic climate in Iran,[573] and that helped in the reconstruction of the Parthian Empire as a whole after his final victory over Osroes, thus reestablishing the civil harmony, and indeed the very survival, of Parthia, despite Hadrian's political schemes with Vologases' rival in Osroes.

Thus despite the military withdrawal, Hadrian's main aim was always to maintain a stake for Rome in the political affairs of the nations beyond the Euphrates and Tigris Rivers. Although he did not use the military, the success that Hadrian's methods brought ensured that those methods, as well as that aim, were to last as some of Hadrian's most important legacies, and would resonate for almost a century after his death on the 10th of July, AD138.

As Rome pursued its interests in the East, commerce with Chara-cene and the Persian Gulf recovered. Characene remained under the Roman sphere of influence[574] and its service to Rome is also indicative of the true loyalty allies east of the Euphrates could provide a Roman emperor. That Characene remained loyal to Rome for so long, despite strong opposition over the years from Parthia, tells us that the loyalty of an ally, even one as far away as Characene, was not nearly as hol-low as the *Historia Augusta*, composed centuries later, might have us believe. Hadrian was certainly not blind to that fact. Although as a new emperor he saw that the allegiances of subjects throughout his own empire extended only so far, he learnt that tactical advan-tages could be accrued by sharing goodwill towards them. The need to stabilize the Roman Empire and deter a Parthian invasion of the eastern provinces after Trajan's death had forced Hadrian to pursue such goodwill. But it was one pursuit that quickly resulted in a large measure of success, both for his and also Rome's interests.

Palmyra and East-West Trade

The peace that the principate of Hadrian ensured saw a flourishing of the trade between the Roman and Parthian Empires and a new trading status quo that would mark Hadrian's reign as a watershed, not a lull. The local commerce centers situated between the Tigris and Euphrates, like Characene, that had maintained East-West trade under Parthia's auspices prior to Trajan's invasion, had declined somewhat,[575] and in their wake, the Roman city of Palmyra took up and embraced its opportunity to exploit the trans-Euphrates trade artery continuing the commercial link between East and West. Demand in Rome for luxury goods from the East had only increased, and the Palmyrenes saw the profitability in meeting such a huge demand.[576]

According to Josephus, Palmyra[577] was founded by the Jewish king Solomon for its springs and central location between Upper Syria to the west and the Euphrates River and Babylonia to the east.[578] It seemed a suitable site to accommodate caravan merchants. By the first century AD Palmyrenes traders operating along the Euphrates was commonplace,[579] and their importance did not go unnoticed in

Rome - Pliny the Elder recognised that Palmyra's location between the Roman and Parthian Empires would mean a prosperous future for its inhabitants.[580]

But Palmyra had been a wealthy trading city for almost a century even before it came under Roman control during the early 1st century AD. Appian stated that when Marc Antony plundered Palmyra at the outset of his Parthian war, the city had already been trading with Rome and Parthia for a long time.[581] It seems that Palmyra's contact with Parthia started in the wake of Crassus' defeat, when Parthian merchants began developing trading ties throughout Syria.[582] That the city came under direct Roman control during the visit to the East by Germanicus is borne by three statues discovered there by archaeologists dedicated to Tiberius, Drusus and Germanicus,[583] and the tax law of Palmyra in 137AD which refers to Germanicus' edicts as legal precedent.[584]

Soon Rome began financially investing in Palmyra's mercantile development, with the result that Palmyra's economy boomed exponentially.[585] Monumental buildings were erected, such as the Temple of Bel and the city's agora[586] The Temple of Bel in itself is a noteworthy demonstration of the extent, but also the limits, of Roman influence over Palmyra. There, a happy mixture of Hellenistic sculpture, Mesopotamian terracottas, and Oriental and Roman architectural practices exist side by side, showing us that while the city had very particular tastes, its inhabitants were content to adopt those particularities from places abroad, such as Rome among other locations. But the Roman influence was still there, and growing.[587] With increased investment Palmyra's population also increased: even if the modern estimate of 150,000 to 200,000 inhabitants[588] in Palmyra at its peak is still too optimistic, it nonetheless remains a reflection on its wealth and influence.

Ruins of the Temple of Bel, at Palmyra, in Syria.
Wikipedia.org

Of the some 2832 inscriptions discovered at Palmyra to date, about 180 are honourific, and about one in six of these refer to trade abroad in one way or another.[589] They tell us that Palmyra's traders operated at Seleucia, Characene, Vologasias, Babylon, and even the Saka kingdoms of north-west India.[590] The profusion of inscriptions between AD130-161 shows that Palmyrene merchants were particularly active at that time. But they are only part of Palmyra's whole story. Given the deep importance of interstate trade in the hearts and minds of the inhabitants of Palmyra as these inscriptions express, there were no doubt more, probably many more, trade missions left unrecorded.

But although much about the lives of those actually involved in the trading life of Palmyra has been lost, the inscriptions left behind do provide us with valuable information about the types of roles they played. One particularly famous character in Palmyra was Soades, son of Boliades. The first inscription to mention his name occurs in the year 132, in which he was honoured for assisting and defending caravans from bandits traveling to and from Vologasias to the point of even not sparing his own life.[591] But for Soades that was not sacrifice enough. In 144 another inscription honours him for taking a force of Palmyrenes, perhaps a troop of Palmyra's famous mounted archers, and no doubt to ensure his life would not be in such danger as it was in 132, and employing them in defending caravans traveling to and from Vologasias.[592] For such bravery Soades was awarded imperial commendations, both by Hadrian and later Antoninus Pius, and in 145 was honoured by decrees and statues in Vologasias, Spasinou Charax, and Gennaes.[593]

There were others too who followed Soades' example, and who also braved the dangers of travel to assist the caravans. Marcus Ulpius Iaraeus was one such notable figure. In 155 he was honoured with an inscription in Palmyra by the caravans traveling there from Spasinou Charax,[594] and two years later he received similar honours from the Characenes again.[595] Amazingly, in 157 he even was honoured for his bravery in helping merchants to and from the Indus region.[596] Other Palmyrenes such as Julius Maximus, a soldier, and one Iariboles, son of Lisamsos, were also honoured with inscriptions in the city, in 135 and 138 respectively.[597]

Inscriptions from Palmyra also tell us that its citizens were not the only ones in the region who took upon themselves the responsibility for defending the caravan trade. One such inscription honours a Characene, one named in Aramaic as NN, son of NN, son of Alexander, and records that he was so honoured not only there but also in Spasinou Charax and Vologasias for his mercenary services.[598] In fact Palmyra had such close relations with their wider world that many of its citizens became politically influential. Inscriptions in Palmyra show that in 131, for instance, one Iarhai Nebouzabados became satrap of Thilouana, in modern Bahrain;[599] while Iariboles, son of Lisamsos, who we have already mentioned (See above) was even sent as an ambassador of Spasinou Charax, to Orodes, king of Elymais.[600] Astonishingly, by 142 Palmyrenes had assumed such a privileged place along the Euphrates trading leg that they even dedicated a temple to the Augusti in Vologasias itself.[601]

Such efforts contributed to Syria becoming one of the most lucrative centers of commerce in the whole of the Roman Empire.[602] Rome took full advantage of these conditions and Syrian wealth was taxed heavily, with Syrian tax posts reaping an enormous 25 percent duty on all goods passing through bound for Ctesiphon to the east, or Tyre, Sidon, and Antioch to the west.[603] As part of Syria, naturally Palmyra was not exempt from such duties; thus an inscription from Palmyra dated to 161 honours Marcus Aemilius Marcianus Asclepiades, the Roman tax-collector of the time based at Antioch.[604] Such a high duty reflects the growing demand in Rome for goods from the East.[605] It also shows the importance that Rome had invested in Syria for its own monetary aspirations. From Palmyra Rome would reap handsome profits, but at this stage Rome's duties were not especially crippling for Palmyra. Rather, instead of investing the city with a garrison, Hadrian was content to allow Palmyra to cooperate, monetarily, freely, as most eastern provincial cities were happy to do.[606] In fact Palmyra was so awash with wealth accrued from trade that it could even afford, on top of duties paid to Rome, to exact its own civic taxes. The Palmyrene tax law of 137 ensured that civic taxes were to be highly regulated; whereas once uncertainty surrounded the level of taxation for each merchant, now the council of Palmyra decreed that the taxable amounts were to be written down in contract form.[607] That gave merchants certainty. It also gave the city of Palmyra heightened legal authority, and the means to reap handsome sums through its own tax, just as Rome had.

This brings us to the critical point that, unlike conditions along Hadrian's Wall in the empire's remote north-west corner, the Euphrates River was never a barrier to Romans or the peoples who lived beyond it. In fact it was just the opposite. The river was a highway of maritime trade and had many wharfs and markets and other infrastructures linked Mesopotamia with Armenia to the north, Syria and Anatolia to the west and the Persian Gulf to the south. Very often in our postcolonial, postmodern age we are tempted to think within borders and boundaries. However, when engaging with the Roman Empire we should leave behind our modern conceptualizations. In essence, the Euphrates was not a confining border separating Romans on one side and Parthians on the other as Hadrian's Wall was. Rather, along the Euphrates Romans and other peoples regularly used it for their business which brought them together. That suited Rome's purposes well, for in the east the Romans were always opportunistic, and whether in war or during times of peace, their intention was rarely to settle for a solid, defensible boundary.[608]

The Parthian response to Rome's growing influence over Parthia's own commercial and political interests by use of Palmyra is difficult to determine for no Parthian literary works have survived. But there no doubt must have been at least some despondency. But misgivings or not the new status quo was emerging regardless.

Palmyra and Princeps

Needless to say, Rome closely monitored the unfolding events. As we have seen, Soades, son of Boliades, received testimonial letters from both Hadrian, and later Antoninus Pius for assisting traders on their journeys to Vologasias.[609] But these were not to be the only imperial honours paid to Palmyra. Hadrian himself visited the city,[610] and one inscription dated to 131AD honours the notable visit of "the god Hadrianus" to Palmyra.[611] Although the full itinerary of the proceedings of Hadrian's visit has not survived, this inscription does note that the emperor's dealings during his visit there were with both Palmyrene citizens and "the foreigners" that he had arranged to meet with while in that city.[612] Therefore it is not hard to find what those plans entailed. The fact that the emperor's visit coincided with the start of Palmyra's flourishing trade proper, as shown by the flurry of its inscriptions, demonstrates that the city's economic prosperity, together with its long-distance trading capabilities, were clearly on Hadrian's official agenda. I think historian Peter Edwell has noted with sharp discernment that the same driving force that lay behind Palmyra's citizens protection of the caravan trade was the same which drove Hadrian to enlarge that city's sizable economic capabilities: that is, the growing demand in Rome for luxury goods from the east.[613]

Needless to say, the new status quo was embraced warmly by Palmyra's entrepreneurs and they worked with it to secure larger profits to cover the high taxes exacted by both Rome and their own city. Thus there existed a mutual-beneficial understanding between Rome and Palmyra for the purpose of conducting trade throughout Mesopotamia that was developed under Hadrian. Where Trajan's invasion had failed to secure for Rome direct control over Mesopotamia by means of war, Hadrian and Palmyra had succeeded in securing influence over it through commerce. Also, whereas Trajan had ultimately failed to secure the Euphrates' riches, Palmyrene traders and the Roman tax-collectors that followed him did not. The Palmyrenes' cultural and geographical conditioning was such that they were driven to voluntarily and wholeheartedly embrace trade and long-distance commerce. Stimulated by Rome's own enthusiasm to invest monetarily in the merits of that conditioning, even if Rome's aims were for the purposes of gaining luxury items from the east and a lucrative tax return, it was that conditioning and investment that ultimately turned Hadrian's dreams for the east into a reality.

Judging Hadrian

Far from being a benign ruler with a benign policy in the east, Hadrian pursued an aggressive diplomatic and economic policy that benefited Rome in several ways. Firstly, it allowed Rome to establish a degree of influence over Parthia through pressure from its allies around Parthia's periphery. Secondly, it contained Parthian imperialist aggression and any resistance it might have considered against Rome's interests in the East. Thirdly, in Palmyra Hadrian was able to develop an economic power that would rival others in the Near East and assume a prominent place commercially. And finally, Hadrian was able to ensure, through Palmyra's contact with the Near and Far East, that Romanisation would flourish beyond the Euphrates, and thus further promote Rome there as an appealing trading partner.

Thus, where Trajan had failed to assert Rome's primary imperialist interests east of the Euphrates, Hadrian succeeded. He had simply recognised, unlike Trajan, the potential to achieve such aims through methods other than war, and seized upon it when the opportunity presented itself. But he was forced to do so. Put simply, war was not an option for Hadrian amidst his struggling empire. It is understandable that after the principate of Trajan who had annexed Arabia, conquered Dacia and Armenia, and attempted to conquer Parthia itself, it seemed to certain contemporaries like Aelius Aristides that under Hadrian there had been a marked and total shift in Roman foreign policy. But those like him had simply failed to notice that Hadrian had resorted to the already well established Roman policy of containment of Parthia in the East, and that he also had a clear economic agenda to uphold Rome's imperial claims there.

In short, it could be said that Hadrian's foreign policy should not be seen as the clean break with the past it is so often considered to be; nor should it be left to the shadows of sweeping and uncertain historical generalisations as it so often is. Through our investigation here for instance, it becomes very clear that the conditions the princeps faced in the east were very different and far removed from Hadrian's Wall in Britain; and that Hadrian was able to capitalise thanks to those conditions with great success. Indeed it was he who was the first Roman princeps ever to recognise the considerable potential for Palmyra to aid in such a lucrative capacity. Its potential as a trading force Hadrian had seen first-hand as a visitor to the city, and its realized success was such that future emperors would continue to nurture the city's trading role for over a century after Hadrian's death. Palmyra's story is one that demonstrates the longstanding Roman policy that existed well before Hadrian and remained well after him: that wealthy and powerful cities around the empire could be successfully developed and exploited so long as they acknowledged the greater power that was Rome. In the case of Palmyra, under the principate of Hadrian that power was in, and guided by, the firm hands of the emperor.

CHAPTER TEN

THE ANTONINE PERIOD

Conditions Under Antoninus Pius

S O LITTLE IS known about the Parthian policy of Hadrian's successor, Antoninus Pius, that it hardly rates even the briefest mention in many history books. But we can recover some of the basic features that molded it throughout his long reign as emperor. For one thing, we know that he continued to conduct Hadrian's containment policy. Pius was determined to confine all of Parthia's imperialist aspirations, and by ensuring the goodwill of Armenia as well as the Pontic and other eastern kingdoms;[614] the princeps was indeed able to effectively keep them in check.

However, Rome's eastern policy of containment was already a source of deep humiliation to Parthians. But worse humiliation was to follow. When, at the beginning of Pius' reign Vologases III dispatched an official embassy to the new emperor seeking his recognition as Parthia's king, which was intended to establish the king's position, and reestablish Parthia itself after another one of its long and bitter civil wars, Pius refused. And he also flatly refused to restore to Parthia its throne, despite Hadrian's previous assurances that it would indeed be returned to it.[615] It was a harsh tone, but not one entirely uncalculated and rash. Pius had seen how both Trajan and then Hadrian had been able to take advantage of Parthia's weaknesses, though in different

179

ways, and he hoped to do the same. But he would be met with disappointment. The eastern legions had not seen active foreign service in some twenty years and Parthia's fortunes were once again on the rise. When Vologases learnt of Pius' rebuttal he prepared for a war.[616] When all was ready Vologases invaded Armenia and deposed Pius' candidate for the throne there.

But then, he backed down and withdrew. This mysterious withdrawal has mystified many historians who can only put it down to some kind of fear the king held for the impending legionary counterattack.[617] But Pius was no military man and while it is true that he sustained Rome's military, he himself had never even seen a legion in his life.[618] Pius had deliberately shirked the provinces and stayed in Rome so that he could receive any pressing news from any part of the empire should the need arise.[619] So, we can rule out that Vologases was scared of the emperor and his armies. Rather, a more pressing threat came from Parthia's north. Pharasmanes, king of the Iberians, had already become a close ally to the Romans during Hadrian's time as emperor, and the *Historia Augusta* tells us that he was closer to Pius himself.[620] We know that this relationship was of great importance to Pius. From 140AD onwards, the emperor had imposed restrictions on the types of embassies he would receive, delegating the vast majority of them to the decision process of the provincial governors and their staff, which meant that only the most important embassies and international representatives were able to have an audience with him.[621] Pharasmanes though, found a ready audience with the emperor whenever he stayed in Rome.[622] Given that this king had had a hand in the Alani invasions of Parthia during Hadian's principate with that princeps' encouragement, it is reasonable to conclude, therefore that Pharasmanes had served his purposes on behalf of a Roman emperor well by once again threatening Parthia with an Alani onslaught. Given the Alani's past track record of overrunning Parthia repeatedly, this is a likely hypothesis.

However relations remained strained when Vologases III died in 147, and in his place, Vologases IV, a more aggressive character, came to the Parthian throne. His silver coinage is very common, indicating that the Parthian Empire was wealthy and prosperous at this time.[623]

It seems the new king used all that money to prepare for war with Rome. But it was slow and meticulous work. It had to be. After the civil wars of the early 2nd century, and the Alani invasions, the Parthian military was still weak. So, Vologases IV played a waiting game, and by gradual preparation, he simply waited for the aging Pius to die and then launch his own onslaught on Rome's eastern provinces. It was a shrewd and calculated tactic. With Pius' dead, the emperor's *auctoritas* and diplomatic influence would erode, and with that any threat Parthia's peripheral neighbours might have posed would too. With that, the Roman Empire would be so weak that Parthia's neighbours would then discard their alliances with Rome and support Parthia instead. Or so Vologases might have thought.

Of course, Pius recognised all of these possibilities. However, because he was not a natural leader of an army, all he could do was wait too, prolong the peace, and suspend the start of the war. But he could not do so indefinitely, and finally, while on his deathbed, he warned those closest to him about the Parthian king's intentions, making plain to all that he was furious with him and certain other kings in the east, and advised those around him not to trust them.[624] In 161AD Antoninus Pius died. The time for Parthia's victory over Rome had finally come.

Marcus Aurelius and Lucius Verus

Immediately upon Antoninus Pius' death in 161AD Vologases IV, declared war and Parthian forces swept over Armenia wiping out the Roman legion that had been dispatched there from nearby Cappadocia. The legion was led by the governor of Cappadocia, M. Sedatius Severianus, but when it was lured into an ambush, he and the remnants of his army had to flee to the nearby town of Elegia, where they were wiped out. Severianus, seeing this all unfold, committed suicide.[625]

Coin of Vologases IV. Legend: 'King of kings, Vologases Arsaces, the Anointed, the Just, the Illustrious, Friend of the Greeks'. Reverse: The king receiving a diadem from the goddess Tyche. c.152AD.
Wikipedia.org

All-victorious the Parthian king then installed his own candidate, one Wa'el, on the Armenian throne. Next, he invaded Syria and defeated yet another Roman force there. The situation was now so chaotic that in response, the new emperor, Marcus Aurelius, gave the order for his younger brother and co-emperor, Lucius Verus, to invade Parthia.[626] It was a tough response sorely required for such a desperate situation. But in the emperor's choice of Verus to take command he showed shrewd calculation and readiness to meet the chaos head-on. The *Historia Augusta* colourfully portrays Verus as a purveyor of luxury and totally inept at matters to do with warfare, and that during his whole time in the East while the war raged, Verus constantly indulged himself in Antioch and Daphne, leaving his army high and dry to do all the necessary work and fighting.[627] That has led some historians believe that Verus' legates, who indeed proved to be gifted and talented, must have been dispatched by Marcus to make up for his brother's lack of such qualities.[628] Some even think that Marcus was ashamed of the kind of licentiousness the *HA* describes in Verus, and that he therefore gave Verus the command in order to remove him from Rome and save the emperor from further embarrassment.[629]

However, such a portrayal is entirely a fourth century fiction. In fact, earlier writers recorded that Verus' capacity as a commander was actually something wonderful to behold. Dio, writing a century before the *Historia Augusta* was composed, described him as a vigorous man well disposed towards all military enterprises, and it was for those admirable qualities, Dio added, that Marcus chose him to conduct the war against the Parthians.[630] Even earlier sources agree with Dio. In 163AD Fronto wrote a letter to Verus praising him for his warlike qualities and military ability;[631] and that same sentiment echoed throughout Fronto's preamble of the history he was writing up about Verus' Parthian war.[632] Although Syme once argued that Fronto deliberately exaggerated Verus' character in the preamble solely to tarnish Trajan's own,[633] such a line of thinking really ignores that Fronto's praises for Verus permeate through all of their private correspondences also. In fact, it is likely that Fronto deliberately tarnished Trajan rather than overestimating Verus. Then, of course, we must consider that there was a real danger presenting itself and a need for a competent commander to handle it. Also, the Antonines were not generally prone to praise there own military exploits; hardly surprising since Rome had not fought a major foreign war for some forty years. Hence they literature from the period typically praises the victories of the past rather than their own.[634] So, by commissioning Fronto to write a history of this war in the first place, the emperor was announcing to all the crucial importance he placed in it as one to rival the great wars of the past, and at its head stood Verus. One wonders whether such a history would have been commissioned at all if Verus was doomed to failure. All such considerations therefore discredit the *Historia Augusta's* notoriously woeful claims about Verus' character, and is a perfect example that when approaching the *HA* as a historical source, we should do so tentatively.[635]

But if the *HA* reflects nothing on Verus' suitability to command, it is also inadequate regarding his actual conduct of the war. Birley believes that its negative portrayal of Verus's character was intentionally over-spiteful.[636] That may be, since it has been shown that its author purposefully chose to contrast his biographies of Marcus Aurelius and Lucius Verus as moral opposites and counter-positioned subjects for the sake of dramatic effect.[637] However, the *HA*'s author can be partly excused for using such literary license. He was after all simply drawing inspiration from popular fourth century writing techniques to characterize Verus. Other writers, like Eutropius, also claimed that Verus was a slave to every passion.[638] But however that may be, the author of the *HA* is blameworthy for going much further than Eutropius did in condemning the young co-emperor. For one thing, Eutropius commended Verus on resisting his passions.[639] The *HA*, on the other hand, claimed that he was simply, and completely, unable to do so.

Verus in the East

According to Fronto, Verus found the eastern legions in a state of total lack of discipline. But shirking any despondency, the co-emperor immediately took the undisciplined Syrian army in hand and through strict training prepared them for war. Results came fast. Up until then, Fronto tells us, the Syrian armies were mutinous, disobedient, and often inebriated.[640] But, upon Verus' arrival, they were quickly restored to the level of discipline required for a prolonged war. Forced marches, exposure to the natural elements, and much encouragement along the way all contributed to the armies' restoration.[641] But Verus was not just a strict disciplinarian - he showed clemency and sympathy for his soldiers when it was due, and painstakingly provided for them all the necessary logistical and medical resources and planning required for their service.[642]

But the danger in the East still loomed large, large enough to warrant the presence of Verus for the duration of the entire war.[643] According to Dio, when the Parthians entered Syria they carried off vast amounts of loot, pillaged from many of its wealthy cities, including Palmyra.[644] To meet the threat Verus dispatched Avidius Cassius ahead to repel the Parthians from Syria, which, just like his republican namesake (See Chapter Four) he successfully carried through to completion.[645]

Meanwhile, Verus was joined by legions and detachments from all over the Roman Empire, including the Legio I Minerva from lower Germany, the Legio V Macedonica from lower Moesia, and the Legio II Adiutrix from lower Pannonia, and many tens of thousands of other troops that all converged upon Syria. It is estimated that up to one-third of the troops stationed around the empire's northern frontier were deployed to the east.[646]

Verus made use of all of these forces immediately and the counter-attack brought immediate results. Once again Avidius Cassius showed off his military abilities, as did Verus' other legates Statius Priscus and Martius Verus. In 163 Priscus invaded Armenia and captured its capital Artaxata. While there, he installed his own candidate, Sohaemus, who was both a Roman Senator and an Arsacid by lineage, upon the Armenian throne.[647] Immediately following this another Roman column, under the command of Cassius, marched south down the Euphrates, and met the Parthians in battle at Sura. It proved a resounding Roman victory. Next, he pressed on and captured the cities of Dausara and Nicephorium.[648] With all of these successes under his belt, Verus then offered Vologases peace terms, but since the king still believed in his own rising star, he refused, and the war continued.

Our evidence for the events of the following year is patchy, but it appears that the Romans once again used their tried and trusted tactic that had so often caught the Parthians out: they opened up two war-fronts. As M. Claudius Fronto advanced east across the Euphrates and Tigris Rivers into Media, Cassius thrust into Mesopotamia, and he, or his colleague Martius Verus, met the Parthians in a great battle near Europos/Carchemish (well to the north of, and not to be confused with, Dura-Europos).[649] Lucian states that the battle involved vast numbers on both sides, and that it was costly to both Romans and Parthians. But, after much bitter fighting on both sides, the Romans again emerged victorious.[650] Buoyed by his success in battle, Cassius then took Edessa and Nisibis, and progressed down the eastern side of the Euphrates. Along the way Cassius took Dura-Europos as well, (Palmyrene inscriptions there begin in 168 with the dedication of its Mithraeum).[651] Finally the general and his army arrived before Ctesiphon and Seleucia. Ctesiphon resisted, but was ultimately captured and sacked. Seleucia too was taken, and when negotiations there broke down between Cassius and its inhabitants it was sacked too.[652]

Vologases, who had had such high hopes for his war against Rome was now at a complete loss. But then a disaster hit the Roman army which changed the course of the whole war and saved Parthia from further damage from Verus' legions: plague. The Parthians had already been suffering heavily from this plague and when the victorious Romans entered Seleucia they contracted it too. In all the army suffered, according to modern estimates, a mortality rate of up to fifteen percent.[653]

By all accounts the Roman army was crippled by this plague. Thus there was a complete halt in the Roman offensive thereafter. As the suffering got worse within the Roman ranks, the Parthians decided to launch a counterattack, and Vologases was able to take Armenia once more. After that the Romans, suffering as badly as they were, decided to cut their losses and withdraw, but not without one final show of force designed to intimidate Vologases and warn him from venturing into Roman territory again. In 166AD Cassius, at the head of a strike force, attacked Media. The ancient sources do not tell us exactly how this attack ended up. Some hypothesise that it was a total failure and that it was consequently hushed over by the Romans so as not to admit defeat at a time when plague was still ravaging their empire and Vologases was still at bay.[654] But on the other hand it is entirely possible that there was rather no failure to speak of and that the attack was merely intended by Verus to be a simple, but effective, show of force. After all, the triumphal procession of Marcus and Verus had already been planned for 12th October that same year and so there was no point in carrying on the war any longer;[655] and then there was the more pressing crisis along the Danubian frontier. There, the Germanic tribes had crossed over into Roman territory and begun looting and pillaging, which they had been allowed to do unchecked thanks to the depletion of the Danubian forces for the Parthian war.

So, sufficiently satisfied with their accomplishments in the East and anxious the meet the threat in the north, Lucius Verus and Marcus Aurelius held their joint triumph through the streets of Rome. But as the *Historia Augusta* relates, signs of the plague that had infected

Verus' army could still be seen on soldiers as they marched in the procession that wound its way throughout the city, tingeing the occasion with much sadness.[656]

After these celebrations were brought to a close Marcus headed north to personally lead the Germanic war. As for the east, the emperor, in recognition for Cassius' military brilliance and personal ability, entrusted it to him. But in time this power went to Cassius' head, and in 175AD he raised the banner of rebellion, proclaiming himself emperor. By that time though Marcus had been active along the Danube for years and had familiarized himself with the arts of war. As his brother Verus had since died as a result of a stroke in 169AD, he prepared to meet Cassius head-on himself. Support was offered to both sides from many quarters, and although our sources are silent on the matter, such support may have also been pledged to Marcus from Vologases himself. But neither Marcus nor Cassius would accept it, because as Marcus was once heard remarking, he did not wish any barbarians to become too familiar with Roman political troubles lest they should begin to exploit them for their own purposes.[657] This civil war was to be an all-Roman contest. But fortunately for the empire the threat of war was snuffed out when Cassius was murdered by his own troops that were loyal to the emperor. But as a sign of respect for his gifted general Marcus could not bring himself to gaze upon his head when it was brought to him. Such was his grief both for an old friend and for the fortunes of the eastern provinces.[658]

However, by failing to conquer Parthia the Romans had left Vologases free to continue defying Rome's interests in the East, which he did so for the duration of Marcus Aurelius' and Commodus' principates. Fortunately for Rome though, Vologases' military forces had been so damaged from the war and the plague that it was unable to reassert Parthia's control along the Euphrates. As a result Vologases could not recover all of Parthia's fortunes, despite his costly capture of Armenia, and Rome, thanks to Verus and his legates, retained a foothold between the Euphrates and Khabur Rivers, and had conquered new territory down the Euphrates as far as Dura-Europos.[659]

Verus' Invasion's Impact on Trade

The impact that Verus' Parthian war had on the Parthian economy is a matter of debate. On the one hand the consistency of geography and minting of Parthian coinage both before and after Verus' invasion shows that Verus did not wreak any substantial havoc on its economy.[660] On the other like all wars this one must have had some effect on the Parthian economy.[661] But whilst numismatic evidence remains critical to the study of Parthian history as a whole, interpretation must be made in light of all evidence. Within the unsophisticated economy of ancient Parthia, a consistent high rate of coinage circulation need not always indicate economic stability, but rather that sometimes the metals needed to strike coins were prolific at certain times.[662] A case in point is the final decades of Parthian history. There was such a profusion of coins then that on the face of it there was no sign of an unhealthy economy, or that Parthian was under any threat from the Persians.[663] However, we know that during that same time there was civil war between Vologases VI (reigned 208-228AD) and his brother Artabanus IV (reigned 216-224AD), and that both of them were overthrown by the Sassanid Persians.[664] Therefore, whilst numismatic evidence is useful when determining some economic patterns, it is clearly not always a reflection of other broader social issues.

What is certain is that by the 130's the Palmyrenes had staked a lucrative claim to the east-west caravan trade,[665] and that was a position they would not give up easily to Parthia. If anything, the consistency of Parthian coinage shows the continuance of that status quo. That was a status quo that Rome invested in too. In fact, during the years following Verus' campaigns, Rome invested so much capital into Palmyra's mercantile wellbeing, that building additions to the temple of Bel were able to be carried out. Also, Rome installed a Roman garrison under C. Vibius Celer, and constructed a new parade ground for Roman armies. Such support sustained Palmyrene mercantile prosperity and economic control in the Near East,[666] and so, as Richmond has put it, the golden age for Palmyra continued.[667] Verus' incursions may not have wreaked too much havoc with Parthia's economy, but

Palmyra certainly made the most of its difficulties and continued to reap a handsome profit.

Palmyrene prominence in the commerce of the region was facilitated in other ways by Rome as well. To return to the numismatic evidence, coinage minted at Edessa after Verus' campaigns feature the epithet *Philoromaios*; at Carrhae too coins were minted with the word *Philoromaioi* in tribute to its inhabitants' political loyalties; and since Singara later bore the title Aurelia, it may have been made a Roman colony using Roman currency at this time as well.[668] That Roman titulature and mercantile relics existed at all in these places is probably silent witness that Palmyrene traders were ever-active in the area. Roman coinage would have been useful for Palmyrene traders as it would have for the Romans who had invested so much into Palmyra economically. Of course, they would not have done so if they did not expect Palmyrene traders to make the most of it. Bu they knew that the Palmyrenes would go on and continue to do what they had done for centuries: trade.

However it cannot be denied that there is little evidence that has survived to teach us about this period with contemporary literature and inscriptions in Palmyra severely lacking. This has leads one to draw the conclusion that the Parthian king, Vologases IV (reigned c.147-191AD) must have barred all further contact with Romans after Verus' invasions in order to rebuild his own power base and reassert Parthia's control over its trade arteries.[669] If correct, that presented the Romans and Palmyrenes with a challenge, but it was one they were ready to accommodate.

Besides Parthia's hostility, there was another force undermining Rome's interests: nomad raids on caravans were on the increase. Although there is no definitive proof for this,[670] some evidence for it is found in the inscriptions at Palmyra dated before Verus', and after Septimius Severus', wars, which state that Palmyrenes were actively guarding caravans from nomad raids.[671] What is clear is that the Palmyrenes continued to provide their own military escorts for caravans to markets along the Euphrates. In the late 2nd century AD, the Palmyrene Aelius Boras, as one inscription relates, was celebrated with statues in the city for his repeated efforts in fighting off nomad raids on caravans as their military escorts' general.[672] Ogelos, another Palmyrene, was also commemorated for leading military expeditions against nomad raiders.[673] At Dura-Europos there is clear evidence that a Palmyrene military force, the cohort XX Palmyrenorum, which was most likely a detachment of archers, was garrisoned there soon after Verus' army had captured the town.[674] By this means the Palmyrenes had tried to maintain the caravan trade.[675] However, with fewer merchants' inscriptions at Palmyra in this period, and fewer caravans from arriving from the East, trade between the Roman Empire and the East had clearly diminished, and with that so too did Palmyra's fortunes. Whereas Trajan's Parthian war may have served Palmyra's commercial interests well, Verus' had not.

Dura-Europos, the so-called 'Pompeii of the Desert', was originally founded as a Seleucid town around 113 BC that was taken over by the Parthians in the late 2nd century BC until its capture by the Romans led by Cassius during Verus' war.[676] It later became famous in the early 1920's when it was discovered and later excavated by archaeologists such as Cumont and Breasted. Although few relics of the Parthian era in Dura have survived, we can say something of its Roman period. During that time it is known, for instance, that the local population's Hellenistic roots were maintained throughout. A parchment found there dated to 180AD makes mention of the cult of Seleucus Nicator,[677] and the town even had its own Temple dedicated to Zeus.[678] But despite its Seleucid appearance, the town was largely made up of Greek and Syrian inhabitants who used Hellenistic civic structures and traditions, but were also deeply loyal to their own unique social identity as well.[679]

Dura-Europos was located on the Euphrates River between Palmyra to the northwest and Mesopotamia to the southeast, and it was heavily influenced by both regions, including with respect to religion. Consequently, Palmyrene-style temple architecture can be seen there alongside Parthian Ahura-Mazda, fire worship, and Parthian king ruler cult buildings.[680] In capturing this town, Rome had secured a site in prime strategic position and social importance to secure and extend Palmyrene, and thus Roman interests as well, into the Parthian empire's Mesopotamian heartland. The presence of a Palmyrene garrison there, serving under Rome's authority, was certainly a statement that Palmyra had a growing vested interest in regional trade passing through Dura and along the Euphrates itself.

Nonetheless, whilst fewer merchants worked the trade routes, those who did were able to translate higher risk into increased profit.[681] Thus, the Palmyrenes, who had much to profit themselves from the ever-increasing market demand in Rome for eastern luxury items, ensured that some semblance of financial continuity remained, and that might go some way in explaining the consistent coinage. However, in reality, they were simply taking advantage of the diminishing presence of Parthian power in the Mesopotamian plains. Parthia's control over the trans-Euphrates leg of the Silk Route was crumbling, and that allowed Rome and Palmyra to capitalise. That trend continued until Vologases' death in 192.[682]

Thus, despite Vologases' embargo, and increasing nomad raids, the Romans and Palmyrenes were ready to respond to the changed conditions. Consequently Vologases' policy to bring trade with the West to a grinding halt ultimately resulted in Parthia's loss, for Rome and Palmyra soon sought out direct trade with China, ignoring the need for Parthian middle-men for the very first time. Marcus Aurelius even sent an embassy to China to open trade negotiations. As the *Han Annals* of China recorded:

> "During the [Chinese] Emperor Huan-ti's reign [166AD] when the king of Ta-ts'in, An-tun [Marcus Aurelius], sent an embassy which, from the frontier of Jih-nan [Annam], offered ivory, rhinoceros horns and tortoiseshell. From that time dates the intercourse with this country."[683]

Although at first glance these gifts appear to be just diplomatic niceties, they actually indicate that Rome was in fact seeking out direct trade with China. Gifts such as these had been an important tribute offered by Parthia to the Chinese court giving as a sign that trade between their empires would be maintained. Hence the eleventh century Chinese historical work, the *Zizhi tongjian*, records that in 105 BC, when China was seeking out trade with western regions, the

Parthians sent an envoy to its court bringing gifts of ostrich eggs and some magicians;[684] and it was precisely at that time that trade began between Parthia and China.[685] Parthia was later to repeat the giving of gifts to ensure trade with China as well. As the *Hou Hanshu* states, in 87AD the Parthians gave a gazelle and some lions as a gift to the Chinese court, and in 101AD they also sent an ostrich and some lions there.[686] In short, the giving of gifts was more than a token gesture when it came to relations with China. Rather, they were signs of economic ties. Marcus Aurelius knew that, and acted accordingly in an effort to bypass Parthia altogether and open up direct trade with China itself.

As a result, despite what the numismatic evidence might suggest to us, it is clear that Verus' invasion caused a total disruption to the Parthian economy.[687] The giving of exotic gifts to the Chinese royalty to secure commerce was traditionally the domain of Parthia. Now, Rome was usurping that position. But Vologases was unable to reverse this trend and could do very little, even with an embargo, to reverse Roman gains.

That was regrettable to many cities which had basked in Parthia's glory days when it controlled the Silk Route throughout its empire. Some of them had hoped that they would return with a reassertion of Parthian power. Statues dedicated in temples throughout Hatra from this time depict their gods in military dress.[688] It is unclear whether or not these statues were petitions for Parthian military remonstration against the Romans, and how entrenched such a sentiment was among Parthia's subjects. But the numismatic, archaeological and Chinese records tell us that Vologases was fighting a losing battle. Rome and Palmyra had invested too much into the enterprise to succumb, and as a result, sought out alternative ways to trade with the East and Far East. By maintaining a military presence along the Euphrates, Palmyra had shown its designs on the trans-Euphrates trade. Rome too, with its sphere of influence as reflected in her coinage in the east, and its success in opening up direct trade with China, showed that it was also determined not to give in to any Parthian resistance.

The End of the Antonine Dynasty

By the death of Marcus Aurelius, Rome had reached a pinnacle that it could only fall from. It is often wondered why the great philosopher-king would allow the succession of his son Commodus when such a move seems to us today as sheer folly. But Marcus was not to know that at the time. Commodus was rightful heir to the principate and seemed innocent enough: even at the outset of his time as emperor he seemed as incorruptible as any man, as Dio assured us,[689] and if Marcus rejected his own son civil war would no doubt have engulfed the whole empire.[690]

Fortunately Commodus' foreign policy exhibited a certain degree of sober-mindedness than did his private life. It had to. Because of the plague's effects on his depleted army, the new emperor could not afford to spend lavishly on many foreign wars, and Vologases was left to rule Parthia in peace.[691] Of course, he did fight some wars, such as those against the Moors and Dacians, but generally, only the putting down of revolts and civil unrests were of this princeps' concern.[692] But while many of Rome's subjects benefited greatly during the peace, Commodus at last began exhibiting signs of his notorious corruptibility, and he began portraying himself as the incarnation of various heroes and gods. Admittedly, that was nothing new in the ancient world among rulers, but when he began believing his own claims himself, it drew the bitter resentment of those who looked upon him as a spoilt youth. So when he refounded Rome in 192AD and named it after himself as the Colonia Antoniana Commodiana,[693] and after spending so lavishly upon himself and his impulses that he even emptied Rome's treasury,[694] he was murdered. With that the civil war that Marcus Aurelius had tried so hard to avoid, even upon his own deathbed, now engulfed the empire. Parthia would not go unaffected by its results.

CHAPTER ELEVEN

SEPTIMIUS SEVERUS TO THE FALL OF PARTHIA

Septimius Severus and Parthia

THE REIGNS OF Septimius Severus and his successors, like last decades of the existence of the Parthian Empire as a whole, were ones of some continuity, but also change. Wars were fought, territories conquered and taxes were reaped. But the Severan period was also one of monumental change as the entire classical world slowly progressed towards a very different age, that of Late Antiquity. The most glaring case in point which demonstrates this time of transition is in the status of Palmyra. As before, it remained a leading trading city, but the increase in Roman military throughout the eastern provinces reflects the developing shift in the method used to maintain that status.

The Roman military machine was sorely needed in the east. In 193AD Parthia had mustered its conscript army and, throwing caution to the wind, made one of its last great acts of defiance against Rome.[695] Once again the Parthians had seized an opportune moment to do so. Civil had erupted after Commodus' assassination and engulfed the Roman Empire. Parthia pledged alliance to one of the war's contenders, Pescennius Niger, against his main rival in the empire, Septimius Severus. Yet as the war raged the new Parthian king, Vologases V, surmised that this was the perfect moment, since Rome's armies were thus preoccupied, to seize back those parts of Mesopotamia that had been lost to Verus. He declared war, and marching his army west, proceeded to lay siege to Nisibis.

However, it Severus eventually emerged victorious over Niger and, all victorious, he immediately marched at the head of an army and counter-attacked, invading Parthia. As a pretext for war, the new emperor claimed Parthia's alliance with Niger. But it appears that Severus was driven by a number of reasons for pressing for a war against Parthia. The Severan historian Herodian wrote that Severus:

> "wanted to win a reputation for himself not just for winning a civil war over Roman armies (which he was ashamed to celebrate as a triumph) but also by raising monuments for victories against the barbarians."[696]

It was an obvious point for Herodian to make, but its worth is mixed. Little is known about the life and identity of Herodian; other than the fact that his work generally reflects Roman elitist attitudes. He often claimed to have had first-hand knowledge, and yet there are passages in his work which he clearly borrowed from other sources including Cassius Dio.[697] But although the claim that Severus hoped to win a reputation for himself other than that of being a contender in a civil war is true, Herodian's other conclusion - that Severus had a fetish for arches - was no doubt drawn on account of the triumphal arches Severus later erected to commemorate his various victories, as all Roman emperors did. These included the famous Arch of Severus which was built in Rome in 203AD to celebrate his successes against Parthia and which can still be seen in the Roman forum today.

In contrast to Herodian, Cassius Dio, who was another contemporary and a Roman Senator, believed that Severus' true motive was simply "a desire for glory", but it was an empty glory Dio believed, because Mesopotamia at that time little to yield, while the cost of keeping a Roman force permanently in the region was too exorbitant for such little gain.[698] This observation does have a ring of truth. There was little to yield in Parthia's Empire at that time: the paucity in issues minted there tells us that Parthia's economy was weak.[699] But that said, it should be remembered that the main motive Dio gives Severus, a desire for glory, was the same that he had already once given to Trajan. One cannot help wonder whether this historian had drawn upon his own impressions of Severus' motives and just projected them onto him and Trajan too. Certainly, Dio admitted that the statement that the war was too costly with too little gain was his own personal complaint.[700] But, it was one that was held by other literati sophists as well.[701] But that did not faze Severus himself. He needed, as a new emperor, a reputation in the field that would cement his place as rightful princeps, not just the glory. Granted, glory always came along with that, but Severus also recognised that a foreign war would bring him many advantages, not glory alone.

However, although Severus sorely needed military distinction,[702] the new princeps, who was well-known for his shrewdness,[703] invaded Parthia over a whole range of other issues too.[704] For one thing, a foreign campaign would boost the morale among the armies on which his legitimacy for the throne rested. For another, it would also paint him in a good light back in Rome. There he needed to impress upon the hearts and minds of his supporters that he was a worthy successor to the emperors that had gone before him.[705] It might also have occurred to Severus while serving as legate of IV Scythia in the East fifteen years earlier that the Euphrates was no effective barrier to armies anyway.[706]

One may add to these motives an acute desire for funds. Of course, we have already seen that Parthia was not rich in coin at that point. But that would have told Severus that Parthia's army could not be sustained for any length of time, and that meant that what funds it did have would be rich pickings for a Roman force intent on looting and pillaging assets. Parthia's poverty also meant that a war would cost Severus little too. No doubt that was one particular deciding factor for the new emperor. After the bitter civil war with Niger the Roman treasury was nearly empty, and unlike when Vespasian was emperor and Parthia's economy was booming, during Severus' principate Parthia had not the resources to fight a prolonged war against Rome. Severus knew that, and as he repeatedly tried to capture cities like Hatra, and succeeded in capturing Seleucia, Babylon, and Ctesiphon,[707] these endeavours replenished the general's coffers and allowed his soldiers to secure valuable loot for themselves as well.[708]

However, loot was not the lone purpose of capturing a city. It also helped secure the loyalty of a general's troops, and increased his popularity and rapport.[709] As the civil war still remained clear in his and his soldiers' minds, for the sake of his empire's stability and his own position, Severus foremost had to earn the loyalty of his armies. By his letting Vologases to escape, and his choosing not to occupy Ctesiphon,[710] Severus was signaling that his war was not just one of conquest, but was also one of accumulation: the accumulation of loot for the troops, which in turn increased their goodwill towards the new emperor, which established his own position, ultimately returned peace to his empire, and rejuvenated it and restored its viability. It was to the cities in Mesopotamia that Severus looked to accumulate these things. Dio and others at the time called that chasing glory. Severus simply saw that as being expedient.

Severus' Parthian War

After sailing from Italy to Asia Minor, Severus marched to Syria and from there he crossed the Euphrates. His first objective was Osrhoene, and at the head of his forces he overran and annexed it. Others kingdoms faired better. The king of Edessa, Abgar, who had welcomed the emperor, was allowed to retain his kingdom, albeit at Roman disposal. Local Arabs and Adiabenes, learning from Abgar's example, quickly also submitted, and so Severus proudly adopted the titles 'Arabicus' and 'Adiabenicus' as displayed on his coinage.[711] These titles also appear on his victory arch in Rome.[712] However, the Arabs and Adiabenes soon grew restless and rebelled. Fierce fighting followed, but ultimately Severus' forces prevailed, and by 195 Severus had been acclaimed *imperator* three times over these enemies on the battlefield.[713]

Up to this point Severus remained virtually unopposed by the Parthian army for good reason: it was occupied in Persia and Media putting down rebellions. According to the Syriac source the Msiha

Zkha, it was Vologases' intention to foment insurrection among the Arabs and Adiabenes for the moment and then later return to the field once the Persians and the Medes in the east were properly dealt with.[714] Severus, too, was content to let the Parthians simply be for the moment, but because he had not yet faced them in battle he refused the title of 'Parthicus' until a more appropriate later date warranted it.

However, because a new civil war was fomenting in the western Empire against Clodius Albinus, Severus had to leave Mesopotamia to deal with that insurrection. Lucius Valerius Valerianus,[715] a trusted equestrian legate of Severus', was left in charge of the army in the East. Valerianus carried on the war but, probably on orders by Severus himself, he did not actually ever engage any Parthian army. Rather, he was content to restore some stability to the region by launching expeditions against local bandit Arabs and other nomads.[716] But then the Parthians, after successfully putting down the insurrections to the east, finally returned to the west and as punishment for the Adiabenes' disloyalty, and as a clear message to other subjects contemplating submission to Rome's armies, they plundered and sacked several Adiabene cities.[717]

In 197, after having won yet another civil war, this time against Clodius, Severus once more took charge of another army made up of two new legions and marched east. He had actually formed three new legions the, I, II, and III Parthica for the task; although he left Legio II Parthica in Italy should need arise anywhere around the empire to use it, while he took Legio I and Legio III with him east. Severus had learnt that Marcus Aurelius' depletion of the Danubian armies for his Parthian war had invited Germanic attacks from across that river. He was determined not to make the same mistake, so he had formed these three new legions precisely for his own Parthian war. Unlike Marcus too, Severus had made plans to permanently conquer Parthian territory, and marched down the Euphrates at the head of his swelling army and a war-fleet.[718] Thus, this life-giving river revealed its double edge: just as it had for so long facilitated trade and friendly human movement for the subjects of Rome and Parthia alike; now it was facilitating yet another war between the two, as Rome's army marched against Parthia's own.

However, once again the Parthian army had to retire before Severus, and the emperor entered both Babylon and Seleucia unopposed on the one-hundredth anniversary of Trajan's succession. Not only was Severus' attack unexpected, but to the east again Vologases was faced with another rebellion. Given that one of his very own brothers had even escorted Severus' army, civil discord frayed his empire.[719]

Civil wars and revolts had plagued the Parthian Empire for much of its history. Indeed the Arsacid monarch's official title 'King of kings' belies the reality that the monarch was a ruler over many other aspiring rulers, the goodwill of whom he relied upon for his own power to last, let alone prosper. In fact, infighting among the Parthian King and his lesser kings was so common throughout the Parthian Empire that Tacitus assumed it was a royal tradition. As Tacitus makes Vologases I say in his *Annals*:

> "By abandoning the tradition of brotherly feuds and family strife, I thought I had settled the affairs of our family satisfactorily."[720]

But of course, even if these words contain a kernel of truth, it is worth noticing that there were indeed Parthian kings like Vologases I who were themselves willing to ignore such dubious 'tradition' for the sake of the stability of their own empire's wellbeing. But all such willingness Severus was now pulling to pieces. Faced with danger in both war and civil war Vologases had no choice but to withdraw before the Romans, contend with the rebellion to the east, and simply hope that Parthia's tried and trusted tactic of withdrawal and counter-attack would confound the Roman attackers one more time. At this point Vologases would have deeply despaired at his earlier impetuosity in attacking Rome when he did years beforehand which had sparked Severus' military onslaughts. Parthian ambition had over-extended itself at a time when consolidation, both economical and military, was most needed.

The way thus cleared, Severus marched onto Ctesiphon which he plundered, then sacked, killing or enslaving its entire population.[721] This was more than just a simple act of war. It was heavy with meaning in the Roman context. Severus was attempting to propagate himself as an extension of previous emperors. Already he had proclaimed himself the son of Marcus Aurelius, as denarii bearing the inscription 'Son of the deified Marcus Pius' demonstrate.[722] He also proclaimed himself adopted brother of Commodus and of divine descent through Nerva.[723] Central to these dynastic claims was essentially the need to control the Roman armies. Severus was still a new princeps and he had already fought several civil wars. Therefore, in order to establish himself properly as emperor he had to show his soldiers that he was its legitimate commander and the empire's legitimate ruler.[724] As a result, Severus was careful to invade only those regions in the east penetrated by his imperial predecessors Trajan and Verus. Larger conquests like those of Alexander the Great were just nowhere near as politically powerful as those more modest ones of his Roman precursors at the time. But for Severus the sacking of Ctesiphon meant more than just a continuum. It was also a culmination. By sacking it Severus was calling a crescendo and an end to the Antonine and pre-Antonine wars that had preceded his own. On the 28th January 198 Severus proclaimed an end to the campaign announcing that Parthia had now been properly conquered, and he adopted the title 'Parthicus Maximus', just as Trajan had done.[725]

Of course, that was not the whole truth. Parthia's empire was not completely subjugated at all, and Severus had to fortify his conquests extensively in preparation for further fighting. But nonetheless, Severus' announcement was a signal to the Roman world that he was intent on maintaining imperial precedence as all reliable emperors did.

Severus then proceeded to return north and besieged Hatra which still held out. Hatra was a fiercely defended Parthian outpost that acted as a frontier fortress between the Euphrates and Tigris Rivers. Its militarism is clearly reflected in its sculpture. Statues dated to this period increasingly depict military dress, and in one inscription found there a suppliant called upon Samya the Eagle patron god of the city to save it from this moment - or one like it - of dire "weakness".[726]

Inevitably, Severus had to abandon the siege and the impregnable Hatra remained Parthian. But if Severus had sought to gain the loyalty and goodwill of his troops by laying siege to this city that was left partly unrealized: at this point there was mutiny fermenting among the troops.[727] According to Dio, Severus had to make another attempt to capture Hatra to please his troops and retain his dignity as a commander but that attempt too proved unsuccessful.[728] Frustrated, the emperor could do little but return west. Nevertheless, he gloried in his new conquests, and Severus loved to boast that he had made a secure "bulwark of Syria" in his new territorial gains east of the Euphrates.[729]

The northern portion of Mesopotamia was now proclaimed the new province of 'Mesopotamia' and placed under the governance of an equestrian prefect, and Nisibis was declared one of three capitals and *colonias*, together with Singara near the Tigris, and Resaina in Mesopotamia's west.[730] But while there was celebration in Rome, there was only humiliation in Parthia. The stationing of Roman forces well east of the Syrian Euphrates was deeply disturbing for the Parthians,[731] and it only added to their woes. What was left of Vologases' loyalists had no option but to make a lackluster withdrawal, and this time there would be no rebellions against Rome from among any of the one-time pro-Parthian territories between the two rivers. The repeated attrition caused by the Romans over the years had had their effect on the region, and among other things they had quickened the demise of Parthian power.[732]

The Arch of Septimius Severus, in the Roman Forum.
Wikipedia.org

But Severus was jubilant. He had at last proved himself a true Roman commander and leader. To celebrate his victory a triumphal arch was erected in the Roman forum in 203AD that features reliefs depicting Roman military actions in Mesopotamia. There are four main reliefs. Section 1 in the southeast part portrays action before a city's walls, sections 2 in the northeast shows the capitulation and surrender of another city, section 3 in the northwest the siege and capitulation of a city by a river (Euphrates or Tigris), and in section 4 in the southwest part the fall of a city. Throughout the twentieth century a number of theories were put forward in order to identify the events those reliefs actually depicted. In has been suggested that section 1 shows the liberation of Nisibis from the Parthian siege, section 2 the submission of Edessa or Seleucia, section 3 the capitulation of Seleucia or Babylon, and section 4 the fall of Ctesiphon.[733] However, all such theories miss the actual motivation behind the erection of the arch, and the fact that it was never intended to be a realistic representation of events in the war. Dio himself states that Seleucia and Babylon surrendered unconditionally without any resistance,[734] so theories about their presence fighting in the artwork are dubious. The truth is that art and architecture were undergoing serious change at this time, whereupon older forms of realistic depictions like those on Trajan's column were giving way to newer ones of defamiliarised modes of expression.[735] Thus, in Severus' arch deliberate use of ambiguity was being employed to communicate a more subtle message than mere representation,[736] so as to simply convince onlookers that Severus' abilities as a commander were not in question. The arch portrayed 'official history', rather than precise actual facts.[737] That was taken for granted at the time too – both the contemporary narratives of Cassius Dio and Herodian are markedly different to the events portrayed on Severus' arch. The message of Severus' arch should be seen therefore, not about actual events that took place during the war, but rather as a case for the legitimacy of Severus' principate as Severus himself wished it to be viewed by his subjects. The timing of the erection of the arch was also of crucial importance – built soon after the tenth anniversary of Severus' accession, the arch reaffirmed his rule and his achievement in rescuing the state from civil war and extending its power over foreign enemies.[738] Therefore, although not a chronicle of Severus' war with Parthia, his arch, and the war it exhibited, served a very tangible political purpose.

Together with his arch, Severus' war with Parthia had served his principate well. Victorious in a foreign war, the Roman treasury replenished and the loyalty of the armies reaffirmed, Severus was able to restore to Rome the stability, pride and imperialist aspirations that had been lacking in it after the chaos of the civil wars. Severus could take credit for that, and the resurgent and united Roman Empire in turn responded with a kind gesture of its own in appreciation: when he died in 211 there would be no civil war and his successor would be Severus' own son, Caracalla.

Severus' Restoration of Palmyrene Trade

With the death of Vologases V in 208AD, Septimius Severus could reassert the presence of Palmyrene commerce in the region. But by doing so with strong Roman military support Severus was signaling that his goal and methods in the East were different to those following Verus' earlier incursions. Whereas once Marcus Aurelius and Commodus had sought to allow the region to be largely under the charge of Palmyra in the face of Parthian and nomad opposition, now Severus sought to directly control his province of Mesopotamia and enforce Palmyro-Roman economical interests there. The bulking up of Rome's military presence in the east signaled an economically resurgent Parthia. In fact by all accounts Parthia's wealth was booming considerably at this time. African Red-Slip dishes and Syrian Easter Sigillate dishes found at Dura-Europos indicate that at the beginning of the third century trade down the Euphrates River had again reestablished itself, and Parthia no doubt profited handsomely once more from its hive of activity.[739] Indeed, the coinage of Vologases VI was profuse enough between the Euphrates and Tigris to indicate thriving trade with the Palmyrenes along this river.[740] But it was also an admission that there was something of a political power-vacuum in the region, and nomad groups who had also recognized the weakness of the region were busy staking their own claims there too. They would be an ongoing obstacle to the Palmyrenes. An inscription from Palmyra dated to 199AD commemorates one Ogelos who had launched a number of forays against nomads in the region. It reads:

> "Ogelos son of Makkaios, son of Ogelos, son of Agegos, son of Seviras, for his complete virtue and courage, for his continuous expeditions he has raised against the nomads, always providing safety for the merchants and caravans on every occasion on which he was their leader."[741]

Indeed, Ogelos' was not a sole case. Severus had established the new province of Mesopotamia,[742] and in c.210 he stationed his Parthica I and III legions in it. He also embarked on a program which thoroughly bolstered his conquests in the east, as he did the whole of the eastern empire. Aerial photography over the Near East shows that Roman fortresses and forts were built from Jordan in the south to Syria and modern-day Iraq in the north and east under Severus. Fortress towns like Dura-Europos and Ana were strengthened, legionary fortresses like Balad Sinjar (in Iraq), Apamaea, Palmyra, and Tayibeh (in Syria) were more heavily fortified, and other, smaller, forts increased dramatically in number.[743]

It was a longstanding Roman military custom to fortify army marching routes at steady intervals so as to supply them with shelter and protection.[744] Hence, the fortifications throughout Scotland were placed 15 miles apart to protect and supply passing armies on the march.[745] Septimius Severus continued this practice.[746] Since soldiers marched far more than they fought in battle it was crucial to their success in war that appropriate resting points and defensive areas were properly established. The result was that the eastern provinces generally, and the province of Mesopotamia in particular, were thoroughly fortified and invested with soldiers, providing both defense for columns under attack, as well as useful staging points for offensives.[747] Severus' establishment of forts throughout the East gave a clear signal of the guarding of his recent conquests, and hailed that future conquests were possible.[748]

The effect on the ground of Severus' program of militarization is seen clearly in the ruins of Dura-Europos. There, the city was turned into something more like that of a fortress with the permanent stationing of vexillations from IIII Scythia and the XVI Flavia Firma, some 500 to 2,000 Roman soldiers; and that was on top of other temporary Roman legion elements and the 1,000 or so Palmyrene soldiers that could be stationed there at any given time.[749] The garrison's headquarters was located in the northern quarter. In fact, the military quarters of Dura-Europos are so distinguishable that Pollard has found serious cause to argue that Roman armies were more isolated, culturally and socially speaking, from the localities they operated in than is often thought.[750] But that said, it would be a mistake to presume that this meant that the garrison's role was purely militaristic, or that it had no contact with civilians at all. In fact, the garrison served a purpose that went beyond the military aspect: in Dura-Europos the garrison constructed baths, an amphitheatre, a temple of Jupiter Dolichenus, and a palace for the Dux Ripae.[751] As much as these were for soldiers, these buildings were for civilian activity as well. These same soldiers were also billeted to private houses right throughout Dura-Europos too.[752]

Indeed, it could be said that Roman soldiers could be just as sociable as anyone else: Roman armies attracted all sorts of retinue and hangers on, among them merchants, soothsayers, prostitutes, allies, and servants.[753] As a result, their social and economic impact on the ground could be, and often was, dramatic.

Roman forts and camps served diplomatic purposes as well as military ones. As can be seen from papyrus from Dura Europos dated to 208AD and written by the Syrian governor to a number of Roman army garrisons, Roman camps often entertained Parthian ambassadors as they traveled along the Euphrates River. It reads:

> "See to it that Goces, the envoy sent by Parthia to our lords the most mighty emperors, is offered the customary hospitality by the quarter-masters of the units through which he passes. And of course write to me what you spend on each unit. [Units at] Gazica, Appadana, Dura, Eddana, Biblada."[754]

Therefore, Roman armies were cultural units that shared their cultural facets with the surrounding populations. Indeed, soldiers under Severus had arguably the greatest social and economic impact on the Near East since the first century: for under Severus Roman soldiers had a rise in pay – their first since the principate of Domitian.[755] These developments served Rome's economic purposes perfectly as new markets were created both within army garrisons and outlying indigenous settlements. These, in turn, facilitated the building of greater infrastructure, urbanization and further furthered monetization replenished Rome's treasury through inevitable taxation.[756]

Severus' army reforms also addressed other social and cultural needs: for the first time in Roman history, soldiers were given the right to marry while on campaign.[757] This gave them the ample opportunity to co-mingle and collaborate with local peoples on a scale unheard of before. Such social and cultural permeation encouraged Romanisation right throughout the entire Near East.[758] Indeed Romanisation was such a success that it seems as though the only people stalling the process were the Romans themselves. But whilst some of Severus' contemporaries, including both Herodian and Dio, disliked these reforms and could not see any sense in them,[759] others saw the value in them as effective means to care for, and encourage a Roman military presence throughout the east.[760]

But despite all of this social reform, soldiers and garrisons remained the effective means by which Rome could exert its military will upon a region. Whatever else the Roman army was, it was first and foremost a military resource. Pollard therefore, is mostly justified in holding his point that the army was a very different creature to ordinary society. Its importance to Dura-Europos was certainly becoming more than just social. The town was still a frontier post of the Roman Empire since the days of Verus, and the bulking up of Roman forces there was an ominous sign that Rome was considering another war with Parthia. In fact the flurry of building there was excellent physical preparation for a fit army, and the fact that it mostly took place there in 211, only several years before the next invasion, under Severus' son Caracalla, took place, tells us that the Euphrates, and Dura-Europos in particular, were becoming increasingly important to Rome's imperial agenda.[761]

Now, it would be too hasty to jump to the conclusion that all of Septimius Severus' reforms were beneficial to the Roman Empire, and any appraisal or judgment of him as an emperor must be passed with the following consideration: one part of his reforms, perhaps to offset to armies' rise in pay, was the measure to lay all of the costs of the maintenance of roads, stations, and the imperial postal service which included countless pack-animals, on the provinces themselves.[762] Although this measure was implemented to boost transport and troop movement around the empire,[763] it actually failed dismally because local communities were simply unable to afford the upkeep that the service entailed. Consequently, corruption set in and the maintenance of the provinces deteriorated.[764]

Severus had aimed to settle his new province and maintain his and Rome's interests there, and he was certainly not backward in coming forward about that. Singara became Aurelia Septimia; Rhesaina became Septimia Rhesaina; and Nisibis, Septimia Nisibis.[765] Carrhae, too, was colonised, and 'colonia' appears on its coinage at this time, and at Rhesaina coins minted there bare the name of the third Parthian legion. To the west of the Euphrates, Palmyra was also granted colonial status.[766] As a result, the whole region from Syria and across the Euphrates was reorganised as a new economical, social, political, as well as military zone.

Severus' reforms were intended to be long lasting. He had calculated that there would be future Roman incursions, as there had been in the past; and perhaps many, into Parthian territory even in the foreseeable future. What he had not calculated on, however, was the failure of his imperial successor, Caracalla, to strike the decisive blow against Parthia. Nor had Severus foreseen the ascendancy of Sassanid Persia, which would succeed where Caracalla had failed. Nonetheless it simply cannot be denied that under Severus, whatever his virtues and despite his failings, a measure of stability in the Middle East was reestablished much to Rome's manifold interests.[767]

Searching for Caracalla

The personality of Caracalla is one that both ancient and modern historians have had difficulty in trying to discover. Part of that difficulty lies in the nature of the ancient sources themselves. Cassius Dio's narrative exists only in epitomes, and even they are fragmentary, while Herodian's narrative, although it is far more extant and detailed, is sometimes unreliable. Yet both Dio and Herodian agreed in their negative tone towards Caracalla, and that has had a marked affect upon modern scholars that are quick to judge and condemn. In keeping with this trend most just surmise that Caracalla sought solely to continue his father's policies and that had no real talent as a ruler in himself. But there is very little detail to back that claim up. I believe, however, that the evidence actually points to a more vibrant Caracalla. Of course, that is a belief made difficult to articulate given: the biases within the ancient literature, and the fact that Caracalla's eastern policy was never a consistent one. But I suspect it was a policy that was far more calculated than what most ancient and modern historians have presumed.

Both Dio and Herodian characterise Caracalla as primarily a fratricide and a ridiculous kind of Alexander the Great imitator who never matched the ability of his father Septimius Severus. In this they are partly right. He did kill his own brother and he did also idolise Alexander. But these facts do not stand him out as being any less violent or fanatical than any of his imperial predecessors. In fact, the option to execute his younger brother Geta was one forced upon Caracalla from the very outset of his succession. Geta was busy making his own moves to do away with Caracalla, and had the backing of "many soldiers"[768] as well as the approval of "the majority" of Romans.[769] Simply in order to survive the older sibling was forced to eliminate his rival and threat. As all historians know, that was nothing new. Most emperors, and most Parthian kings, had neutralized contenders for the purple including their own relatives. It was a risky thing to contend for the principate, and Caracalla, understandably and unsurprisingly, chose to win it outright at the cost of Geta rather than being killed off himself.

Caracalla's love for Alexander the Great was also anything but new. Many Romans were inspired by his military prowess in both republican and imperial times. Pompey is a case in point, but there are many other examples including Augustus,[770] Nero,[771] and Trajan.[772] Indeed, lots of Romans admired and sought to emulate something of Alexander's famous achievements.[773]

As for the thematic claim that Caracalla was outshined by his father; such a theme was a common classical writing device designed for dramatic affect. Perhaps the most famous case in point is Tacitus' negative portrayal of Tiberius against his predecessor Augustus.[774] Tacitus claimed that it was Augustus who chose Tiberius as his successor to show up his own principate, but given the popularity of Tiberius' principate with those of his contemporaries including Velleius Paterculus, the truth was certainly otherwise. Most likely, any positive portrayal of Augustus against his successor was entirely of Tacitus' own license.[775] Certainly Tacitus was not alone in using it, and he did not invent the device. In fact it is traceable to fifth century BC Greek tragedy wherein the theme of the ideal deteriorating into chaos was very popular. Like other ancient writers Tacitus did not escape being affected by a literary fashion as effective as this. Neither, it appears, could Dio or Herodian.

But this all begs the question: why were Dio and Herodian so hostile to Caracalla in particular? Dio stated that he hated Caracalla's public violence, drunkenness, and lavish spending,[776] but such qualities were not unique to this princeps either. Most likely, the answer lies in Caracalla's treatment of Dio's and Herodian's political climate. According to both Dio and Herodian, upon his succession Caracalla had the senators who had supported Geta assassinated, and he expelled every governor and procurator who had ties with Geta from their provinces.[777] In fact the emperor had executed or killed some twenty-thousand men and women who he perceived as a threat to his rule.[778] But of course, Caracalla's hard line with the Senate and the empire as a whole was not of his own invention. His father Septimius Severus was also firm with the Senate,[779] and famously drew upon the violent precedents exemplified by Marius, Sulla and Augustus and their notoriously cruel dealings with that institution.[780] But Dio was a second or third generation Senator who lived precisely during Caracalla's rule, so it could be said that his negative reception of that princeps was inevitable.[781] Herodian was also part of the Roman elite, although in what capacity is still debated, and he was naturally affected by Caracalla's hard-line too.[782] These facts must be kept in mind when evaluating these authors' accounts of Caracalla's principate.

Both Dio and Herodian expressed the sighing relief felt by Senators when Caracalla was assassinated in April 217, and how they believed their very lives were in constant danger while Caracalla was still alive.[783] Such a climate affected both authors deeply too, and inspired them to reflect, and form their views, about the emperor, the way they did. It was not the first time Dio had preserved something of popular sentiment following the death of an emperor. His reasoning for Trajan's motives for his Parthian war were heavily influenced by conditions following immediately upon Trajan's death when Hadrian sought to publicly denigrate them as folly and thus justify his own foreign policy.[784] Another example is Tacitus, who was ultimately influenced by the general mood in Rome immediately after the deaths of Augustus and Claudius in his damning estimations of their characters and principates.[785]

Caracalla's First Parthian War

According to Cassius Dio, by the time of Caracalla's succession all military ventures across the Euphrates cost Rome vast sums but yielded very little.[786] Such ventures were thus far less appealing in the eyes of the Romans. Not only that, as Roman armies campaigned further and further east they became fresh targets for new enemies like the Medes and Persians. As Dio put it:

> "...now that we have reached out to peoples who are neighbours of the Medes and Parthians rather than of ourselves, we are always, one might say, fighting the battles of those peoples."[787]

But Caracalla had seen the political benefits of a Parthian war during his father's time as emperor, and so, despite the dangers and emptiness of war in the east, he still sought to equal him. The distribution and profusion of Parthian coins from this time show that Parthia's economy was still strong, thus making the control of it appear all the more alluring.[788] Consequently, by 213 Caracalla was inciting dynastic struggle in Parthia with a view to Roman intervention.[789] Vologases VI and his brother Artabanus VI were both of the royal Arsacid family, and while Artabanus controlled Media and most of Mesopotamia, minting coinage at Ecbatana, Vologases held out within Seleucia and minted his own there.[790] This division of the brothers' mintage is certain proof that both Artabanus and Vologases were intent on exerting total control over the Parthian Empire despite the other's claims.[791] Caracalla watched on with his eye on the right moment to invade.[792] He had seen what chaos his own previous dynastic dispute with Geta had caused and he no doubt had the same result in mind when he began to play off one Parthian contender against the other. In the meantime he prepared for war. An army recruitment drive was implemented, and by the time of his eventual invasion he had amassed seven legions.[793] There was also an increase in minting in the eastern provinces, and the emperor summoned the vassal kings of Armenia and Osrhoene to Rome to be recognized as Roman nominees in their kingdoms under Roman control.[794]

Finally, when the Parthians refused to hand over to the emperor certain wanted persons, Antiochus the Cynic philosopher and Tiridates the Armenian, Caracalla dispatched his general Theocritus with an army to invade Armenia. He was resoundingly defeated, but that only infuriated Caracalla's and whetted his appetite to assert his rule over the East.[795] Caracalla's next move was to make an offer of a marriage to the daughter of the Parthian king Artabanus VI, but when this was flatly refused he took that as justification for war.

We have seen that Caracalla held Alexander the Great in high regard. But Caracalla's next move shows that he did not place too high a regard in his hero. When Artabanus soon returned Antiochus and Tiridates, Caracalla called the war off.[796] With that Caracalla's first Parthian War came to an abrupt, premature end. Now that was not the kind of behaviour one would expect from a fanatical emulator of Alexander. Caracalla was his own man.

Herodian, however, stated that Caracalla really only sought military glory and the title 'Parthicus'.[797] But one should be weary not to take comments such as this too literally – it was a standard charge made against Roman emperors who campaigned against Parthia.[798] But, that said, it is very true that Caracalla was exploiting Roman symbolism and imperial protocol. In fact, Caracalla's first expedition against Parthia was launched on the centenary of Trajan's own Parthian war, and Trajan had himself assumed the title 'Parthicus'. By recalling his predecessor's grandeur within his own principate Caracalla was in essence establishing his own. In fact, Trajan was central to Caracalla's motivations. As we have seen already, his father, Severus, had himself proclaimed an end to his own Parthian War and adopted the title 'Parthicus' on the 28th January 198 which was the centenary of Trajan's accession.[799] Far from emulating Alexander then, Caracalla was, like his immediate predecessor, invoking the fame and popularity of his Roman imperial forbears. Thus, although much has been made of Caracalla's admiration for Alexander in the sources, Trajan's own fame was equally appealing. By campaigning as Trajan had done only through Mesopotamia and east of the Tigris, on the one-hundred year anniversary of Trajan's Parthian war, Caracalla was signaling the nature and purpose of his own principate, but also its imperialist limits. Thus when Caracalla did assume the title Parthicus in 217AD when the emperor was awarded triumphal honours,[800] (although the *Historia Augusta* records that Caracalla took it up after his first expedition in 215AD)[801] he was showing off to the world that he was far from being the naive tyrant of Dio and Herodian. He was far more politically astute than he was given credit for.

Caracalla's Second War

Caracalla's second war in Parthia was forced upon him by external circumstances. Leading up to it he actually had the best interests of his empire and those of Parthia's too in mind when in 217 he made an offer of marriage to the daughter of Artabanus. According to Herodian, Caracalla held out the hope that if the two empires were united then both would benefit greatly and there would be no more war between them. With his proposal Caracalla added that if they worked together, the Roman infantry and Parthian cavalry could fight off and conquer all enemies come what may. It was an offer of monumental meaning, and if pulled off would have had an immensity of repercussions for the entire ancient world. After all the wars, centuries of them in fact, after all the political battles and real battles, and after all the symbolic and otherwise successes of each side over the years, as well as all the military failures and waste of life on the battlefield, here was a chance for both Rome and Parthia to put all of that behind them and take on the world together. Or was it? In the past, historians have believed the authenticity of this proposal on Caracalla's part to be dubious, and an improbable tale.[802] But actually, it may have had substance. Certainly, Romans like Herodian himself admired the idea, and although his claim that Macrinus later sought out a similar alliance with Parthia is total fabrication, it still remains that the author himself thought it real and sensible.[803] Why he would attach the idea, which he esteemed, to an emperor he hated without good reason is thus strange. In fact, Dio also reported the offer,[804] and Caracalla's later desecration of the royal Parthian tombs after the proposal's rejection reflects a personal spite for Artabanus that could have stemmed from his rebuttal.[805] Caracalla's offer of marriage then is a likely one.

Make no mistakes though; there were also other dynamics to the offer, including both economic and political aspects. If the empires had combined, then the spices and garments and other goods so loved in Rome could be traded for Roman metals and manufactured goods with far more ease.[806] Furthermore, Caracalla also had much to personally gain by the marriage arrangement. He would be privy to Parthian political issues and have a claim to the Parthian succession.[807] But, Artabanus also had much to gain from it. His own claim to the Parthian throne against Vologases' would be strengthened with Rome's support, as would Parthia's own security against other military threats. Not surprisingly, according to ancient writers Artabanus agreed to Caracalla's offer.

According to Herodian, it was during nuptial celebrations that Caracalla attacked unarmed members of the Parthian court and then led a Roman force throughout Mesopotamia and beyond the Tigris, looting and pillaging as he went.[808] This story is often regarded as spurious because at times Herodian is notoriously not the most reliable source we have.[809] But, the story might not be as dubious as some presume: our fragments of Dio tell us that Caracalla did in fact make his offer of marriage and that soon after its rejection he did also ravage parts of Media.[810] Now, although the nuptial celebrations are not mentioned in our fragments of Dio, they certainly allow for the possibility that Caracalla did in fact take part in some kind of betrothal celebration in Parthia. Not only that, but given Caracalla's speedy appearance in Media immediately after Artabanus' rejection of the emperor's offer, he must have already been in the East for some pressing reason - not unlike that of a royal nuptial celebration.

But although both Dio and Herodian condemn outright Caracalla's military response to the rejection as savage and unnecessary,[811] the error was really with Artabanus. He had initially agreed to the marriage after all as well as the alliance it implied. It would have ensured peace and economical prosperity for both the Parthian and Roman Empires, but at the last minute Artabanus rejected it,[812] and that rejection may have been delivered during official wedding celebrations of global importance. According to Dio, he ultimately rejected the alliance because he did not wish to see Caracalla hold a stake in Parthia's affairs.[813] Artabanus had fought his own brother for the Parthian throne. Now he would fight the Roman emperor for it too.

Caracalla's humiliation was complete and so his military response is more understandable than what Dio and Herodian acknowledged. It seems that Caracalla had accounted for the possibility of a last-minute refusal of marriage and alliance, and so he therefore anticipated condemnation for any military response. But he knew he could put something of a positive spin on things by evoking Trajan's fame once again: one hundred years earlier Trajan announced his own victory over Parthia. Thus despite the wedding's ultimate failure, Caracalla's military vengeance helped to successfully turn public humiliation on a global scale into one justifying the Roman pursuit of military glory. Caracalla the strategist was certainly a prodigious one.

As for Artabanus, by rejecting the offer, he was not only rejecting Caracalla's involvement in Parthian political and court affairs, but was also rejecting an offer of peace. In the carnage Caracalla left in his wake throughout Media, Artabanus' popularity suffered. That only added to his many woes: Vologases was still holding out, and Ardashir, king of Sassanid Persia, who would later exert Sassanid control over what remained of the Parthian empire by 228AD, was growing in power.

To Caracalla the rejection of marriage was a decision for war over peace. No doubt it appeared that way to many others too. Yet, Artabanus' rejection reflects a cultural disdain for Rome that the Romans, after so many wars over the centuries, had brought upon themselves. Indeed Caracalla himself and his father Septimius Severus had both wrought havoc on Parthia. The Parthian nobility too must have made refusal appear the only option available for Artabanus. Whatever his concerns for peace were, Artabanus' position ultimately rested upon his nobility's support as a Parthian king's always did; a nobility that preferred a weak ruler like Artabanus to rule though rather that a strong willed emperor like Caracalla.

As Severus had done, Caracalla proclaimed victory, and his commemorative coins were struck with 'VIC(TORIA) PART(HICA)' to mark his success over Parthia.[814] Also, as Verus and Severus had done, Caracalla promoted the colonial Romanisation of the lands between the Euphrates and Tigris Rivers. Thus Carrhae became known as Antoniana Aurelia Alexandriana, Dura-Europos was refounded and became Aurelia Antoniniana, and Edessa's coins at this point also began bearing the titles Aurelia Antoniniana, signifying that Caracalla had refounded it as well.[815]

Caracalla also enacted a return to his predecessors' policy to promote private and public trade ventures among Rome's subjects: between 213 – 217AD Zeugma and many cities of the Levant were minting their own coinage.[816] Thus, locals were encouraged to look to their own devices and initiatives for riches while the imperial treasury awaited the inevitable taxes that would be accrued through those same means.

Upon Caracalla's attack in 217 Artabanus withdrew before the invading army. Roman troop movements at this time suggest that Caracalla believed the fighting was now largely over, for he returned a large part of his army back to Pannonia.[817] However, Artabanus had simply crossed over the Zagros Mountains to recruit and train an army within the Parthian heartland to launch a counter-attack. In 217 he invaded Roman Mesopotamia. According to Dio, Caracalla planned to retaliate, but before he could muster a response he was assassinated in April 217AD.[818]

The Demise of Rome and the Fall of Parthia

The response among Roman Senators to Caracalla's assassination was one of jubilation at the death of a person they hated bitterly, and one that affected Cassius Dio deeply.[819] In the aftermath, Macrinus assumed the purple, and tried to fight off the Parthian army. Near Nisibis the Roman and Parthian armies finally met and a fierce battle lasted for three days. This was the final battle to be fought between Roman and Parthian armies and a description of it has survived in Herodian's narrative. It is illuminating. Artabanus was equipped with a vast army of horse-cavalry, horse-archers, and many camel-lancers. The morning after the two sides came into contact, Artabanus offered sacrifice to the sun, and then charged the Roman line that had also drawn up opposite his army's own position. As usual, the Parthian

archers were very effective and killed many within the Roman legionary ranks, while in close combat the legionnaires were most destructive. Eventually, however, the Romans were forced back, and they
began fortifying their positions with earth-spikes and other devices
so as not to be outflanked and destroyed as Crassus' army was under
similar circumstances. These methods maimed many Parthian horses,
so the Parthians, too, were forced to withdraw.[820]

Both sides thus proved themselves a worthy match for the other,
and the stalemate on the battlefield lasted another two days. But on
the third day, after much fierce fighting which saw Parthian cavalry
pitted against Roman legions one last time, the battle was finally
decided simply by the Parthians' numerical advantage. During the
battle here was a huge loss of life; according to Herodian there were so
many huge piles of corpses left on the battlefield that moving amongst
the dead bodies was near impossible.[821] Severely depleted in numbers,
by that time the Romans' limited numbers allowed the swift moving
cavalry of the Parthians to encircle them and begin a wholesale massacre of the enemy legionnaires unable to counter-maneuver at all on
account of the vast piles of the dead. Macrinus fled for his life. Such
was the end to one of the largest battles ever fought between Romans
and Parthians. It was to be their last against each other.[822]

As for Macrinus, his soldiers now despised him, but there was a
faint glimmer of hope for him. Artabanus' army was weary and was
eager to return home. So Macrinus sued for peace, or rather bought
peace, at the cost of 20 million sesterces.[823] But just as Macrinus was
no true Severan in warfare, so too was he desperate to cover over his
defeat in battle. He even tried to convince the Senate that he was actually victorious, and his coins even bear the inscription VICT(ORIA)
PART(HICA) as Caracalla's had previously done.[824] But such mimicry
for Caracalla's military exploits reflects a deeper need by Macrinus to
recapture his appeal to his soldiers - soldiers that had served under
Caracalla with far greater success. But it was all too little, too late.
His defeat on the battlefield was a humiliation that led the armies to
mutiny and Rome's population generally to regret Caracalla's downfall.[825] For all his faults and failings, as a military leader Caracalla, not
Macrinus, had proved that he alone was Septimius Severus' successor.

In fact, the light of Severus and Caracalla was not to be quickly put out. On 16th May 218AD Macrinus was killed by his own troops who then raised Elagabalus, a fourteen year-old youth who was Severan by descent, to the imperial throne. The legitimacy of the Severans had certainly not passed away. But Elagabalus' succession was more a warning of the crisis that was to come than the hailing in of a golden age for the empire. Four years after he became emperor this boy-princeps was also murdered, and his cousin, Severus Alexander, was in turn proclaimed emperor in his place. Unfortunately, the use of such coups and counter-coups had set in to Roman politics deeply, and would predominantly feature right throughout the whole of the third century until Diocletian, and then the House of Constantine reestablished some stability to the empire once again. But until then, becoming emperor did not mean safety or strength; rather, it brought dangers and murderous intrigue with it. Severus Alexander would not be immune. On the 21st March 235AD Severus Alexander fell victim to his own assassins. The Severan dynasty and the glories of classical Rome were finally brought to a close.

As for Artabanus, he would contend for the Parthian throne until c.222/3AD. In that year the very last of Vologases' coins were minted in Seleucia which says to us that Artabanus had finally prevailed in the civil war with his brother. Or had he? There happen to be several coins minted later in 228/9 that are almost identical to Vologases' earlier issues. Was Vologases' disappearance the result of his actually being captured by the Persians in 222/3, whereupon he escaped in 228/9 and started minting his own coins once again?[826] We have no way of knowing for sure. But a more likely explanation may simply be that there was a short-lived counter movement in Seleucia against the Sassanid conquerors, and that they used the rallying iconography of the Arsacids like those on recent coins.[827] Indeed resistance against Persia would continue in Armenia,[828] and large numbers of Parthian soldiers did feel so much animosity towards the new Sassanid regime that many even enlisted in the Roman army; the famous Parthian stronghold of Hatra even established an alliance with Rome rather than surrender to Ardashir.[829] But the cause was already lost. Artabanus, the last Parthian king, died in battle fighting the Sassanid armies in c.226AD.[830] In the aftermath, Ardashir founded the Sassanid Persian Empire, which covered even more territory than the Parthian Empire had done. It would last some four hundred years until when it was finally conquered by Muslim armies in the seventh century.

Despite Caracalla's possible hopes for peace, after his death Parthia crumbled and ceased to exist. Hence the ancients' few remarks upon this final period in Parthian history reflect the desperate conditions in Parthia at the time. Debevoise described conditions in Parthia as a whole at that time as a "senile wreck whose ruler had no more power than tradition or his individual prowess could command".[831] For that Caracalla must shoulder part of the blame: just when Parthia's fortunes were increasing, he had exploited its internal conflict for his own purposes. But he should not bear all of the blame. Caracalla's lust for military glory was the same lust that all other Roman emperors possessed. Tacitus himself noted that throughout Rome's entire history Roman armies always created desolation and called that peace.[832]But even that duly acknowledged, it must also be pointed out that it was that very thirst for power which ultimately dashed Rome's hopes of finally conquering Parthia, for since it was so severely weakened by Roman onslaughts it lay vulnerable and the way was open for the Sassanids to succeed where Rome had failed.

In a startling paradox, Rome had tried to undermine its Parthian rival, but that by doing so it would bring to the fore the power of Sassanid Persia that would pose an even more dangerous threat. Sassanid Persia, under the leadership of Ardashir, had been expanding its control over neighbouring kinglets since 212AD, and by 220AD it was in open revolt against Parthia, together with the Medes, Adiabenes and Kirkuk. Then, Ardashir overthrew both the Arsacid contenders Vologases and Artabanus and took control of the whole region for himself.[833] A new period, the Sassanid period, had finally begun.

In an added irony, it was the Romans themselves who were partly responsible for the galvanizing of the strength of Persia's coalition: it was they who had been drawn into conflict with Parthia, Media, and their neighbours,[834] and it was they, who by having penetrated ever further east, became the common enemy of Persia, Media and their allies. That standing as an enemy was one that established a common cause that ultimately resulted in the strengthening of Persian popularity and zeal, the overthrow of Parthia, and the bitter warfare between Rome and Sassanid Persia that was to last for centuries. But perhaps the error was not altogether with Roman individuals, but in the very nature of imperialism itself which is never satisfied, and never entirely open to possibilities other than warfare and exploitation. But, whatever cultural forces were at work, to the Roman elite Parthia was all too often seen as a weaker and conquerable neighbour, with the result that individual Romans within imperial, Senatorial and military circles, enthusiastically chose to be taken in by that same imperialism. In their hopes of conquest they were always disappointed, and the wealth they hoped to accrue by the wagonload was realised only in fractions. But it was they who by gradually weakening and destroying Parthian power had ultimately brought to the fore an enemy that history shows proved to be and even more dangerous foe than what the Parthians ever were.

CONCLUSION

THE STORY OF Rome and Parthia is an entertaining one, of that there is no doubt. Wars, battles, revenge, plots and intrigue all make for incredibly entertaining reading. But like any good story this one has deeper moral lessons to teach us.

Firstly there is the lesson of power. Neither Rome nor Parthia were able to prevail over the other for any length of time no matter what devices they employed against each other. They were simply too powerful to be overcome entirely by war. It is another strange paradox that the one thing that drove their armies onward to conquer others – thirst for power – was the same thing which ensured that neither side could conquer the other. They were simply too powerful. Repeatedly, both tried to take Armenia for themselves but neither could succeed without some concession by the other. Moreover, all attempts to conquer the other ultimately failed. So in the end it was the common pursuit of power that placed a limitation upon the realization of that same power for any one people.

Likewise, when we turn to the sphere of politics we get a similar result. For all of Augustus' brilliance, Tiberius' sense, and the abilities and giftedness of so many other Roman politicians, their efforts met their match in Parthia. Parthia, too, had its own politicians in the form of kings and nobility, but once again they met their own match in Rome.

Finally, then, we come to profit. This was one area in which Romans and Parthians were willing to cooperate, at least during certain periods. But in yet another paradox it was the result of such cooperation, the accumulation of wealth, which spurred Roman and Parthian commanders on to make to make war with each other in the never-ending quest to monopolise the market.

So, with all of this in mind, what, we might ask ourselves, were the rewards of Roman and Parthian imperialism in the end? The obvious answer is course, for the ordinary man and woman, very few. In a rigid class-structured world, power, politics and profit were the domains of the ruling elite. But that is not to say that the average person benefited nothing at all. As happens so often today, those three things – power, politics and profit – if used wisely, can prove invaluable to the defense of one's own kind against external threats and in extending one's nations interests at home and overseas. This book proves that if indeed used wisely, such things can take a city on the Mediterranean coast like Rome to world empire status or for that matter a nomadic tribe like the Parthians to the heights of international influence. Fortunately, for Rome and Parthia, they had the leaders who could use them wisely and did for generations. But as these two ancient superpowers each maintained sharp social inequality there was always a very real danger of uprising and civil war. When they finally increased and erupted on a growing scale it became clear that neither Parthia nor Rome could recapture the glories of their classical pasts. Thus Parthia was overthrown by their Persian subjects, and Rome descended into a century-long crisis of civil war after civil war. That is why it could be said that for all of their power, politics and wealth, it was the glaring inequalities in these societies which ultimately destabilized Rome's and Parthia's vast empires and hastened their demise. That inequality is a legacy handed on by Romans and Parthians to us living today, but if we are to preserve something our peoples' greatness, such inequalities must be addressed and freedoms must be respected, or else this world might go the same way as that of the classical world and also fall. Such an address is not something to be feared. It is when the brevity of humanity is respected and honoured that we as people are truly empowered, as well as politically enfranchised, and enriched – not only monetarily, but on far deeper levels.

NOTES

Chapter One

[1] Plutarch, *Sulla*, 5.

[2] Keaveney, A., (1982) *Sulla: The Last Republican.* Croom Helm Ltd. Beckenham. p39.

[3] Florus, 1. 46. 4.

[4] Orosius, 6. 13. 2.

[5] Sherwin-White, (1977) 'Ariobarzanes, Mithridates and Sulla', in *The Classical Quarterly*, 5. 27, pp173-183.

[6] Plutarch, *Sulla*, 5.

[7] On Gnaeus Manlius' reception in Rome on his homecoming from Galatia, see Livy, *History of Rome*, 38. 44-50.

[8] Livy, 33. 49., 36. 7.

[9] Compare, for instance, Livy's description of the various nationalities of Hannibal's forces at the Battle of Cannae in 12. 46., with his catalogue of Antiochus' forces at the Battle of Magnesia in 37. 40.

[10] On the general Legacy in the east left by Hannibal in the minds of Romans, see Ball, W., (2000) *Rome in the East: The Transformation of an Empire.* Routledge. London. pp9f.

[11] On the possibility that Romans and Parthians had considerable knowledge of each other, see Schlude, J., (2009) *Rome, Parthia and Empire: The First Century of Roman-Parthian Relations.* PhD Dissertation. University of California. Berkeley. p12.

[12] Plutarch, *Sulla*, 5.

[13] Sidebottom, H., (2007) 'International Relations', in *The Cambridge History of Greek and Roman Warfare*, Vol 2, p19.

[14] Valerius Maximus, 5. 7.

[15] Mathiesen, H., (1992) *Sculpture in the Parthian Empire*. Aarhus University Press. Fig 1, no 1, p120.

[16] Mathiesen, H., (1992) no 95, p174.

[17] Mathiesen, H., (1992) Fig 25, no 20, p142.

[18] Mathiesen, H., (1992) Fig 26, no 21, p143.

[19] On the use of the title 'Arsaces' on Parthian coinage, see Sellwood, D., (1983) 'Parthian Coins', in *The Cambridge History of Iran*, 3 (1), p281f.

[20] Debevoise, N., (1938) *A Political History of Parthia*. The University of Chicago Press. p46.

[21] Sherwin-White, A., (1977) pp173-183.

[22] Assar, (2006) 'A Revised Chronology of the Period 165-91 BC', in *Electrum*, Vol 11, pp87-158. For a detailed discussion of Parthian chronology see also Assar (2011) 'Iran Under the Arsacids', in *Numismatic Art of Persia. The Sunrise Collection*. Part 1: Ancient – 650 BC toAD650, pp113-171.

[23] Appian, *Mithridatic War*, 15. For a discussion on the Armenian marriage see also Debevoise, N., (1938) pp47-48, note 70.

[24] Assar, G., (2006) pp145-149.

[25] Mathiesen, H., (1992) p173.

[26] Bivar, A., (1983) 'The Political History of Iran Under the Arsacids', in *The Cambridge History of Iran*, 3 (1) p39.

[27] Tacitus, *Annals*, 15. 2.

Chapter Two

[28] Hind, G., (1992) 'Mithridates', in *Cambridge Ancient History*, Vol 9, ch 5, p129.

[29] Hind, G., (1992) pp129-163.

[30] Plutarch, *Lucullus*, 6. Sherwin-White, A., (1992) 'Lucullus, Pompey and the East', in *Cambridge Ancient History*, Vol 9, p234.

[31] Strabo, 2. 12. 4., Tacitus, *Annals*, 15. 5. 2.

[32] Bivar, A., (1983) p46.

[33] Plutarch, *Pompey*, 24. Sherwin-White, A., (1992) p233.

[34] Plutarch, *Pompey*, 30. Cassius Dio, 36. 45. 1f. Seager, R., (1979) *Pompey the Great: A Political Biography*. Blackwell. London. p51.

[35] On Manilius and Pompey, see Plutarch, *Pompey*, 30., Cicero, 9. Seager, R., (1979) pp49, 64.

[36] Strabo, 12. 3. 28., Plutarch, *Pompey*, 32., Cassius Dio, 36. 4. 8.

37 Strabo, 2. 1. 15., 11. 2. 17., 3. 5., 7. 3. Pliny the Elder, *Natural History*, 6. 52. Sherwin-White, A., (1992) p257.

38 Pliny the Elder, *Natural History*, 7. 99.

39 On the limitations of Pompey's army's capacity to conquer any further east, see Leach, J., (1978) *Pompey the Great*. Croom Helm Ltd. London. p83. On Pompey's influence on Crassus, see Greenhalgh, P., (1981) *Pompey: The Republican Prince*. Weidenfeld and Nicolson. London. pp60f.

40 Appian, *Mithridatic War*, 106. Debevoise, N., (1938) *A Political History of Parthia*. University of Chicago Press. p74. Bivar, A., (1983) p48.

41 Plutarch, *Pompey*, 36.

42 Cassius Dio, 37. 5. 2-5.

43 Plutarch, *Pericles*, 1., *Alexander*, 1.

44 Sidebottom, H., (2007) 'Severan Historiography: Evidence, Patterns and Arguments', in Swain, S., Harrison, S., Elsner, J., (eds.) *Severan Culture*. Cambridge University Press. p76.

45 Plutarch, *Crassus*, 18.

46 Seager, R., (1979) pp79-80. Beard, M., (2007) *The Roman Triumph*. Belknap Press. London. pp7-42.

47 Pliny the Elder, *Natural History*, 37. 16-17.

48 On Pompey's wealth on his return to Rome, see Green, P., (1990) *Alexander to Actium: The Historical Evolution of the Hellenistic Age*. University of California. Berkeley. pp659-661.

49 *Gospel of Matthew*, 24. 28.

50 Plutarch, *Pompey*, 31.

51 *Commentary on Habakkuk*, 1QpHab III.

52 Strabo, 12. 3. 34.

53 Green, P., (1990) p651.

54 Balsdon, J., (1949) 'Long-Term Commands at the End of the Republic', in *The Classical Review*, Vol 63, No 1, p15.

55 Botsford, G., (1918) 'Roman Imperialism', in *The American Historical Review*, Vol 23, No 4, pp772-778.

56 Galtung, J., (1971) 'A Structural Theory of Imperialism', in *Journal of Peace Research*, Vol 8, No 2, p116.

57 See Harris, (1979) *War and Imperialism*. Oxford. North, J., (1981) 'The Development of Roman Imperialism', in *The Journal of Roman Studies*, Vol 71, pp1-9.

58 Barroll, M., (1980) 'Toward a General Theory of Imperialism', in *Journal of Anthropological Research*, Vol 36, No 2, pp174-195.

59 See the same views as Barroll's held by Woolf, G., (1992) 'Imperialism, Empire and the Integration of the Roman Economy', in *World Archaeology*, Vol 23, No 3, pp283-293.

[60] For mention of these opponents see Plutarch, *Pompey*, 30. Seager, R., (1979) pp44f, 49f.

[61] Plutarch, *Crassus*, 16.

Chapter Three

[62] Braund, D., (1993) 'Dionysiac Tragedy in Plutarch, Crassus', in *The Classical Quarterly*, New Series, Vol 43, No 2, p468.

[63] Homer, *The Iliad*, 2. 8-9. On this inflection see Zadorojniy, A., (1997) 'Tragedy and Epic in Plutarch's 'Crassus'', in *Hermes*, Vol 125, No 2, pp176-177.

[64] Mattern-Parkes, S., (2003) 'The Defeat of Crassus and the Just War', in *The Classical World*, Vol 96, No 4, pp393-396.

[65] Zadorojniy, A., (1997) p170.

[66] Simpson, A., (1938) 'The Departure of Crassus for Parthia', in *Transactions and Readings of the American Philological Association*, Vol 69, pp532-538.

[67] Keaveney, A., (1982) 'The King and the War-Lords: Romano-Parthian Relations Circa 64-53 BC', in *The American Journal of Philology*, Vol 103, No 4, p428.

[68] Adcock, F., (1966) *Marcus Crassus, Millionaire*. W. Heffer and Sons Ltd. Cambridge. p49. Ward, A., (1977) *Marcus Crassus and the Late Republic*. University of Missouri Press. Columbia. p281.

[69] Plutarch, *Crassus*, 16. Keaveney, A., (1982) p427.

[70] Canfora, L., (2007) *Julius Caesar: The Life and Times of the People's Dictator*. University of California Press. pp17-18.

[71] That a Parthian War was in the air in Rome at this time, see Marshall, B., (1976) *Crassus: A Political Biography*. Adolf M. Hakkert. Amsterdam. p146.

[72] Simpson, A., (1938) pp536-537, 541.

[73] Velleius Paterculus, 2. 46. 3.

[74] Appian, *Civil Wars*, 2. 18. Cassius Dio, 39. 4. 7-8.

[75] Colledge, M. A. R., (1967) *The Parthians*. Frederick A. Praeger. pp 216-217.

[76] 'Wall of an Unknown Parthian Fortress Visible After Rainfall' in CAIS News, 4th May 2006. www.cais-soas.com/News/2006/May2006/04-05-wall.htm

[77] 'Discovery of Six Residential Units in Parthian Fortress at Yazdegerd' in CAIS News, 8th May 2008. www.cais-soas.com/News/2008/May2008/08-05-discovery.htm

[78] Grimal, P., (1983) *Roman Cities*. University of Wisconsin Press. London. pp10-11.

[79] Colledge, M. A. R., (1967) pp16-17.

[80] Colledge, M. A. R., (1967) pp217ff.

[81] Plutarch, *Crassus*, 17.

[82] Plutarch, *Crassus*, 18.

[83] Sampson, G., (2008) *The Defeat of Rome: Crassus, Carrhae and the Invasion of the East*. Pen and Sword. Barnsley. pp119-120.

84 Ammianus Marcellinus, 23. 3. 1.

85 Pubilius Syrus, 235.

86 Plutarch, *Crassus*, 23.

87 On Crassus' tactics generally, see Sampson, G., (2008) p110.

88 Plutarch, *Crassus*, 24.

89 Rostovtzeff, M., (1943) 'The Parthian Shot', in *American Journal of Archaeology*, Vol 47 No 2 (April-June) pp180-183.

90 Coulston, J., (1986) 'Roman, Parthian and Sassanid Tactical Developments' in Freeman and Kennedy (eds.) *The Defence of the Roman and Byzantine East: Proceedings of a Colloquium Held at the University of Sheffield in April 1986*. British Archaeological Reports. Oxford. pp59-75.

91 Plutarch, *Crassus*, 26.

92 Plutarch, *Crassus*, 32.

93 Plutarch, *Crassus*, 33.

94 Mattern-Parkes, S., (2003) pp393, 396.

Chapter Four

95 Everitt, A., (2003) *Cicero: The Life and Times of Rome's Greatest Politician*. Random House. New York. pp193-194.

96 On Parthian coinage in this period, see Sellwood, D., (1983) 'Parthian Coins', in *The Cambridge History of Iran*, 3 (1), p290.

97 Plutarch, *Cicero*, 36. Everitt, A., (2003) p193.

98 Cicero, *To Atticus*, 5. 18.

99 Cicero, *To Atticus*, 5. 20. Everitt, A., (2003) p194.

100 Cicero, *To Atticus*, 5. 21., *To Atticus*, 6. 1.

101 Cicero, *To Atticus*, 6. 6., *To Atticus*, 7. 1.

102 Horace, *Epodes*, 7. 1-3.

103 On Horace's use of dramatic license in this instance, see Mankin, D., (1995) *Horace: Epodes*. Cambridge University Press. p144.

104 Caesar, *Civil War*, 3. 82., Cassius Dio, 41. 55f. Debevoise, N., (1938) pp104-105.

105 Sellwood, D., (1983) p290.

106 Sheldon, R., (2010) *Rome's Wars in Parthia: Blood in the Sand*. Vallentine Mitchell. London. pp55-56.

107 Cassius Dio, 40. 30. Justin, 42. 4. 5. Debevoise, N., (1938) pp103-104.

108 On the effect that Crassus' death had on relations between Pompey and Caesar, and on Roman politics in general, see Holland, T., (2003) *Rubicon: The Triumph and Tragedy of the Roman Republic*. Abacus. London. pp288f.

[109] Fuller, J., (1998) *Julius Caesar: Man, Soldier and Tyrant*. Wordsworth editions. Ware. Hertfordshire. p300.

[110] Plutarch, *Pompey*, 56. Plutarch, *Caesar*, 29. Appian, *Civil War*, 2. 29. 114-115. Cassius Dio, 40. 65. 2 – 66. 1.

[111] Cicero, *To Atticus*, 13. 27.

[112] Cicero, *In Support of Marcus Claudius Marcellus*, 3. 9f. Everitt, A., (2003) p247.

[113] Suetonius, *Julius Caesar*, 44.

[114] Fuller, J., (1998) p300.

[115] Plutarch, *Antony*, 12.

[116] However, for an alternative view, see Billows, R., (2009) *Julius Caesar: The Colossus of Rome*. Routledge. London. p248.

[117] Canfora, L., (2007) *Julius Caesar: The Life and Times of the People's Dictator*. University of California Press. Berkeley. pp281-285.

[118] This is certainly the view of Billows, R., (2009) p248.

[119] Suetonius, *Caesar*, 79. Plutarch, *Caesar*, 60.

[120] On Alexander's adoption of Iranian practice, see Balsdon, J., (1950) 'The 'Divinity' of Alexander', in *Historia*, 1, pp363-388, especially p373f. On the offense this caused among his Macedonian officers, see Badian, E., (1981) 'The Deification of Alexander the Great', in *Ancient Macedonian Studies in Honour of Charles F. Edson*. Thessaloniki. pp27-71, especially p52f.

[121] This view is shared by Billows, R., (2009) p246.

[122] Fuller, J., (1998) p300.

[123] Plutarch, *Caesar*, 58.

[124] Appian, 3. 7-58. Scullard, H., (1988) *From the Gracchi to Nero: A History of Rome 133 BC to AD68*. Routledge. London. pp155-156.

[125] Syme, R., (1939) *The Roman Revolution*. Oxford University Press. p196.

[126] On Roman matrons' economic and artistic influence, see especially Pomeroy, S., (1994) *Goddesses, Whores, Wives and Slaves: Women in Classical Antiquity*. Pimlico. London. pp163-171. On women's roles in Roman religion, see Kraemer, R., (1992) *Her Share of the Blessings: Women's Religions Among Pagans, Jews and Christians in the Greco-Roman World*. Oxford University Press. pp50-70.

[127] Valerius Maximus, 8. 3., Quintilian, 1. 1. 6. Pomeroy, S., (1994) p175.

[128] Livy, 34. 1f. Pomeroy, S., (1994) pp178-179.

[129] Appian, 4. 33.

[130] On Roman the socio-political conditions of this period, see especially Alfoldy, G., (1988) *The Social History of Rome*. Translated by Braund, D., and Pollock, F. Routledge. London. pp73-93.

[131] Appian, 4. 133.

[132] Appian, 4. 63.

[133] Cassius Dio, 48. 39-40.

[134] Cassius Dio, 48. 41.

[135] Plutarch, *Marc Antony*, 34.

[136] Cassius Dio, 49. 19.

[137] Cassius Dio, 49. 20., Plutarch, *Marc Antony*, 34.

[138] Plutarch, *Marc Antony*, 34.

[139] Cassius Dio, 49. 20.

[140] Appian, 5. 75. Southern, P., (2010) *Mark Antony: A Life*. Amberley. Stroud. p210.

[141] On Herod's securing of power in Jerusalem and Judaea, see Josephus, *Jewish Antiquities*, 14. 14. 1 - 14. 16. 4. *Jewish War*, 1. 248-260.

[142] Cassius Dio, 49, 23-24.

[143] Cassius Dio, 49. 24. Plutarch, *Marc Antony*, 37. Southern, P., (2010) p212.

[144] Appian, 5. 132-133.

[145] See, for instance, Southern, P., (2010) p210.

[146] Huzar, E., (1978) *Mark Antony: A Biography*. University of Minnesota Press. Minneapolis. pp176-177.

[147] Cassius Dio, 49. 25.

[148] Southern, P., (2010) p212.

[149] Cassius Dio, 49. 27.

[150] Plutarch, *Marc Antony*, 37. Southern, P., (2010) p213.

[151] Lindsay, J., (1937) *Marc Antony: His World and His Contemporaries*. E P Dutton and Company. New York. p265.

[152] The slowness of the siege equipment baggage-trains is noted by Huzar, E., (1978) p177.

[153] Plutarch, *Marc Antony*, 39.

[154] Plutarch, *Marc Antony*, 40.

[155] Plutarch, *Marc Antony*, 50.

[156] Cassius Dio, 49. 31. Plutarch, *Marc Antony*, 50.

[157] Appian, 5. 133, 136. Huzar, E., (1978) p180. Southern, P., (2010) p222.

[158] Cassius Dio, 49. 33.

[159] Bivar, A., (1983) p64.

[160] Plutarch, *Marc Antony*, 53.

[161] Cassius Dio, 49. 40.

[162] On the Alexandrian triumph as consolation for Antony's failed Parthian war, see Huzar, E., (1978) p184.

[163] Cassius Dio, 49. 40-41. Plutarch, *Marc Antony*, 53-54. For a modern recount and detailed description of Antony's triumph and the Donations, see Fletcher, J., (2008)

Cleopatra the Great: The Woman Behind the Legend. Hodder and Stoughton. London. pp274f.

[164] On Antony's plans for further foreign conquests, see Huzar, E., (1978) p180.

[165] Cassius Dio, 49. 44 – 50. 1.

[166] On the triumph in general, and as a source of Roman identity, see Beard, M., (2007) *The Roman Triumph*. Belknap Press. London. p314.

[167] Scullard, H., (1988) p268. Goodman, M., (1997) *The Roman World: 44 BC-AD180*. Routledge. London. p38.

[168] Plutarch, *Marc Antony*, 66. On Roman writers' animosity towards Cleopatra following Actium, see especially Maehler, H., (2003) 'Roman Poets on Egypt', in Matthews, R., and Roemer, C., (eds.) *Ancient Perspectives on Egypt* UCL Press. London. pp203-315.

[169] For a description of the battle, see Plutarch, *Antony*, 66.

[170] Syme, R., (1939) pp305f. Green, P., (1990) pp679-682. Maehler, H., (2003) pp205f.

Chapter Five

[171] Cassius Dio, 51. 5-6.

[172] Cassius Dio, 51. 16.

[173] Horace, *Epodes*, 7. 1-10.

[174] Mankin, D., (1995) *Horace: Epodes*. Cambridge University Press. p144.

[175] Watson, L., (2003) *A Commentary on Horace's Epodes*. Oxford University Press. p275.

[176] White, P., (2005) 'Poets in the New Milieu: Realigning', in Galinsky, K., (ed.) *The Cambridge Companion to the Age of Augustus*. Cambridge University Press. pp322, 366.

[177] Cassius Dio, 51. 20., 53. 7.

[178] Horace, *Odes*, 1. 19. 11-12., 3. 5. 1-12., 3. 6. 9-12.

[179] Nisbet, R., and Rudd, N., (2004) *A Commentary on Horace: Odes Book III*. Oxford. pp80-82. Syndikus, H., (2010) 'The Roman Odes', in Davis, G., (ed.) *A Companion to Horace*. Wiley-Blackwell. London. p203.

[180] Suetonius, *Augustus*, 22., Cassius Dio, 53. 33.

[181] Hubbard, M., (1974) *Propertius*. Duckworth. London. pp94, 104.

[182] Propertius, 3. 4. 1f. Stahl, H., (1985) *Propertius: Love and War*. University of California Press. Los Angeles. pp192-195.

[183] Heyworth, S., and Morwood, J., (2011) *A Commentary on Propertius: Book III*. Oxford University Press. p130.

[184] Suetonius, *Tiberius*, 9., Cassius Dio, 54. 9. As to who exactly received the standards has confounded many historians, including Levick, who has argued that Tiberius had no hand in it given Velleius Paterculus' silence on the matter and that

Suetonius' statements that both Augustus and Tiberius received the standards is spurious. See Levick, B., (1976) *Tiberius the Politician*. Croom Helm. London. p234, note 38. However, Vellieus did not serve under Tiberius until a later date, and Suetonius' evidence is solid if Tiberius received the standards *on behalf* of Augustus. The Prima Porta statue of Augustus also portrays the receipt of the standards by a Roman not Augustus. This shows that the princeps recognized the exchange as carried out by another agent, but it was ultimately as his own coup.

[185] Cassius Dio, 54. 9.

[186] *Res Gestae Divi Augusti*, 29. 2. Galinsky, K., (1996) *Augustan Culture*. Princeton University Press. p155.

[187] Tacitus, *Annals*, 2. 25f.

[188] Horace, *Odes*, 4. 15. 1-9.

[189] Thomas, R., (2011) *Horace: Odes Book IV and Carmen Saeculare*. Cambridge University Press. p263.

[190] On this statue in general, see Galinsky, K., (1996) pp24f, 155f.

[191] Schneider, R., (2007) 'Friend and Foe: The Orient in Rome', in *The Age of the Parthians*. I. B. Tauris & Co. Ltd. London. pp61, 75, 78, 79.

[192] Schneider, R., (2007) pp58, 61, 62.

[193] Butterworth, A., Laurence, R., (2005) *Pompeii: The Living City*. Weidenfeld and Nicolson. London. p143.

[194] Beard, M., (2009) *Pompeii: The Life of a Roman Town*. Profile Books. London. p234.

[195] On this observation, see Braund, S., (2002) *Latin Literature*. Routledge. London. pp82f.

[196] Cassius Dio, 51. 20.

[197] Syme, R., (1939) p473f. Jones, A. H. M., (1977) *Ancient Culture and Society: Augustus*. Chatto and Windus. London. p150.

[198] Sellwood, D., (1983) pp284f.

[199] Curtis, V., (2000) 'Parthian Culture and Costume', in *Mesopotamia and Iran in the Parthian and Sasanian Periods*. British Museum Press. London. pp26-27.

[200] Research Centre for Conservation of Cultural Relics, (1998) *SALTMAN: Scientific Investigations Carried Out on the Saltman Mummified Remains and Its Artefacts*. RCCCR. Tehran. See also, Ramaroli, V., Hamilton, J., Ditchfield, P., Fazeli, H., Aali, A., Coningham, R., Pollard, A., (2010) *The chrhr Abad "Salt Men" and the Isotopic Ecology of Humans in Ancient Iran*. Calle Larga Santa Marta. Venizia.

[201] Mathiesen, H., (1992) *Sculpture in the Parthian Empire*. Aarhus University Press. Vol 2, p120.

[202] Josephus, *Jewish Antiquities*, 20. 3. 1-3.

[203] *Gospel of Luke*, 2. 1-3.

[204] Mounce, W., (1999) *Basics of Biblical Greek: Grammar*. Zondervan. Grand Rapids. Michigan. p70. Barnett, P., (2004) *Is the New Testament History?* Aquila Press. Sydney. p111.

[205] On the dating of the census in Egypt, see Ramsey, W., (1915) *The Bearing of Recent Discovery on the Trustworthiness of the New Testament*. Hodder and Stoughton. London. p255f. On Cyrene, see Lewis, N., and Reinhold, M., (1990) *Roman Civilization: Selected Readings*, Vol 2. Columbia University Press. New York. p589. On Spain, see Lewis, N., and Reinhold, M., (1990) pp589-590. On Paphlagonia, see Lewis, N., and Reinhold, M., (1990) pp588-589.

[206] *Res Gestae Divi Augusti*, 8. See also Cooley, A., (2009) *Res Gestae Divi Augusti: Text, Translation and Commentary*. Cambridge University Press. pp142-143.

[207] Josephus, *Jewish Antiquities*, 17. 2. 4.

[208] On year-long duration of this census in the provinces, see Ramsey, W., (1915) p255, note 10.

[209] Marco Polo, *The Travels*. (1958) Penguin. London. p58.

[210] This is a common view taken up by Henry, M. (1974) *Matthew Henry's Commentary: The Four Gospels*. Hodder and Stoughton. London. p8.

[211] 'The Magi's Gifts – Tribute or Treatment?' *Biblical Archaeology Review*, Jan/Feb 2012, Vol 38, No 1, p16.

[212] On this line in general, see Kidger, M., (1999) *The Star of Bethlehem: An Astronomer's View*. Princeton University Press.

[213] Virgil, *Eclogues*, 9. 47-49. On this see Galinsky, K., (1996) p159.

[214] Jenkins, R., (2004) 'The Star of Bethlehem and the Comet of AD 66', in *The Journal of the British Astronomy Association*, 114, (June) pp336-343.

[215] On the magi generally, see Colledge, M., (1967) pp98-103.

[216] See, for instance, Neusner, J., (1999) *A History of the Jews in Babylonia: 1. The Parthian Period*. Wipf and Stock. Eugene. Oregon. pp10f.

[217] *Book of Daniel*, 1. 3-5.

[218] *Numbers*, 24. 17.

[219] On these astrological and astronomical details, see Kaufmanis, K., (2003/2004) 'The Star of Bethlehem', in *The Minnesota Astronomy Review*, Vol 18, pp2-3.

[220] *Gospel of Matthew*, 2. 1-2.

[221] BM 35429.

[222] Yarshater, E., (1983) 'Introduction', in *The Cambridge History of Iran*, 3 (1) pxxi.

[223] Josephus, *Jewish Antiquities*, 14. 14. 1f.

[224] *1 Samuel*, 16. 4., *Gospel of Matthew*, 1. 1-16., *Gospel of Luke*, 3. 23-38.

[225] *Gospel of Matthew*, 2. 13-18.

[226] On Herod as Jesus' successor, see Richardson, P., (1996) *Herod: King of the Jews and Friend of the Romans*. University of South Carolina Press. p298. On the need

for political importance within Palestine, see Fenn, R., (1992) *The Death of Herod: An Essay on the Sociology of Religion*. Cambridge University Press. p189.

[227] On these political conditions and Herod's own deterioration, see Perowne, S., (1956) *The Life and Times of Herod the Great*. Hodder and Stoughton. London. pp103-108, 179-180.

[228] Josephus, *Jewish Antiquities*, 17. 2. 4., 17. 6. 1f.

[229] Josephus, *Jewish Antiquities*, 18. 2. 4.

[230] Bivar, A., (1983) p68.

[231] Josephus, *Jewish Antiquities*, 18. 2. 4., Strabo, 6. 4. 2., Justin, 42. 5. 12.

[232] See, for instance, Suetonius, *Tiberius*, 25., Tacitus, *Annals*, 1. 2., Cassius Dio, 55. 10., 56. 30. On Livia's promotion of Tiberius during the principate of Augustus, see Dennison, M., (2010) *Empress of Rome: The Life of Livia*. Quereus. London. pp175, 193, 218., and Freisenbruch, A., (2010) *The First Ladies of Rome: The Women Behind the Caesars*. Jonathan Cape. London. p61.

[233] On Nero's and Agrippina's relations, see Tacitus, *Annals*, 12. 41, 57., 13. 58f., Suetonius, *Nero*, 29. On Agrippina's use of affection for political power, see Barrett, A., (1996) *Agrippina: Sex, Power and Politics in the Early Roman Empire*. B T Batsford Limited. London. pp182-183.

[234] Rich, J., (1998) 'Augustus' Parthian Honours, The Temple of Mars Ultor and the Arch in the Forum Romanum', in *The Papers of the British School in Rome*, 66, p72. Syndikus, H., (2010) p203.

[235] Horace, *Odes*, 4. 5. 25-28., 4. 14. 43., 4. 15. 1-9.

[236] Virgil, *The Aeneid*, 8. 686-689. Morwood, J., (2008) *Virgil: A Poet in Augustan Rome*. Cambridge university Press. p134.

[237] Morwood, J., (1991) 'Aeneas, Augustus, and the Theme of the City', in *Greece and Rome*. 2nd series, Vol 38, No 2, (October) pp212-223, esp. 221.

[238] Livy, *History of Rome*, 1. 16. 7.

[239] Griffin, J., (1984) 'Augustus and the Poets: 'Caesar Qui Cogere Posset'', in Millar, F., and Segal, E., (eds.) *Caesar Augustus: Seven Aspects*. Clarendon Press. Oxford. pp189-217. Powell, A., (1992) 'The Aeneid and the Embarrassments of Augustus', in Powell, A., (ed.) *Roman Poetry and Propaganda in the Age of Augustus*. Bristol Classical Press. London. pp143, 147, 162.

[240] Hannah, R., (1997) 'The Temple of Mars Ultor and 12 May', in *Mitteilungen Des Deutschen Archaeologischen Instituts Roemische Abteilung*, Vol 104, pp527-535.

[241] Galinsky, K., (1996) p198f.

[242] Zanker, P., (1990) *The Power of Images in the Age of Augustus*. University of Michigan Press. Ann Arbor. p195.

[243] On the identification of Charax as being an intelligence gatherer, see the evidence in Pliny the Elder, *Natural History*, 6. 141., and Athenaeus, *Deipnosophists*, 3. 46/93d-94b. For a discussion of this evidence, see Austin, N., (1998) *Exploratio: Military and Political Intellegence in the Roman World from the Second Punic War to the Battle of Adrianople*. Routledge. London. p116.

[244] Suetonius, *Augustus*, 43. Ovid, *The Art of Love*, 1. 171-2.

[245] Pliny the Elder, *Natural History*, 6. 141.

[246] Rose, C., (2005) 'The Parthians in Augustan Rome', in *The American Journal of Archaeology*, Vol 109, pp21-75, esp. pp46f.

[247] Velleius Paterculus, *History of Rome*, 2. 101. 1-3.

[248] Josephus, *Jewish Antiquities*, 18. 2. 4. Tacitus, *Annals*, 2. 2.

[249] *Res Gestae Divi Augusti*, 33.

[250] Cooley, A., (2009) p255.

[251] Suetonius, *Augustus*, 23.

[252] Cassius Dio, 56. 25.

Chapter Six

[253] Syme, R., (1959) *Tacitus*. Clarendon Press. Oxford. pp498, 530.

[254] Syme, R., (1959) p494.

[255] Juvenal, *Satires*, 10. 68-81. Barr, W., (1991) 'Introduction', in *Juvenal: The Satires*. Oxford University Press. xxiv. As Barr points out, Juvenal's negative portrayal of Tiberius stemmed from his satirical theme of the folly of mankind. But that is no doubt a variation of the popular disgust Tiberius was held in at that time. Walters also reminds us that Juvenal's satires were intentionally theatrical in their presentation of historical individuals. It is perhaps safe to argue that Tiberius seemed a suitable candidate for satire in Juvenal's mind not for that emperor's capacity to be altered but to be popularly recognized as old and benign among his audience. See Walters, J., (2009) 'Making a Spectacle: Deviant Men, Invective, and Pleasure', in Plaza, M., (ed.) *Persius and Juvenal*. Oxford University Press. pp349f.

[256] Tacitus, *Annals*, 1. 11.

[257] For a praise of Tiberius, see Velleius Paterculus, 2. 126. Schmitzer U., (2011) 'Roman Values in Velleius', in Cowan, E., (ed.) *Velleius Paterculus: Making History*. The Classical Press of Wales. Swansea. pp177-202, esp. p184.

[258] This is reflected in Manilius, *Astronomica*, 4. esp. 50f. The precise dating of Manilius' works is problematic, but historical references in it and language style indicate that from book 4 onwards his *Astronomica* was composed sometime soon after Tiberius' succession. See Goold, G., (1977) *Manilius: Astronomica*. Harvard University Press., and Boyle, A., and Sullivan, J., (1991) 'Introduction', in *Roman Poets of the Early Empire*. Penguin. London. p382., and Volk, K., (2009) *Manilius and His Intellectual Background*. Oxford University Press. p1.

[259] Tacitus, *Annals*, 3. 47., 4. 30.

[260] Tacitus, *Annals*, 1. 69f.

[261] Velleius Paterculus, 2. 94.

[262] Tacitus, *Annals*, 2. 1.

[263] Tacitus, *Annals*, 2. 1. Syme, R., (1959) p237.

264 Tacitus, *Annals*, 2. 50. On the pomp of Roman princes in the east, see Maranon, G., (1956) *Tiberius: A Study in Resentment*. Hollis and Carter. London. p99.

265 Levick, B., (1976) *Tiberius the Politician*. Croom Helm. London. p145.

266 Smith, C., (1972) *Tiberius and the Roman Empire*. Kennikat Press. London. p82.

267 Tacitus, *Annals*, 2. 56. Smith, C., (1972) p92.

268 Tacitus, *Annals*, 2. 55.

269 Smith, C., (1972) pp92-93.

270 On Piso and Tiberius, see Smith, C., (1972) pp92-94.

271 Seager, R., (2005) *Tiberius*. Blackwell Publishing. London. p82.

272 On Artaxias' death see, Tacitus, *Annals*, 6. 28. On Tiberius' fascination for smooth administration, see Maranon, G., (1956) p179.

273 Tacitus, *Annals*, 6. 28. Smith, C., (1972) p195.

274 Seager, R., (2005) p203.

275 Tacitus, *Annals*, 6. 31.

276 Tacitus, *Annals*, 6. 31f.

277 Tacitus, *Annals*, 6. 38.

278 Tacitus, *Annals*, 6. 38. Smith, C., (1972) p197., Seager, R., (2005) p205.

279 On Tiberius' successes in these matters, see Levick, B., (1976) p147., and Seager, R., (2005) p205.

280 Tacitus, *Annals*, 6. 30.

281 Syme, R., (1959) p530.

282 Suetonius, *Caligula*, 13.

283 Suetonius, *Caligula*, 14. Cassius Dio, 69. 27. 3f.

284 Cassius Dio, 69. 27. 3f.

285 For another example of Artabanus' prostration, see Josephus, *Jewish Antiquities*, 20. 3. 56.

286 Cassius Dio, 69. 27. 3f.

287 On this event, see Suetonius, *Caligula*, 19. Cassius Dio, 69. 17. On Caligula's whimsical vanity, see Ferrill, A., (1991) *Caligula: Emperor of Rome*. Thames and Hudson. pp116-117

288 Cassius Dio, 69. 17.

289 Caligula, of course, never lived to attack Parthia. He did make plans for war with Britain and Germany, but his premature death cut short any imperial projects he may have had. It is clear though, that had he lived on Caligula would probably have sooner or later attacked Parthia. See Barrett, A., (1989) *Caligula: The Corruption of Power*. B T Batsford Ltd. London. pp63-64.

290 Ferrill, A., (1991) p153.

[291] Josephus, *Jewish Antiquities*, 18. 9. 1f. For a modern discussion of the Jewish population of Babylonia in this period, see Neusner, J., (1999) *The History of the Jews in Babylonia: Part 1. The Parthian Period.* Wipf and Stock. Eugene, Oregon. pp53f.

[292] Josephus, *The Jewish War*, 2. 388. On the Jews of Adiabene, see Neusner, J., (1999) p61f.

[293] Levick, B., (1990) *Claudius.* Yale University Press. London. pp159-161.

[294] Tacitus, *Annals*, 11. 6f.

[295] Tacitus, *Annals*, 11. 10f.

[296] Josephus, *Jewish Antiquities*, 20. 3. 4.

[297] Tacitus, *Annals*, 11. 10f.

[298] Tacitus, *Annals*, 11. 10f.

[299] Tacitus, *Annals*, 12. 14.

[300] On Gotarzes' assassination, see Josephus, *Jewish Antiquities*, 20. 74. On his death by illness, see Tacitus, *Annals*, 12. 14. Bivar is undecided as to which side is the correct one, but the calm following Gotarzes' death suggests there was no assassination. See Bivar, A., (1983) p79.

[301] Tacitus, *Annals*, 12. 44f.

[302] Tacitus, *Annals*, 12. 44f.

[303] On Tacitus' intent to excite his readership, see Griffin, M., (1990) 'Claudius in Tacitus', in *The Classical Quarterly*, New Series, Vol 40, No 2, p499.

[304] Keital, E., (1978) 'The Role of Parthia and Armenia in Tacitus Annals 11 and 12', in *The American Journal of Philology*, Vol 99, No 4 (winter) pp462-473.

[305] Andrade, N., (2012) 'Seducing Autocracy: Tacitus and the Dynasts of the Near East', in *The American Journal of Philology*, Vol 133, No 3, pp441-475.

[306] Levick, B., (1990) p90.

[307] On the delegation as relics by Roman historians of Foreign histories, see Potter, D., (1999) *Literary Texts and the Roman Historian.* Routledge. London. See esp. pp98f.

[308] Suetonius, *Claudius*, 25.

[309] On the conquest of Britain, see Cassius Dio, 60. 19f.

[310] For this view, see Momigliano, A., (1981) *Claudius: The Emperor and His Achievement.* Greenwood Press. Connecticut. p54., and Levick, B., (1990) p161.

[311] Tacitus, *Annals*, 13. 1f.

[312] Tacitus, *Annals*, 13. 1f. Hammond, M., (1934) 'Corbulo and Nero's Eastern Policy', in *Harvard Studies in Classical Philology*, Vol 45, pp81-104.

[313] Syme, R., (1970) 'Domitius Corbulo', in *The Journal of Roman Studies*, Vol 60 pp27-39.

[314] For more discussion on the psychological conditions of each side on the eve of war, see Gillmartin, K., (1973) 'Corbulo's Campaigns in the East: An Analysis

of Tacitus' Account', in *Historia: Zeitschrift fur Alte Geschichte*, Vol 22, No 4, (4th Quarter) pp583-626.

[315] Tacitus, *Annals*, 13. 34f.

[316] On the arch, see Tacitus, *Annals*, 13. 41f. For discussion of the ancient images depicting the arch on coins and other media, see Kleiner, F., (1985) *The Arch of Nero in Rome: A Study of the Roman Honorary Arch Before and Under Nero*. Giorgio Bretschneider Editore. Rome. On the artistic and historical importance of the arch itself, see Kleiner, F., (1985) pp72f, 85f, 92f.

[317] Tacitus, *Annals*, 15. 1f.

[318] Tacitus, *Annals*, 15. 28.

[319] Cassius Dio, 63. 1.

[320] Champlin, E., (2003) *Nero*. Belknap Press. London. p225.

[321] Cassius Dio, 63. 6. 1.

[322] Seneca, *Apocolocyntosis*, 4. Sullivan, J., (1986) *Petronius: The Satyricon. Seneca: The Apocolocyntosis*. Penguin. London. p235, note 13.

[323] Calpurnius Siculus, *Eclogues*, 1. 40-45., 4. 5f, 29. Keene, C., (1969) *The Eclogues of Calpurnius Siculus and Nemesianus*. Georg Olms Verlag. Hildesheim. pp2f, 97. See also the Einsiedeln Eclogues, 2. 35 for a similar allusion to a golden age under Nero.

[324] Manning, C., (1975) 'Acting and Nero's Conception of the Principate', in *Greece and Rome*, 2nd Series, Vol 22, No 2, pp164-169.

[325] Cassius Dio, 62. 17. 5.

[326] Rubies, J., (1994) 'Nero in Tacitus and Nero in Tacitism: The Historian's Craft', in Elsner, J., and Masters, J., (eds.) *Reflections of Nero: Culture, History and Representation*. Duckworth. London. p37. Barton, T., (1994) 'The invention of Nero: Suetonius' in Elsner, J., and Masters, J., (eds.) op cit. pp52, 58.

[327] Syme, R., (1958) *Tacitus*. Clarendon Press. Oxford. p437.

[328] Lucan, 1. 36f.

[329] Braund, S., (2008) *Lucan: Civil War*. Oxford University Press. ppxviii-xv.

[330] See for instance, Lucan, 1. 102f., 2. 550f.

[331] Lucan, 7. 440f.

[332] Morford, M., (1967) *The Poet Lucan: Studies in Rhetorical Epic*. Basil Blackwell. Oxford. p87. Ahl, F., (1976) *Lucan: An Introduction*. Cornell University Press. London. p35.

[333] Tacitus, *Annals*, 15. 48f. For discussion and construction of these events, see Ahl, F., (1976) p352.

[334] On Lucan's opposition to civil war, see Leigh, M., (1997) *Lucan: Spectacle and Engagement*. Clarendon Press. Oxford. p291. On Lucan's acceptance of the principate, see Bartsch, S., (1997) *Ideology in Cold Blood*. Harvard University Press. London. p59.

[335] On Nero's inconsistent and unsatisfactory public image, see Griffin, M., (1984) *Nero: The End of a Dynasty*. Yale University Press. London. p234.

[336] Tacitus, *Histories*, 1. 7., Suetonius, *Nero*, 19.

[337] Warmington, B., (1981) *Nero: Reality and Legend*. Chatto and Windus. London. p98f.

Chapter Seven

[338] Ball, W., (2000) *Rome in the East: The Transformation of an Empire*. Routledge. London. pp2, 12.

[339] On the Grand Strategy see Luttwak, (1976) *The Grand Strategy of the Roman Empire From the First Century AD to the Third*. Baltimore. John Hopkins University Press. For Kagan's revised version of the strategy see Kagan, K., (2006) 'Redefining Roman Grand Strategy', in *The Journal of Military History*, Vol 70, No 2, (April) pp333-362. For Gruen's quote and review of Luttwak's claims see Gruen, E., (1978) 'Reviews: The Grand Strategy of the Roman Empire from the First Century AD to the Third', in *The Journal of Interdisciplinary History*, Vol 8, No 3, (Winter) p563.

[340] Josephus, *The Jewish War*, 7. 93ff.

[341] Josephus, *The Jewish War*, 7. 93ff.

[342] See Beard, M., (2007) *The Roman Triumph*. The Belknap Press of Harvard University Press, London. p314., where Beard observes, "Rome was a triumphal city from its very birth; there was no Rome without the triumph, no triumph without Rome."

[343] Levick, B., (1999) *Vespasian*. Routledge. London. pp155, 165.

[344] Cody, J., (2003) 'Conquerors and Conquered on Flavian Coins', in Boyle, A., Dominik, W., (eds.) *Flavian Rome: Culture, Imagery, Text*. Brill. London. pp115-116.

[345] Jones, B., (1984) *The Emperor Titus*. Croom Helm. London. p56.

[346] Josephus, *The Jewish War*, 6. 356, 7. 39ff, 7. 59.

[347] On these matters see Jones, B., (1984) pp56-57.

[348] Rawlinson, G., (1893) *Parthia*. T. Fisher Unwin. London. pp292-296.

[349] Josephus, *The Jewish War*, 2. 377-396.

[350] Suetonius, *Vespasian*, 6.

[351] Syme, R., (1958) p30. Syme argued for the existence of an understanding between Rome and Parthia "for the common interests of the two empires" that resulted virtually no "threat of war". See also Luttwak, E., (1976)., and Campbell, B., (1993) 'War and Diplomacy: Rome and Parthia, 31 BC-AD235', in Rich, J., and Shipley, G., (eds.) *War and Society in the Roman World*. Routledge. London. pp233-234.

[352] Pliny the Younger, *Panegyricus*, 9, 14, 16.

[353] *Supplementum Epigraphicum Graecum (SEG)* 20. 112. McCrum, M., and Woodhead, A., (1962) *Select Documents of the Principates of the Flavian Emperors*. Cambridge University Press. p72. Number 237. Compare Levick, B., (1999) p169, with Debevoise, N., (1938) pp201-202.

[354] Isaac, B., (1990) *The Limits of Empire. The Roman Army in the East*. Clarendon Press. Oxford. pp67, 416.

[355] Whittaker, C., (2000) 'Frontiers', in *The Cambridge Ancient History*, Vol 11, p309.

[356] Jones, B., (1992) *The Emperor Domitian*. Routledge. London. pp155, 231 note 54.

[357] Whittaker, C., (2000) p309.

[358] On the functions of forts in general, see Southern, P., (2007) *The Roman Army: A Social and Institutional History*. Oxford University Press. London. p178f.

[359] Campbell, B., (1993) p234.

[360] Woolf, G., (1993) 'Roman Peace', in Rich, J., and Shipley, G., (eds.) *War and Society in the Roman World*. Routledge. London. pp180-181.

[361] Levick, B., (1999) p166.

[362] Suetonius, *Vespasian*, 8.

[363] Levick, B., (1999) p166.

[364] Levick, B., (1999) pp167-169.

[365] Sartre, M., (2005) *The Middle East Under Rome*. Belknap Press. London. p65.

[366] Syme, R., (1958) p31.

[367] Isaac, B., Roll, I., (1976) 'A Milestone of A D 69 from Judaea: The Elder Trajan and Vespasian', in *The Journal of Roman Studies*, Vol 66, p15.

[368] Isaac, B., Roll, I., (1976) p18.

[369] Bowersock, G., (1973) 'Syria Under Vespasian', in *The Journal of Roman Studies*, Vol 63, p140.

[370] Strabo, 16. 1. 27.

[371] Sarte, M., (2005) p267.

[372] On duties in Syria in Roman times, see Sartre, M., (2005) p256-257. For ancient reference to customs procedures along the Euphrates see Philostratus, *The Life of Apollonius of Tyana*, 1. 20.

[373] Jones, A. H. M., (1974) *The Roman Economy*. Basil Blackwell. Oxford. pp171-172.

[374] Isaac, B., (1990) p110.

[375] Bivar, A., (1983) pp82-83.

[376] Sellwood, D., (1967) 'A Die-Engraver Sequence for Later Parthian Drachms', in *The Numismatic Chronicle*, pp18-19, and plate 1, type 59 C (early) and 59 E (late). Sellwood, D., (2000) p295.

[377] On the resurgence of Parthian art and Iranian culture during the Parthian period in general, see Yarshater, E., (2000) 'Introduction' in *The Cambridge History of Iran* 3 (1) ppxvii-lxxv.

[378] Bivar, A., (1983) p86.

[379] Keall, E., (1975) 'Parthian Nippur and Vologases' Southern Strategy: A Hypothesis', in *Journal of the American Oriental Society*, Vol 95, No 4, (October-December) pp620-626.

[380] Josephus, *The Jewish War*, 8. 230f.

[381] Cassius Dio, 78. 19. 1.

[382] On Josephus' Roman audience and Josephus generally, see Mason, S., (2003) 'Flavius Josephus in Flavian Rome: Reading On and Between the Lines', in Boyle, A., Dominik W, op cit., pp559-590.

[383] *Res Gestae Divi Augusti*, 32.

[384] Valleius Paterculus, 94. 4.

[385] On hostages in general see Sidebottom, H., (2007) 'International Relations', in Sabin, P., Wees, H., and Whitby, M., (eds.) *The Cambridge History of Greek and Roman Warfare*, Vol 2, Rome From the Late Republic to the Late Empire, pp22-24.

[386] For examples of this, see Tacitus, *Annals*, 2. 4, 2. 56, 11. 16, 12. 14. On hostages in general see Sidebottom, H., (2007) pp22-24.

[387] Dessau no 9,200, in Lewis, N., and Reinhold, M., (1990) *Roman Civilization: Selected Readings. The Empire*. Vol 2. Columbia University Press. p49.

[388] Cassius Dio, 65. 11. 3.

[389] Levick, B., (1999) p145.

[390] Josephus, *The Jewish War*, 8. 250ff.

[391] Suetonius, *Vespasian*, 16.

[392] Levick, B., (1999) p95.

[393] Goldsworthy, A., (2003) *In the Name of Rome: The Men Who Won the Roman Empire*. Phoenix. London. p375. Goldsworthy, A., (2007) *Roman Warfare*. Phoenix. London. p143.

[394] 'Hadrian', *Historia Augusta*, 17, 21.

[395] Levick, B., (1999) p169.

[396] Cassius Dio, 65. 15. 3.

[397] Cassius Dio, 75. 3. 3.

[398] Cassius Dio, 75. 3. 3.

[399] On Dio's sources and literati peers see Moscovich, M., (2004) 'Cassius Dio's Palace Sources for the Reign of Septimius Severus', in *Historia: Zeitschrift fur Alto Geschichte*, Vol 53, No 3, pp356-368.

[400] Cassius Dio, 75. 21., 76. 8. 1. Cooley, A., (2007) 'Septimius Severus: The Augustan Emperor', in Swain, S., Harrison, S., Elsner, J., (eds.) Severan Culture. Cambridge University Press. pp385, 389. On Dio's life and career see Millar, F., (1964) A Study of Cassius Dio. Oxford. pp8f.

[401] Sidebottom, H., (2007) p76.

[402] Whittaker, C., (2000) p309.

403 Jones, B., (1992) pp155f.

404 Jones, B., (1992) pp155-157.

405 Bivar, A., (1983) p86. See also Sellwood, D., (1983) pp296-297.

406 Statius, *Silvae*, 4. 4., Southern, P., (1997) *Domitian: Tragic Tyrant*. Routledge. London. pp112, 153 note 7.

407 Statius, *Silvae*, 4. 2. 49., 4. 3. 110., 4. 3. 154.

408 Suetonius, *Domitian*, 2.

409 On this see Nauta, R., (2008) 'Statius in the Silvae', in Smolenaars, J., Dam, H., Nauta, R., (eds.) *The Poetry of Statius*. Brill. Boston. p149. See also Gibson, B., (2006) 'The Silvae and Epic', in Nauta, R., Dam, H., Smolenaars, J., (eds.) *Flavian Poetry*. Brill. Boston. pp171-172.

410 Isaac, B., (1990) p44, and see note 169.

411 Cody, J., (2003) p116.

412 Suetonius, *Domitian*, 2.

413 Cassius Dio, 62 (63). 8. 1-2. Tacitus, *Histories*, 1. 6.

414 On Domitian's assassination, see Suetonius, *Domitian*, 18. Cassius Dio, 67. 15. 1ff.

Chapter Eight

415 Cassius Dio, 68. 7. 5, 17. 1. Fronto, *Princ Hist*, 2. 213 para 14, 207 para 10.

416 Although, see Ferguson, R., (2005) 'Rome and Parthia: Power Politics and Diplomacy Across Cultural Frontiers'. Bond University. School of Humanities and Social Sciences: Centre of East-West Cultural and Economic Studies. (December) p11. http://epublications.bond.edu.au/cewces_papers/10.

417 Bennett, J., (1997) *Trajan: Optimus Princeps*. Routledge. London. pp189-190.

418 Bowersock, G., (1983) *Roman Arabia*. Cambridge University Press. London. pp82, 85.

419 Sheldon, R. M., (2010) p127.

420 Lepper, F., (1948) Trajan's Parthian War. Oxford University Press. London. p188f.

421 Griffin, M., (2000) 'Nerva to Hadrian', in *The Cambridge Ancient History*, Vol 11, p126.

422 Lepper, F., (1948) pp207-209. Birley, A., (1997) *Hadrian: The Restless Emperor*. Routledge. London. p70.

423 Plutarch states that the Romans had learnt that lesson with the defeat of Crassus in 53 BC: "...they [the Roman army] had believed that the Parthians were just the same as the Armenians or even the Cappadocians whom Lucullus had gone on plundering until he was tired of it... now, however, they found themselves in the unexpected position of having to face real fighting and great danger [in the Parthians]." (Plutarch, *Crassus*, 18.) Furthermore, Suetonius, and many other Romans also knew that Julius Caesar had laid tentative plans to gain intelligence and invade Parthia before his assassination: "...an attack on Parthia by way of Lesser Armenia;

but he decided not to risk a pitched battle until he had familiarized himself with Parthian tactics." (Suetonius, *Julius Caesar*, 44.)

[424] Arrian, *Parthica*, frag. 41.

[425] On the various theories for Pliny's appointment as governor and for Levick's own conclusions see Levick, B., (1979) 'Pliny in Bithynia – And What Followed', in *Greece and Rome*, 2nd Series, Vol 26, No 2 (October) pp122, 125, 126-130.

[426] Cuntz, O., (1926) 'Zum Briefwechsel des Plinius mit Traian', in *Hermes*, Vol 61, p192f.

[427] Lepper, F., (1948) pp165-170.

[428] Lepper, F., (1948) p169.

[429] Griffin, M., (2000) pp100-101.

[430] Cassius Dio, 68. 7. 5., 68. 17. 1., 68. 29. 1.

[431] Cassius Dio, 68. 29. 1.

[432] See Sheldon, R., (2010) pp126-127., and Bennett, J., (1997) p189.

[433] Guey, J., (1937) *Essai sur la Guerre Parthique de Trajan*. Bibliotheque d'Istros. No 2. Bucharest.pp27-28.

[434] 'Hadrian', *Historia Augusta*, 4. 1.

[435] Cassius Dio, 68-69. See Lepper, F., (1948) pp171-172. Birley agrees with the *Historia Augusta* as well as Dio. According to Birley, between Hadrian's first legateship and his commission during the Parthian war, he spent time in Rome and Athens in recreation, until the influence of Plotina secured Hadrian a place in Trajan's staff as the princeps passed through Athens on his way to the East. See Birley, A., (1997) pp67-68.

[436] Strack, P., (1931) *Untersuchungen zur romischen Reichspragung des zweiten Jahrhunderts*. W. Kohlhammer. Stuttgart. On FORT[una] RED[ux] coins see pp215-216. On coins commemorating Traianus' deification see pp199-202.

[437] Cassius Dio, 55. 24. 4.

[438] Lepper, F., (1948) p173.

[439] Lepper, F., (1948) pp164-165.

[440] Lepper, F., (1948) pp173-178.

[441] Cassius Dio, 68. 17. 2.

[442] Plutarch, *Crassus*, 18.

[443] Ball, W., (2000) p16.

[444] On this see Cassius Dio, 68. 28. 2-4.

[445] There were at that point three contestants for the Arsacid throne – Pacorus, Vologases and Osroes. See Birley, A., (1997) p65.

[446] Cassius Dio, 68. 26. 4(2).

[447] Bivar, A., (1983) p88. On the coinage minted at Seleucia at this time, see Sellwood, D., (1983) p296.

[448] Isaac, B., (1990) p140.

[449] Jones, A. H. M., (1974) p127. Garnsey, P., Saller, R., (1987) *The Roman Empire: Economy, Society and Culture.* Duckworth. London. pp55, 56, 62.

[450] Jones, A. H. M., (1974) p129.

[451] Jones, A. H. M., (1974) p127, 129.

[452] Garnsey, P., Saller, R., (1987) p53.

[453] For an ancient description of the Silk Route, see Isidore of Charax, *Parthian Stations.* For a modern discussion of the Silk Route, see Colledge, M., (1967) pp79ff.

[454] Isidore of Charax, *Parthian Stations*, 1-19.

[455] On China's trade with Parthia and Rome in general, see Hill, J., (2009) *Through the Jade Gate to Rome: A Study of the Silk Routes During the Later Han Dynasty 1st to 2nd Centuries CE.* Booksurge.

[456] Tao, W., (2007) 'Parthia in China: A Re-Examination of the Historical Records', in Curtis, V., and Stewart, S., (eds.) *The Age of the Parthians.* I. B. Tauris. London. p96.

[457] Tao, W., (2007) p98.

[458] Tao, W., (2007) p98.

[459] On Parthian steel and leather see Pliny the Elder, *Natural History*, 34. 145. On rhubarb see, 37. 128. On the peach see 15. 44.

[460] On the trade of these and other goods between Rome and Parthia see Kurz, O., (1983) 'Cultural Relations Between Parthia and Rome' in *The Cambridge History of Iran*, Vol 3, No 1, pp560f.

[461] Kurz, O, (2006) p564.

[462] Wheeler, M., (1955) *Rome Beyond the Imperial Frontiers.* Philosophical Library. New York.

[463] Wheeler, M., (1955) p154.

[464] Colledge, M., (1967) p80.

[465] Tao, W., (2007) pp100-101.

[466] Tomber, R., (2008) *Indo-Roman Trade: From Pots to Pepper.* Duckworth. London. p114.

[467] Keall, E., (1975) pp620-624.

[468] Al Salihi, Wathiq I., (1987) 'Palmyrene Sculptures Found at Hatra' in *Iraq*, Vol 49.

[469] Abadie-Reynal, C., Ergec, R., et al. (1997)'Mission de Zeugma-Moyenne Vallee de l'Euphrate' in *Anatolia Antiqua* 5 in Sartre, M., (2007) p180.

[470] On the use of Greek titles in Dura-Europos, see Pollard, N., (2007) 'Colonial and Cultural Identities in Parthian and Roman Dura-Europos', in Alston, R., Lieu, S., (eds.) *Aspects of the Roman East: Papers in Honour of Fergus Millar FBA.* Brepols Publishers. Turnhout. pp81-101. On the use of Parthian titles, see Welles, C., Fink, R., Gilliam, J., (eds.) *The Excavations at Dura-Europos, Final Report, Volume V,*

Part 1: The Parchments and Papyri. Yale University Press. New Haven. (1959) 20. On Parthia's control through existing hierarchies and civic structures, see Edwell, P., (2008) *Between Rome and Persia: The Middle Euphrates, Mesopotamia and Palmyra Under Roman Control.* Routledge. London. p113.

471 Rostovzeff, M., (1932) 'The Caravan-Gods of Palmyra', in *Journal of Roman Studies*, Vol 22, Part 1, pp107-116. See especially pp108 and 113, and plates 25, 26 and 27.

472 Sartre, M. (2007) p171.

473 Oates, D., (1956) 'The Roman Frontier in Northern Iraq', in *The Geographical Journal*, Vol 122, No 2 (June) p193.

474 Oates, D., (1956) p193.

475 Isidore of Charax, *Parthian Stations*, 19. "As far as this place [north-west India] the land is under the rule of the Parthians."

476 For a full discussion of Persian Gulf Parthian ports see Tomber, R., (2008) pp109ff.

477 Sartre, M., (2007) p242.

478 Sartre, M., (2007) p243.

479 Turner, P., (1989) *Roman Coins From India.* Institute of Archaeology Occasional Publication. London. 12. pp5, 59-60. See also Tomber, R., (2008) p139.

480 Tomber, R., (2008) p117f.

481 Radhakrishnam, M., (2009) 'First Century Spanish Pottery Found in Pattanam', in *India Today*, (7th December) www.indiatoday.intoday.in/site/story/First+century+spanish+pottery+found+in+Patternam/1/73920.html

482 On the red Sea as a trade route to the Indian Ocean see Tomber, R., (2008) pp57-87.

483 Starr, C., (1993) *The Roman Imperial Navy 31 BC-AD324.* Ares Publishers, Inc. Chicago. p175.

484 Juvenal, *Satires*, 3. 62.

485 Barr, W., (1991) *Juvenal: The Satires.* Oxford World's Classics. pxvii.

486 Knoche, U., (2009) 'Juvenal's Canons of Social Criticisms', in Plaza, M., (ed.) *Persius and Juvenal.* Oxford University Press. p276.

487 Mattingly, D., (2011) *Imperialism, Power and Identity.* Princeton University Press. pp204, 215.

488 Gilliver, C., (1999) p108.

489 Cassius Dio, 68. 17-19.

490 Cassius Dio, 68. 23. 2.

491 Cassius Dio, 68. 26.

492 Bivar, A., (1983) p88.

493 Cassius Dio, 68. 26. 4(1).

494 Bivar, A., (1983) p89.

[495] Debevoise, N., (1938) p232.

[496] Ammianus Marcellinus, 24. 2.

[497] Zosimus, 3. 15.

[498] Lightfoot, C., (1990) 'Trajan's Parthian War and the Fourth-Century Perspective', in *The Journal of Roman Studies*, Vol 80, pp115-126.

[499] Festus, *Breviarium of the Accomplishments of the Roman People*, 10, 20., Ammianus Marcellinus, *Roman History*, 23. 6. 15-23.

[500] Bivar, A., (1983) p89.

[501] Cassius Dio, 68. 28. 3.

[502] Cassius Dio, 68. 29. 3.

[503] Cassius Dio, 68. 26.

[504] On this numismatic evidence and its implications, see Keall, E., (1975) p629.

[505] Cassius Dio, 68. 26.

[506] Keall, E., (1975) p632. Gawlikowski, M., (1994) 'Palmyra as a Trading Centre', in *Iraq*, Vol 56, pp27-33.

[507] Gawlikowski, M., (1994) p29. See also Wenke, R., (1981) 'Elymeans, Parthians, and the Evolution of Empires in Southwestern Iran', in *The Journal of the American Oriental Society*, Vol 101, No 3, (July-September) p310.

[508] Festus, 20. 2.

[509] Ammianus Marcellinus, 23. 6. 15.

[510] Ammianus Marcellinus, 23. 6. 20.

[511] Eutropius, *Abridgement of Roman History*, 8. 3. 2., 6. 2.

[512] Cameron, A., (1993) *The Mediterranean World in Late Antiquity* AD395-600. Routledge. London. p136.

[513] For examples of such coins see Mattingly, H., (1923) *Roman Imperial Coinage*. Spink. London. *RIC* II, 326, 331, 332. Mattingly, H., (1976) *Coins of the Roman Empire in the British Museum*. British Museum Publications. 2nd Ed. BMCRE 626.

[514] Cassius Dio, 68. 28. 4 - 29. 1.

[515] Stark, F., (1966) *Rome on the Euphrates: The Story of a Frontier*. Harcourt, Brace and World, Inc. New York. p213.

[516] Cassius Dio, 68. 29.

[517] Fronto, 'Preamble to History', 7.

[518] Cassius Dio, 31. 4.

[519] Gilliver, C., (1999) p129.

[520] On the issue of the succession of Hadrian after Trajan's death, see Birley, A., (1997) *Hadrian: The Restless Emperor*. Routledge. London. pp77f. See also Bennett, J., (1997) p202f.

[521] Sheldon, R. M., (2010) p141, Neusner, J., (1999) p58ff.

[522] On this disdain as well as the revolts in general, see Smallwood, E., (1981) *The Jews Under Roman Rule: From Pompey to Diocletian*. Brill. Leiden. pp389ff., and Zeev, M., (2005) *Diaspora Judaism in Turmoil 116/117CE: Ancient Sources and Modern Insights*. Peeters. Leuven. pp209f.

Chapter Nine

[523] For an example of Campbell's modest evaluations of Roman-Parthian relations during the period after Trajan's death, see Campbell, B., (1993) 'War and Diplomacy: Rome and Parthia, 31 BC-AD 234', in Rich, J., and Shipley, G., (eds.) *War and Society in the Ancient World*. Routledge. London. p236.

[524] A notable proponent of this is Lintott, A., (1993) *Imperium Romanum: Politics and Administration*. Routledge. London. p14. See also Colledge, M., (1967) pp56, 166.

[525] Lintott, A., (1993) p14.

[526] Aelius Aristides, *Letter to Rome*, 29-33. 40.

[527] Aelius Aristides, *Letter to Rome*, 11-13.

[528] Lepper, F., (1948) pp212-213. Syme, R., (1958) p495.

[529] 'Hadrian', *Historia Augusta*, 4. 10f. Birley, A., (1997) *Hadrian: The Restless Emperor*. Routledge. London pp78f.

[530] On the political circumstances surrounding Hadrian's succession, see Everitt, A., (2009) *Hadrian and the Triumph of Rome*. Random House. New York. pp169f.

[531] Syme, R., (1983) *Historia Augusta Papers*. Clarendon Press. Oxford. pp38-39. Syme, R., (1979) *Roman Papers*. Clarendon Press. Oxford. Vol 2, pp642-652.

[532] Birley, A., (1997) pp3-4. Birley consistently draws upon Hadrian's biography in the *Historia Augusta* throughout much of this monograph of indispensable expertise.

[533] 'Hadrian', *Historia Augusta*, 4. 10f.

[534] Champlin, F., (1980) *Fronto and Antonine Rome*. Harvard University Press. pp2, 29, 44, 95.

[535] Fronto, 'Preamble to History', 10.

[536] Tacitus, *Annals*, 4. 32. On Syme's argument for references to Hadrian in Tacitus' account of Tiberius' reign see Syme, R., (1958) *Tacitus*. Oxford. London. pp490-498. See also Birley, A., (1997) pp104, 116.

[537] Syme, R., (1958) pp470-471.

[538] Gawlikowski, M. (1994) 'Palmyra as a Trading Centre', in *Iraq*, Vol 56, p29.

[539] Goodyear, F., (1972) *The Annals of Tacitus*, 1. Cambridge. pp127-8, 183-4.

[540] Syme, R., (1974) 'History or Biography: The Case of Tiberius Caesar', in *Historia: Zeitschrift fur Alte Geschichte*, Vol 23, No 4, (4th Quarter) p482.

[541] Bowersock, G., (1993) *Tacitus and the Tacitean Tradition*. Princeton University Press. p5.

[542] Bowersock, G., (1993) pp5, 10.

[543] Tacitus, *Annals*, 2. 67f.

[544] Sailor, D., (2008) *Writing and Empire in Tacitus*. Cambridge University Press. p256.

[545] Tacitus, *Annals*, 4. 32.

[546] Tacitus, *Histories*, 1. 1.

[547] Birley, A., (1997) p5. Wallace-Hadrill, A., (1983) *Suetonius: The Scholar and his Caesars*. Duckworth. London. p62.

[548] Suetonius, *Domitian*, 23.

[549] Martial, *Epigrams*, 5. 7.

[550] Gibbon, E., (1970) *The Decline and Fall of the Roman Empire*. Phoenix. London. p34.

[551] Plutarch, *Sulla*, 5.

[552] Plutarch, *Pompey*, 33.

[553] Plutarch, *Caesar*, 58.

[554] Plutarch, *Marc Antony*, 43-50.

[555] Konstan, D., (2009) 'Reading Politics in Suetonius', in Dominik, W., Garthewaite, J., and Roche, P., (eds.) *Writing Politics in Imperial Rome*. Leiden. Boston. pp458, 459.

[556] Lamberton, R., (2001) *Plutarch*. Yale University Press. London. p72. Stadter, A., (2000) 'The Rhetoric of Virtue in Plutarch's Lives', in Stockt, L., (ed.) *Collection D'Etudes Classiques: Rhetorical Theory and Praxis in Plutarch*. Peeters. Louvain. pp493-501.

[557] Plutarch, *Pericles*, 1-2., *Demetrius*, 1.

[558] Plutarch, *Alexander*, 1.

[559] Fronto, 'Preamble to History', 10.

[560] 'Hadrian', *Historia Augusta*, 21.

[561] Lepper, F., (1948) p204.

[562] 'Hadrian', *Historia Augusta*, 13, 21.

[563] 'Hadrian', *Historia Augusta*, 17, 21.

[564] 'Hadrian', *Historia Augusta*, 17, 21.

[565] Whittaker, C., (2000) 'Frontiers', *The Cambridge Ancient History*, Vol 11, p310.

[566] Jones, B., (1992) pp155-157.

[567] Cassius Dio, 58. 26.

[568] Josephus, *Jewish War*, 7. 244-51.

[569] On these matters, see Debevoise, N., (1938) pp242-244.

[570] 'Hadrian', *Historia Augusta*, 13.10., 17. 3f.

[571] 'Hadrian', *Historia Augusta*, 13. 6f., Bivar, A., (1983) p93.

[572] Bivar, A., (1983) p93.

[573] Sellwood, D., (1980) p248.

[574] Gawlikowski, M., (1994) p29.

[575] Wenke, R., (1981) 'Elymeans, Parthians, and the Evolution of Empires in Southwestern Iran', in *The Journal of the American Oriental Society*, Vol 101, No 3 (July-September) p306. Wenke draws upon numismatic studies in Mesopotamia on this period which indicate a sharp decline in the circulation of local coinage after Trajan's war.

[576] On this see Edwell, P., (2008) *Between Rome and Persia: The Middle Euphrates, Mesopotamia and Palmyra Under Roman Control*. Routledge. London. pp32, 33, 202.

[577] On Palmyra, see Seyrig, H., (1950) 'Palmyra and the East', in *The Journal of Roman Studies*, Vol 40., Richmond, I., (1963) 'Palmyra Under the Aegis of Rome', in *The Journal of Roman Studies*, Vol 53., Matthews, J., (1984) 'The Tax Law of Palmyra: Evidence for Economic History in a City of the Roman East', in *The Journal of Roman Studies*, Vol 74., and for a more detailed and recent treatment of Palmyra, see Edwell, P., (2008).

[578] Josephus, *Jewish Antiquities*, 8. 6. 1.

[579] See the following inscriptions from Palmyra from the first century recording the trading links with the east: PAT 02070, PAT 1324, PAT 1366, PAT 1376, PAT 1421, PAT 1584. On these inscriptions see, Gardner, I., Lieu, S., Parry, K., (2005) *From Palmyra to Zayton: Epigraphy and Iconography*. Brepols. Turnhout.

[580] Pliny the Elder, *Natural History*, 5. 88.

[581] Appian, *Civil War*, 5. 9.

[582] Seyrig, H., (1950) p1.

[583] Richmond, I., (1963) p44.

[584] Matthews, J., (1984) p161. See also page 164 for Palmyrene economic boom coinciding with Roman investment in Palmyra.

[585] Richmond, I., (1963) p44.

[586] Richmond, I., (1963) pp44, 48.

[587] On the Temple of Bel, and Roman influence over Palmyra's religious building, see Drijvers, H., (1976) *The Religion of Palmyra*. E. J. Brill. Leiden. p9., Teixidor, J., (1979) *The Pantheon of Palmyra*. E. J. Brill. Leiden. pp1-28.

[588] Crouch, D., (1972) 'A Note on the Population and Area of Palmyra', in *Mélanges de l'Universite Saint Joseph*, Vol 47, pp241-250. Admittedly, Matthews states that Crouch's methods are speculative, but he adds that his results are plausible.

[589] On Palmyra's honourific inscriptions, see Gianto, A., (2005) 'Variation in the Palmyrene Honorific Inscriptions', in Cussini, E., (ed.) *A Journey to Palmyra: Collected Essays to Remember Delbert R. Hillers*. Brill. Boston. pp74-88.

[590] For an overview of publications of these particular inscriptions, see Matthews, J., (1984) pp157-158. For a recent, thorough, description and discussion of these 34 inscriptions, see Gawlikowski, M., (1994) pp28-33.

[591] *PAT* 0197.

[592] *JSS* S4 pp34-36. See Gardner, I., et al, (2005) pp106-107. On Palmyra's archers, see *PAT* 0253. Edwell, P., (2008) p32.

[593] *PAT* 1062.

[594] *PAT* 0274.

[595] *PAT* 1411.

[596] *PAT* 2763.

[597] See Julius Maximus: *PAT* 1395. Iariboles: *PAT* 1414.

[598] *PAT* 1412.

[599] *PAT* 1374.

[600] *PAT* 1414.

[601] Matthews, J., (1984) p166.

[602] Sartre, M., (2007) p267.

[603] Sartre, M., (2007) pp256-257. For ancient commentary on customs procedures along the Euphrates see Philostratus, *The Life of Apollonius of Tyana*, 1. 20.

[604] *PAT* 1373. Butcher, K., (2003) *Roman Syria and the Near East*. British Museum Press. London. pp191-194.

[605] Jones, A. H. M., (1974) *The Roman Economy*. Basil Blackwell. Oxford. pp171-172.

[606] Browning, I., (1979) *Palmyra*. Chatto and Windus. London. p25. On cooperation eastern provincial cities generally provided Rome, see Elton, H., (1996) *Frontiers of the Roman Empire*. Indiana University Press. Indianapolis. p39.

[607] *PAT* 0259 lines 7-11. Gardner, I., Lieu, S., Parry, K., (2005) pp36-38.

[608] Isaac, B., (1990) *The Limits of Empire. The Roman Army in the East*. Clarendon Press. Oxford. pp67, 416.

[609] Matthews, J., (1984) p166.

[610] 'Hadrian', *Historia Augusta*, 13. 10f. Birley, A., (1997) p230f.

[611] *PAT* 0305

[612] *PAT* 0305

[613] Edwell, P., (2008) p32, 33, 202.

Chapter Ten

[614] 'Antoninus Pius', *Historia Augusta*, 9. 6f.

[615] 'Antoninus Pius', *Historia Augusta*, 9. 6f.

[616] 'Antoninus Pius', *Historia Augusta*, 7. 10f.

[617] Bryant, E., (1895) *The Reign of Antoninus Pius*. Cambridge University Press. p77.

[618] Wilkes, J., (1985) 'Review of Lawrence Keppie 'The making of the Roman Army: From R*e*public to Empire', in *The Journal of Roman Studies*, Vol 75, p242.

[619] 'Antoninus Pius', *Historia Augusta*, 7. 6f.

[620] 'Antoninus Pius', *Historia Augusta*, 9.6.

[621] Williams, W., (1967) 'Antoninus Pius and the Control of Provincial Embassies', in *Historia: Zeitschrift fur Alte Geschichte*, 16, 4, p475.

[622] 'Antoninus Pius', *Historia Augusta*, 9. 6.

[623] Sellwood, D., (1980) p268.

[624] 'Antoninus Pius', *Historia Augusta*, 12. 7. On this see also Birley, A., (2012) 'The Wars and Revolts', in Ackerman, M., (ed.) *A Companion to Marcus Aurelius*. Wiley-Blackwell. London. p217.

[625] Cassius Dio, 71. 2. 1.

[626] Cassius Dio, 71. 2. 1.

[627] 'Marcus Aurelius' *Historia Augusta*, 9.

[628] Sheldon, R., (2010) p156.

[629] McLynn, F., (2010) *Marcus Aurelius: Warrior, Philosopher, Emperor*. Vintage Books. London. p139.

[630] Cassius Dio, 71. 3.

[631] Fronto, *Ad Verum Imp.* 2. 1.

[632] Fronto, 'Preamble to History', 13f.

[633] Syme, R., (1979) *Roman Papers*. Clarendon Press. Oxford. Vol 3, p1436.

[634] Kemesis, A., (2010) 'Lucian, Fronto, and the Absence of Contemporary Historiography Under the Antonines', in *The American Journal of Philology*, Vol 131, No 2, (Summer) pp285-325.

[635] On the reliability of the *Historia Augusta* as an historical source, see Birley, A., (1966) *Marcus Aurelius*. Eyre and Spottiswoode. London. pp19-20. Syme, R., (1983) *Historia Augusta Papers*. Clarendon Press. Oxford. pp12f.

[636] Birley, A., (1966) p166.

[637] Birley, A., (1966) p215. Barta, G., (1971) 'Lucius Verus and the Marcomannic Wars', *Acta Class. Univ. Sc. Dedrecen.* Vol 7, pp67-71. On the *HA* Life of Verus see section 2. 1. c. Stanton, G., (1975) 'Marcus Aurelius, Lucius Verus, and Commodus: 1962-1972', in *Aufstieg Und Niedergang Der Romischen Welt*. Walter de Gruyter. Berlin. Vol 2, Part 2, pp539-540.

[638] Eutropius, 8. 10.

[639] Eutropius, 8. 9-10.

[640] Fronto, 'Preamble to History', 12.

[641] Fronto, 'Preamble to History', 12-13.

[642] Fronto, 'Preamble to History', 13.

[643] Birley, A., (1966) p165.

[644] Cassius Dio, 71. 2. 1.

[645] Cassius Dio, 71. 2. 3.

[646] McLynn, F., (2010) p141.

[647] Cassius Dio, 71. 3. 1.Oates, D., (1968) p72.

[648] Fronto, *Ad Verum Imp.*, 2. 1. 3. Birley, A., (1966) pp176.

[649] It was Birley who assumed that the site of this battle was Dura-Europos. Birley, A., (1966) p140. However, that assumption has now been discarded in favour of Europos/Carchemish near where much of the rest of the heavy fighting in this war took place. See Edwell, P., (2008) p116.

[650] Lucian, *History*, 20, 24, 28., Birley, A., (1966) p189., Millar, F., (1993) p113.

[651] Rostovtzeff, M., Bellinger, A., Hopkins, C., Welles, C., (eds.) *The Excavations at Dura Europos: Preliminary Report of the Seventh and Eighth Seasons 1933-1934 and 1934-1935.* Yale University Press. New Haven. (1936) pp83-84. Inscription number 845. Edwell, P., (2008) p116.

[652] Cassius Dio, 71. 2. 3., 'Verus', *Historia Augusta*, 7. Birley, A., (1966) p189.

[653] For a detailed discussion on the plague itself, see Littman, R., and Littman, M., (1973) 'Galen and the Antonine Plague', in *The American Journal of Philology*, Vol 94, No 3, pp243-255. For mortality rate figures in the Roman army see especially p255.

[654] McLynn, F., (2010) p164.

[655] Birley, A., (2012) p221.

[656] 'Verus', *Historia Augusta*, 7. 3ff., 'Marcus Antoninus', *Historia Augusta*, 12ff.

[657] Cassius Dio, 72. 27. 1f, 1a.

[658] Cassius Dio, 72. 27. 1a.

[659] Sheldon, R., (2010) pp161-162, see also notes 69 and 70.

[660] Sellwood, D., (2000) p297.

[661] Ferguson, R., (2005) p12.

[662] Sellwood, D., (1980) p248.

[663] Sellwood, D., (1980) pp286, 290.

[664] Debevoise, N, (1938) pp263ff.

[665] Keall, E., (1975) p632.

[666] Richmond, I., (1963) 'Palmyra Under the Agis of Rome', in *The Journal of Roman Studies*, Vol 53, parts 1 and 2, p50.

[667] Richmond, I., (1963) p53.

[668] On coins at Edessa and Carrhae, and conditions at Singara, see Oates, D., (1968) p72-73.

[669] Gawlikowski, M., (1994) p31.

[670] Sartre, M., (2005) pp70, 238f.

[671] For Palmyrene guides before Verus' invasions, see Matthews, J., (1984) p165, Seyrig, H., (1950) p6. For Palmyrene military escorts following Severus' Parthian wars, see Matthews, J., (1984) p168.

[672] Matthews, J., (1984) p168.

[673] Matthews, J., (1984) p168.

[674] On the garrisoning of Dura-Europos with Palmyrene archers, and later the Cohort XX Palmyrenorum, see James, S., (2004) *The Excavations at Dura-Europos: Final Report VII – The Arms and Armour and Other Military Equipment*. British Museum Press. London. p16f. See also Edwell, P., (2008) pp32, 117.

[675] Matthews, J., (1984) p169.

[676] Hopkins, C., (1979) *The Discovery of Dura Europos*. Yale University Press. New Haven. p256.

[677] Millar, F., (1998) p473f.

[678] On religious interaction between Palmyra and Dura-Europos, see Dirven, L., (1999) *The Palmyrenes of Dura-Europos. A Study of Religious Interaction in Roman Syria*. E. J. Brill. Leiden. On the Temple of Zeus in Dura-Europos, see Dirven, L., (1999) p294.

[679] Pollard, N., (2007) 'Colonial and Cultural Identities in Parthian and Roman Dura-Europos', in Alston, R., and Lieu, S., (eds.) *Aspects of the Roman East: Papers in Honour of Professor Fergus Millar FBA*. Brepols Publishers. Turnhout. pp81-101.

[680] Hopkins, C., (1931) 'The Palmyrene Gods at Dura-Europos', in *The Journal of the American Oriental Society*, Vol 51, No 2 (June) pp119, 124f, 127, 128, 131-132, 134.

[681] Sartre, M., (2007) p272.

[682] Gawlikowski, M., (1994) p31.

[683] *The Western Regions According to the Hou Hanshu: The Xiyu chuan (Chapter on the Western Regions)*. See discussion of this source in Wheeler, M., (1955) p174.

[684] Zizhi tongjian, juan 21. Tao, W., (2007) p100.

[685] Watson, W., (1983) 'Iran and China', in *The Cambridge History of Iran*, 3 (1) , p542.

[686] Tao,, W., (2007) pp100-101.

[687] Keall, E., (1975) p632.

[688] Oates, D., (1956) p194.

[689] Cassius Dio, 73. 1. 1.

[690] Birley, A., (1966) p308.

[691] Hekster, O., (2002) *Commodus: An Emperor at the Crossroads*. J. C. Gieben. Amsterdam. p45.

[692] On Dacia, see Cassius Dio, 73. 8. 1f. On Commodus' wars around the empire generally, see Cassius Dio 73. 8. 1f., 'Commodus', *Historia Augusta*, 12. 1 – 14. 8f.

[693] Cassius Dio, 73. 15. 2f. 'Commodus', *Historia Augusta*, 7. 1 – 9. 6. Hekster, O., (2002) p136.

[694] Cassius Dio, 73. 16. 1f.

Chapter Eleven

[695] On Septimius Severus' Parthian war see Birley, A., (1988) *Septimius Severus: The African Emperor.* Yale University Press. pp115f, 129f. See also Sheldon, R., (2010) pp163-171.

[696] Herodian, 3. 9. 1.

[697] Sidebottom, H., (2007) pp78-82.

[698] Cassius Dio, 75. 1-3.

[699] Sellwood, D., (1980) p281.

[700] Cassius Dio, 75. 3. 3.

[701] Moscovich, M., (2004) 'Cassius Dio's Palace Sources for the Reign of Septimius Severus', in *Historia: Zeitschrift fur Alte Geschichte*, Vol 53, No 3, p368.

[702] Campbell, B., (2005) 'The Severan Dynasty', in *The Cambridge Ancient History*, Vol 12, p5.

[703] Cassius Dio, 74. 15. 1.

[704] Birley, A., (1988) pp115f.

[705] Baharal, D., (1996) *Victory of Propaganda. The Dynastic Aspect of the Imperial Propaganda of the Severi: The Literary and Archaeological Evidence A D193-235.* Tempus Reparatum. BAR International Series 657. p34.

[706] Birley, A., (1988) p115.

[707] Cassius Dio, 76. 9. 3-4.

[708] Gilliver, C., (1999) p129.

[709] Gilliver, C., (1999) p129.

[710] Cassius Dio, 76. 9. 4.

[711] Coinage see *RIC* 4 50, 51, 55, 62, 63, 690, 690b, 691, 696. *RIC* 40. 118. *BMCRE* 40. 120, 557, 137. 555. Birley, A., (1988) p116.

[712] *Arch of Septimius Severus.* Birley, A., (1988) p116.

[713] Birley, A., (1988) p116.

[714] Msiha Zkha, in Birley, A., (1988) p117.

[715] On L. Valerius Valerianus, see Speidel, M., (1985) 'Valerius Valerianus in Charge of Septimius Severus' Mesopotamian Campaign', in *Classical Philology*, Vol 80, No 4, (October) p323-324. See also Birley, A., (1988) pp98, 113, 117, 246 note 13.

[716] Speidel, M., (1985) p323-324.

[717] Msiha Zkha, in Debevoise, N., (1938) p259.

[718] Smith, R., (1972) 'The Army Reforms of Septimius Severus', in *Historia: Zeitschrift fur Alte Geschtiche*, Vol 21, No 3 (3rd Qtr) pp482-485.

[719] Campbell, B., (2005) p6.

[720] Tacitus, *Annals*, 15. 2.

[721] Cassius Dio, 75. 9. 3-4, Herodian, 3. 9. 9-11. See also Birley, A., (1988) p130. Sheldon, M., (2010) p167.

[722] Birley, A., (1988) p117.

[723] Birley, A., (1988) p118.

[724] Baharal, D., (1996) p21.

[725] Birley, A., (1988) p130.

[726] Oates, D., (1956) p194.

[727] Cassius Dio, 76. 10. 2-3.

[728] Cassius Dio, 76. 10. 1.

[729] Cassius Dio, 75. 3. 2.

[730] Birley, A., (1988) pp115, 117, 132.

[731] Kennedy, D., (1996) *The Roman Army in the East*. Journal of Roman Archaeology, Supplementary Series 18. Ann Arbor. Kennedy, D., (1987) 'The Garrisoning of Mesopotamia in the Late Antonine and Early Severan Period', in *Antichthon*, Vol 21, pp57-58.

[732] Debevoise, N., (1938) p262.

[733] See Hulson, C., (1906) *The Roman Forum: Its History and its Monuments*. Ermanno Loescher and Company. Platner, S., (1927) *A Topographical Dictionary of Ancient Rome*. Oxford University Press. Brilliant, R., (1967) *The Arch of Septimius Severus in the Roman Forum*. Rome. Bober, P., (1971) 'Review: The Arch of Septimius Severus in the Roman Forum', in *The Art Bulletin*, Vol 53, No 2 (June) p243.

[734] Cassius Dio, 76. 9. 3.

[735] Huskinson, J., (2005) 'Art and Architecture a.d.193-337', in *Cambridge Ancient History*, Vol 12, p679.

[736] Bober, P., (1971) p243.

[737] Brilliant, R., (1967) p171.

[738] Campbell, B., (2005) p7.

[739] Heath, S., (2012) 'Trading at the Edge: Pottery, Coins, and Household Objects at Dura-Europos', in Chi, J., Heath, S., (eds.) *Edge of Empires: Pagans, Jews and Christians at Roman Dura-Europos*. Institute for the Study of the Ancient World. New York. pp63f.

[740] Sellwood, D., (2000) p297.

[741] *PAT* 1378.

[742] See Birley, A., (1988) p132f. Sartre, M., (2005) p135-136.

[743] Kennedy, D., and Riley, D., (1990) *Rome's Desert Frontier: From the Air.* B. T. Batsford Limited. London. pp111-138.

[744] Gilliver, C., (1999) pp59f., 63f.

[745] Gilliver, C., (1999) pp46f.

[746] On Septimius Severus' camps, see Gilliver, C., (1999) p49. Kennedy, D., and Riley, D., (1990) pp111-138.

[747] On the roles of fortifications in the Roman army, see Gilliver, C., (1999) pp63-88.

[748] Gilliver, C., (1999) On Agricola and Severus see p49. On the use of forts for protection as well as future attacks see pp60-62.

[749] James, S., (2004) p18-19.

[750] Pollard, N., (2000) *Soldiers, Cities and Civilians in Roman Syria.* Ann Arbor. Michigan. pp7, 44, 167.

[751] Downey, S., (1998) p163-164.

[752] James, S., (2004) p18.

[753] Gilliver, C., (1999) pp29-31, 82.

[754] Welles, C., et al., (1959) Papyrus Number 60B.

[755] Smith, R., (1972) p492.

[756] Roth, J., (2002) 'The Army and the Economy in Judaea and Palestine', in Erdkamp, P., (ed.) *The Roman Army and the Economy.* J C Gieben. Amsterdam. pp386, 388, 397.

[757] On Septimius Severus' army reforms, see Smith, R., (1972) p485ff.

[758] Roth, J., (2002) pp386, 388, 397.

[759] Cassius Dio, 75. 2. 3. Herodian, 3. 8. 5. On Dio's literati peers, see Moscovich, M., (2004) p368.

[760] Smith, R., (1972) p493.

[761] Edwell, P., (2008) p202.

[762] Duncan-Jones, R., (1994) *Money and Government in the Roman Empire.* Cambridge University Press. pp3, 15, 56.

[763] Wells, B., (1923) 'Trade and Travel in the Roman Empire', in *The Classical Journal,* Vol 19, No 1 (October) p16.

[764] Wells, B., (1923) p16.

[765] Jones, A., (1971) pp220-221.

[766] Jones, A., (1971) pp220-221. On Palmyra see p266.

[767] Smith, R., (1972) p489.

[768] Cassius Dio, 78. 2. 2.

[769] Herodian, 4. 2.

[770] Suetonius, *Augustus*, 18.

[771] Suetonius, *Nero*, 19.

772 Cassius Dio, 68. 29. 1.

773 On the influence Alexander the Great's fame and legacy had on Roman emperors, see Ball, W., (2000) pp8f., Sartre, M., (2005) pp65f.

774 Tacitus, *Annals*, 1. 9-11.

775 For discussion of negative portrayals of Tiberius contemporary with Tacitus, see Syme, R., (1958) pp420f.

776 Cassius Dio, 78. 6. 2., 78. 9. 8., 78. 17. 4.

777 Cassius Dio, 78. 3. 4f. Herodian, 4. 5. 7ff.

778 Cassius Dio, 78. 3. 4.

779 On the continuity of economic policy from Septimius Severus to Caracalla, see De Blois, L., (2002) 'Monetary Policies, the Soldiers' Pay and the Onset of Crisis in the First Half of the Third Century AD', in Erdkamp, P., (ed.) *The Roman Army and the Economy*. J. C. Gieben. Amsterdam. p96. On Caracalla's continuity of Septimius' military lifestyle, see Birley, A., (1988) *Septimius Severus: The African Emperor*. Yale University Press. p190. On Septimius' cruelty to the Senate see Birley, A., (1988) p199.

780 Cassius Dio, 76. 8. 1. Cooley, A., (2007) pp385, 389.

781 On Cassius Dio's life and career, see Millar, F., (1964) pp8-10. See also Sidebottom, H., (2007) pp76f.

782 Whittaker, C., (1969) *Herodian: History of the Empire, Books 1-4*. Harvard University Press. ppxixff., lxivff.

783 Cassius Dio, 79. 9. 3. Herodian, 5. 2. 2.

784 Lepper, F., (1948) p202.

785 For Tacitus' thematic use of mood following Augustus' death see Tacitus, *Annals*, 1. 9-11., and that following Claudius' see Tacitus, *Annals*, 13. 1-4. According to Syme, Tacitus relied on first-hand documentation as his chief sources, so his portrayals of Julio-Claudian dynasts were heavily influenced by both individual response and collective mood. See Syme, R., (1958) p421.

786 Cassius Dio, 75. 3. 3.

787 Cassius Dio, 75. 3. 3.

788 On Parthia's coinage and economy during this period, see Sellwood, D., (1983) p297. See also Sellwood, D., (1980) p286.

789 Herodian, 4. 10. 1. Cassius Dio, 78. 19. 1.

790 McDowell, R., (1935) *Coins From Seleucia on the Tigris*. Ann Arbor. Michigan. pp94, 199f, 235. Wroth, W., (1964) *A Catalogue of Greek Coins in the British Museum: Catalogue of the Coins of Parthia*. Arnaldo Forni. Bologna. pp247-50. Sellwood, D., (1983) pp297f.

791 Sellwood, D., (1983) p298.

792 Campbell, B., (1993) 'War and Diplomacy: Rome and Parthia, 31 BC-AD235', in Rich, J., Shipley, G., (eds.) *War and Society in the Ancient World*. Routledge. London. p236.

793 Debevoise, N., (1938) pp263-4.

794 Campbell, B., (2005) p19.

795 Cassius Dio, 78. 19.

796 Cassius Dio, 78. 21. 1.

797 Herodian, 4. 10. 1.

798 Whittaker, C., (1969) pp428-429, note 3.

799 Birley, A., (1988) p130.

800 Herodian, 4. 11. 9.

801 'Caracallus', *Historia Augusta*, 6. 7f., 11. 2f.

802 Debevoise, N., (1938) p265.

803 Herodian, 5. 1. 4.

804 Cassius Dio, 79. 1. 1f.

805 See Cassius Dio, 79. 1. 1., 'Caracalla', *Historia Augusta*, 6. 4f., Debevoise, N., (1938) p265.

806 Herodian, 4. 10. 3-4.

807 Bivar, A., (1983) p95.

808 Herodian, 4. 11. 1-8.

809 Sheldon, R., (2010) p173.

810 Cassius Dio, 79. 1. 1-3.

811 Cassius Dio, 79. 1. 1-3. Herodian, 4. 11. 1-8.

812 Cassius Dio, 79. 1. 1.

813 Cassius Dio, 79. 1. 1-3.

814 Debevoise, N., (1938) p266.

815 Jones, A. H. M., (1971) *The Cities of the Eastern Roman Provinces*. Clarendon Press. Oxford. p221.

816 Butcher, K., (1998) 'The Mint at Zeugma', in Kennedy, D., (ed.) *The Twin Towns of Zeugma on the Euphrates: Rescue Work and Historical Studies*. Journal of Roman Archaeology: Supplementary Series Number Twenty-Seven. p234.

817 Campbell, B., (2005) p19.

818 Cassius Dio, 79. 4. 1.

819 Cassius Dio, 79. 9. 1f. Moscovich, M., (2004) 'Cassius Dio's Palace Sources for the Reign of Septimius Severus', in *Historia: Zeitschrift fur Alte Geschichte*, Vol 53, No 3, pp356-368. See particularly p369.

820 Herodian, 4. 15. 1-3.

821 Herodian, 4. 15. 4-5. Sheldon, R., (2010) p175.

822 Herodian, 4. 15. 4-6.

823 Cassius Dio, 79. 27-28. Bivar, A., (1983) p95.

[824] Regling, K., (1903) 'Romische aurei aus dem Funde von Karnak', in *Festschrift zu Otto Hirschfelds, 60, Geburtstage*. Berlin. p297, note 60. Debevoise, N., (1938) p267.

[825] Cassius Dio, 79. 28. 1ff, Herodian, 5. 2. 3f. Birley, A., (1988) p192.

[826] Colledge, M., (1967) p173.

[827] On Vologases' coinage see Bivar, A (1983) p96., Sellwood, D., (1983) p297.

[828] Colledge, M., (1967) p173.

[829] Oates, D., (1968) 'East Against West: 1. Rome and Parthia', in *Studies in the Ancient History of Northern Iraq*. Oxford. pp67-92.

[830] Colledge, M., (1967) p173.

[831] Debevoise, N., (1938) p269.

[832] Tacitus, *Agricola*, 30.

[833] On the Sassanid ascendancy see Debevoise, N., (1938) pp268-9. Bivar, A., (1983) pp96-97. Frye, R., (1983) 'The Political History of Iran Under the Sasanians', in *The Cambridge History of Iran*, 3 (1) pp116-180.

[834] Cassius Dio, 75, 3. 3.

BIBLIOGRAPHY

Abadie-Reynal, C., Ergec, R., et al. (1997)'Mission de Zeugma-Moyenne Vallee de l'Euphrate' in *Anatolia Antiqua*, 5, pp349-470.

Ahl, F., (1976) *Lucan: An Introduction*. Cornell University Press. London.

Al Salihi, Wathiq I., (1987) 'Palmyrene Sculptures Found at Hatra' in *Iraq*, Vol 49, pp53-61.

Alfoldy, G., (1988) *The Social History of Rome*. Translated by Braund, D., and Pollock, F. Routledge. London.

Andrade, N., (2012) 'Seducing Autocracy: Tacitus and the Dynasts of the Near East', in *The American Journal of Philology*, Vol 133, No 3, pp441-475.

Assar, G., (2006) 'A Revised Chronology of the Period 165-91 BC', in *Electrum*, Vol 11, pp87-158.

Assar, G. (2011) 'Iran Under the Arsacids', in *Numismatic Art of Persia. The Sunrise Collection*. Part 1: Ancient – 650 BC to AD650, pp113-171.

Austin, N., (1998) *Exploratio: Military and Political Intellegence in the Roman World from the Second Punic War to the Battle of Adrianople.* Routledge. London.

Badian, E., (1981) 'The Deification of Alexander the Great', in *Ancient Macedonian Studies in Honour of Charles F. Edson.* Thessaloniki. pp27-71.

Ball, W., (2000) *Rome in the East: The Transformation of an Empire.* Routledge. New York.

Balsdon, J., (1949) 'Long-Term Commands at the End of the Republic', in *The Classical Review*, Vol 63, No 1, pp14-15.

Balsdon, J., (1950) 'The 'Divinity' of Alexander', in *Historia*, 1, pp363-388.

Barnett, P., (2004) *Is the New Testament History?* Aquila Press. Sydney.

Barr, W., (1991) 'Introduction', in *Juvenal: The Satires.* Oxford University Press.

Barrett, A., (1989) *Caligula: The Corruption of Power.* B T Batsford Ltd. London.

Barrett, A., (1996) *Agrippina: Sex, Power and Politics in the Early Roman Empire.* B T Batsford Limited. London.

Barroll, M., (1980) 'Toward a General Theory of Imperialism', in *Journal of Anthropological Research*, Vol 36, No 2, pp174-195.

Barta, G., (1971) 'Lucius Verus and the Marcomannic Wars', *Acta Universitatus. Scientiarum. Dedreceniensis.* Vol 7. pp67-71.

Barton, T., (1994) 'The invention of Nero: Suetonius' in Elsner, J., and Masters, J., (eds.) *Reflections of Nero: Culture, History and Representation.* Duckworth. London.

Bartsch, S., (1997) *Ideology in Cold Blood*. Harvard University Press. London.

Beard, M., (2007) *The Roman Triumph*. The Belknap Press of Harvard University Press, London.

Beard, M., (2009) *Pompeii: The Life of a Roman Town*. Profile Books. London.

Bennett, J., (1997) *Trajan: Optimus Princeps*. Routledge. London.

Billows, R., (2009) *Julius Caesar: The Colossus of Rome*. Routledge. London.

Birley, A., (1966) *Marcus Aurelius*. Eyre and Spottiswood. London.

Birley, A., (1988) *Septimius Severus: The African Emperor*. Yale University Press. London.

Birley, A., (1997) *Hadrian: The Restless Emperor*. Routledge. London.

Birley, A., (2012) 'The Wars and Revolts', in Ackerman, M., (ed.) *A Companion to Marcus Aurelius*. Wiley-Blackwell. London. pp217-233.

Bivar, A., (1972) 'Cavalry Equipment and Tactics on the Euphrates Frontier', in *Dumbarton Oaks Papers*, Vol 26, pp271-291.

Bivar, A., (1983) 'The Political History of Iran Under the Arcasids', in *The Cambridge History of Iran*. Cambridge University press. Vol 3. (1) pp21-99.

Bober, P., (1971) 'Review: The Arch of Septimius Severus in the Roman Forum', in *The Art Bulletin*, Vol 53, No 2 (June), pp242-244.

Botsford, G., (1918) 'Roman Imperialism', in *The American Historical Review*, Vol 23, No 4, pp772-778.

Bowersock, G., (1973) 'Syria Under Vespasian', in *The Journal of Roman Studies*, Vol 63, pp133-140.

Bowersock, G., (1993) *Tacitus and the Tacitean Tradition*. Princeton University Press.

Braund, S., (2002) *Latin Literature*. Routledge. London.

Braund, S., (2008) *Lucan: Civil War*. Oxford University Press.

Brilliant, R., (1967) *The Arch of Septimius Severus in the Roman Forum*. Rome.

Browning, I., (1979) *Palmyra*. Chatto and Windus. London.

Bryant, E., (1895) *The Reign of Antoninus Pius*. Cambridge University Press.

Butcher, K., (1998) 'The Mint at Zeugma', in Kennedy, D., (ed.) *The Twin Towns of Zeugma on the Euphrates: Rescue Work and Historical Studies*. Journal of Roman Archaeology: Supplementary Series Number Twenty-Seven. pp233-236.

Butcher, K., (2003) *Roman Syria and the Near East*. British Museum Press. London.

Butterworth, A., Laurence, R., (2005) *Pompeii: The Living City*. Weidenfeld and Nicolson. London.

Cameron, A., (1993) *The Mediterranean World in Late Antiquity* AD395-600. Routledge. London.

Campbell, B., (1993) 'War and Diplomacy: Rome and Parthia, 31 BC-AD234', in Rich, J., and Shipley, G., (eds.) *War and Society in the Ancient World*. Routledge. London. pp213-240.

Campbell, B., (2005) 'The Severan Dynasty', in *The Cambridge Ancient History*, Vol 12, pp1-27.

Canfora, L., (2007) *Julius Caesar: The Life and Times of the People's Dictator*. University of California Press. Berkeley.

Champlin, E., (2003) *Nero*. Belknap Press. London.

Champlin, F., (1980) *Fronto and Antonine Rome*. Harvard University Press.

Cody, J., (2003) 'Conquerors and Conquered on Flavian Coins', in Boyle, A., Dominik, W., (eds.) *Flavian Rome: Culture, Imagery, Text*. Brill. London.

Colledge, M. A. R., (1967) *The Parthians*. Frederick A. Praeger Publishers. New York.

Cooley, A., (2007) 'Septimius Severus: The Augustan Emperor', in Swain, S., Harrison, S., Elsner, J., (eds.) *Severan Culture*. Cambridge. pp381-393.

Cooley, A., (2009) *Res Gestae Divi Augusti: Text, Translation and Commentary*. Cambridge University Press.

Crouch, D., (1972) 'A Note on the Population and Area of Palmyra', in *Melanges de l'Universite Saint Joseph*, Vol 47, pp241-250.

Curtis, V., (2000) 'Parthian Culture and Costume', in *Mesopotamia and Iran in the Parthian and Sasanian Periods*. British Museum Press. London. pp23-34.

Curtis, V., and Stewart, S., eds. (2010) *The Age of the Parthians*. I. B. Tauris. London.

Debevoise, N., (1938) *The Political History of Parthia*. University of Chicago Press. Chicago.

Dennison, M., (2010) *Empress of Rome: The Life of Livia*. Quereus. London.

De Blois, L., (2002) 'Monetary Policies, the Soldiers' Pay and the Onset of Crisis in the First Half of the Third Century AD', in Erdkamp, P., (ed.) *The Roman Army and the Economy*. J. C. Gieben. Amsterdam. pp90-107.

Dirven, L., (1999) *The Palmyrenes of Dura-Europos. A Study of Religious Interaction in Roman Syria*. E. J. Brill. Leiden.

Downey, S., (1998) 'The Transformation of Seleucid Dura-Europos', in Fentress, E., (ed.) *Romanization and the City: Creation, Transformations and Failures. Proceedings of a Conference Held at the American Academy in Rome, May 14-16 1998*. Journal of Roman Archaeology Supplementary Series 38. Portsmouth. Chapter 10.

Drijvers, H., (1976) *The Religion of Palmyra*. E. J. Brill. Leiden.

Duncan-Jones, R., (1994) *Money and Government in the Roman Empire*. Cambridge University Press.

Edwell, P., (2008) *Between Rome and Persia: The Middle Euphrates, Mesopotamia and Palmyra Under Roman Control*. Routledge. London.

Elton, H., (1996) *Frontiers of the Roman Empire*. Indiana University Press. Indianapolis.

Everitt, A., (2003) *Cicero: The Life and Times of Rome's Greatest Politician*. Random House. New York.

Everitt, A., (2009) *Hadrian and the Triumph of Rome*. Random House. New York.

Fenn, R., (1992) *The Death of Herod: An Essay on the Sociology of Religion*. Cambridge University Press.

Ferrill, A., (1991) *Caligula: Emperor of Rome*. Thames and Hudson.

Fletcher, J., (2008) *Cleopatra the Great: The Woman Behind the Legend*. Hodder and Stoughton. London.

Freeman, P., and Kennedy, D., (1986) *The Defense of the Roman and Byzantine East: Proceedings of a Colloquium Held at the University of Sheffield in April 1986*. British Archaeological Reports, International Series. 292. 1 and 2. London.

Freisenbruch, A., (2010) *The First Ladies of Rome: The Women Behind the Caesars*. Jonathan Cape. London.

Frye, R., (1983) 'The Political History of Iran Under the Sasanians', in *The Cambridge History of Iran*, 3 (1) pp116-180.

Fuller, J., (1998) *Julius Caesar: Man, Soldier and Tyrant*. Wordsworth editions. Ware. Hertfordshire.

Galinsky, K., (1996) *Augustan Culture*. Princeton University Press.

Gardner, I., Lieu, S., Parry, K., (2005) *From Palmyra to Zayton: Epigraphy and Iconography*. Brepols. Turnhout.

Galtung, J., (1971) 'A Structural Theory of Imperialism', in *Journal of Peace Research*, Vol 8, No 2, pp81-117.

Garnsey, P., Saller, R., (1987) *The Roman Empire: Economy, Society and Culture*. Duckworth. London.

Gawlikowski, M., (1994) 'Palmyra as a Trading Centre', in *Iraq*, Vol 56, pp27-33.

Gianto, A., (2005) 'Variation in the Palmyrene Honorific Inscriptions', in Cussini, E., (ed.) *A Journey to Palmyra: Collected Essays to Remember Delbert R. Hillers*. Brill. Boston. pp74-88.

Gibbon, E., (1970) *The Decline and Fall of the Roman Empire*. Phoenix. London.

Gibson, B., (2006) 'The Silvae and Epic', in Nauta, R., Dam, H., Smolenaars, J., (eds.) *Flavian Poetry*. Brill. Boston. pp163-183.

Gilliver, C., (1999) *The Roman Art of War*. Tempus Publishing Ltd. Gloucestershire.

Gillmartin, K., (1973) 'Corbulo's Campaigns in the East: An Analysis of Tacitus' Account', in *Historia: Zeitschrift fur Alte Geschichte*, Vol 22, No 4, (4th Quarter) pp583-626.

Goldsworthy, A., (2003) *In the Name of Rome: The Men Who Won the Roman Empire*. Phoenix. London.

Goldsworthy, A., (2007) *Roman Warfare*. Phoenix. London.

Goodman, M., (1997) *The Roman World 44 BC – AD180*. Routledge. London.

Goodyear, F., (1972) *The Annals of Tacitus*, 1. Cambridge.

Goold, G., (1977) *Manilius: Astronomica*. Harvard University Press.

Green, P., (1990) *Alexander to Actium: The Historical Evolution of the Hellenistic Age*. University of California. Berkeley.

Greenhalgh, P., (1981) *Pompey: The Republican Prince*. Weidenfeld and Nicolson. London.

Griffin, J., (1984) 'Augustus and the Poets: 'Caesar Qui Cogere Posset'', in Millar, F., and Segal, E., (eds.) *Caesar Augustus: Seven Aspects*. Clarendon Press. Oxford. pp189-217.

Griffin, M., (1984) *Nero: The End of a Dynasty*. Yale University Press. London.

Griffin, M., (1990) 'Claudius in Tacitus', in *The Classical Quarterly,* New Series, Vol 40, No 2, pp482-501.

Griffin, M., (2000) 'Nerva to Hadrian', in *The Cambridge Ancient History,* Vol 11, pp84-131.

Gruen, E., (1978) 'Reviews: The Grand Strategy of the Roman Empire from the First Century AD to the Third', in *The Journal of Interdisciplinary History,* Vol 8, No 3, (Winter) pp563-566.

Hammond, M., (1934) 'Corbulo and Nero's Eastern Policy', in *Harvard Studies in Classical Philology,* Vol 45, pp81-104.

Hannah, R., (1997) 'The Temple of Mars Ultor and 12 May', in *Mitteilungen Des Deutschen Archaeologischen Instituts Roemische Abteilung,* Vol 104, pp527-535.

Harris, (1979) *War and Imperialism.* Oxford.

Heath, S., (2012) 'Trading at the Edge: Pottery, Coins, and Household Objects at Dura-Europos', in Chi, J., Heath, S., (eds.) *Edge of Empires: Pagans, Jews and Christians at Roman Dura-Europos.* Institute for the Study of the Ancient World. New York. pp62-73.

Hekster, O., (2002) *Commodus: An Emperor at the Crossroads.* J. C. Gieben. Amsterdam.

Henry, M. (1974) *Matthew Henry's Commentary: The Four Gospels.* Hodder and Stoughton. London.

Heyworth, S., and Morwood, J., (2011) *A Commentary on Propertius: Book III.* Oxford University Press.

Hind, G., (1992) 'Mithridates', in *Cambridge Ancient History,* Vol 9, ch 5, pp129-163.

Holland, T., (2003) *Rubicon: The Triumph and Tragedy of the Roman Republic*. Abacus. London.

Hopkins, C., (1931) 'The Palmyrene Gods at Dura-Europos', in *Journal of the American Oriental Society*, Vol 51 No 2 (June), pp119-137.

Hopkins, C., (1979) *The Discovery of Dura Europos*. Yale University Press. New Haven.

Hubbard, M., (1974) *Propertius*. Duckworth. London.

Hulson, C., (1906) *The Roman Forum: Its History and its Monuments*. Ermanno Loescher and Company.

Huskinson, J., (2005) 'Art and Architecture a.d.193-337', in *Cambridge Ancient History*, Vol 12, pp672-703.

Huzar, E., (1978) *Mark Antony: A Biography*. University of Minnesota Press. Minneapolis.

Isaac, B., Roll, I., (1976) 'A Milestone of AD69 from Judaea: The Elder Trajan and Vespasian', in *The Journal of Roman Studies*, Vol 66, pp15-19.

Isaac, B., (1990) *The Limits of Empire: The Roman Army in the East*. Clarendon Press. Oxford.

James, S., (2004) *The Excavations at Dura-Europos: Final Report VII – The Arms and Armour and Other Military Equipment*. British Museum Press. London.

Jenkins, R., (2004) 'The Star of Bethlehem and the Comet of AD66', in *The Journal of the British Astronomy Association*, 114, (June) pp336-343.

Jones, A. H. M., (1971) *The Cities of the Eastern Roman Provinces*. Clarendon Press. Oxford.

Jones, A. H. M., (1974) *The Roman Economy*. Basil Blackwell. Oxford.

Jones, A. H. M., (1977) *Ancient Culture and Society: Augustus*. Chatto and Windus. London.

Jones, B., (1992) *The Emperor Domitian*. Routledge. London.

Kagan, K., (2006) 'Redefining Roman Grand Strategy', in *The Journal of Military History*, Vol 70, No 2, (April) pp333-362.

Kaufmanis, K., (2003/2004) 'The Star of Bethlehem', in *The Minnesota Astronomy Review*, Vol 18, pp2-3.

Keall, E., (1975) 'Parthian Nippur and Vologases' Southern Strategy: A Hypothesis' in *Journal of the American Oriental Society*, Vol 95, No 4 (October-December), pp620-632.

Keaveney, A., (1982) *Sulla: The Last Republican*. Croom Helm Ltd. Beckenham.

Keene, C., (1969) *The Eclogues of Calpurnius Siculus and Nemesianus*. Georg Olms Verlag. Hildesheim.

Keital, E., (1978) 'The Role of Parthia and Armenia in Tacitus Annals 11 and 12', in *The American Journal of Philology*, Vol 99, No 4 (winter) pp462-473.

Kemesis, A., (2010) 'Lucian, Fronto, and the Absence of Contemporary Historiography Under the Antonines', in *The American Journal of Philology*, Vol 131, No 2, (Summer) pp285-325.

Kennedy, D., (1987) 'The Garrisoning of Mesopotamia in the Late Antonine and Early Severan Period', in *Antichthon*, Vol 21, pp57-66.

Kennedy, D., and Riley, D., (1990) *Rome's Desert Frontier from the Air*. B. T. Batsford. London.

Kennedy, D., (1996) *The Roman Army in the East.* Journal of Roman Archaeology, Supplementary Series 18. Ann Arbor.

Kennedy, D., (1998*) The Twin Towns of Zeugma on the Euphrates: Rescue Work and Historical Studies.* Journal of Roman Archaeology: Supplementary Series Number Twenty-Seven.

Kidger, M., (1999) *The Star of Bethlehem: An Astronomer's View.* Princeton University Press.

Kleiner, F., (1985) *The Arch of Nero in Rome: A Study of the Roman Honorary Arch Before and Under Nero.* Giorgio Bretschneider Editore. Rome.

Knoche, U., (2009) 'Juvenal's Canons of Social Criticisms', in Plaza, M., (ed.) *Persius and Juvenal.* Oxford University Press.

Konstan, D., (2009) 'Reading Politics in Suetonius', in Dominik, W., Garthewaite, J., and Roche, P., (eds.) *Writing Politics in Imperial Rome.* Leiden. Boston. pp447-462.

Kraemer, R., (1992) *Her Share of the Blessings: Women's Religions Among Pagans, Jews and Christians in the Greco-Roman World.* Oxford University Press.

Kurz, O., (1983) 'Cultural Relations Between Parthia and Rome', in *The Cambridge History of Iran.* Cambridge University Press, Vol 3 (1), pp559-567.

Lamberton, R., (2001) *Plutarch.* Yale University Press. London.

Leach, J., (1978) *Pompey the Great.* Croom Helm Ltd. London.

Leigh, M., (1997) *Lucan: Spectacle and Engagement.* Clarendon Press. Oxford.

Lepper, F., (1948) *Trajan's Parthian War.* Oxford University Press. London.

Levick, B., (1976) *Tiberius the Politician.* Croom Helm. London.

Levick, B., (1979) 'Pliny in Bithynia – And What Followed', in *Greece and Rome*, 2nd Series, Vol 26, No 2 (October), pp119-131.

Levick, B., (1990) *Claudius.* Yale University Press. London.

Levick, B., (1999) *Vespasian.* Routledge. London.

Lewis, N., and Reinhold, M., (1990) *Roman Civilization: Selected Readings. The Empire.* Vol 2. Columbia University Press.

Lightfoot, C., (1990) 'Trajan's Parthian War and the Fourth-Century Perspective', in *The Journal of Roman Studies*, Vol 80, pp115-126.

Lindsay, J., (1937) *Marc Antony: His World and His Contemporaries.* E P Dutton and Company. New York.

Lintott, A., (1993) *Imperium Romanum: Politics and Administration.* Routledge. London.

Littman, R., and Littman, M., (1973) 'Galen and the Antonine Plague', in *The American Journal of Philology*, Vol 94, No 3, pp243-255.

Luttwak, (1976) *The Grand Strategy of the Roman Empire From the First Century AD to the Third.* Baltimore. John Hopkins University Press.

Maehler, H., (2003) 'Roman Poets on Egypt', in Matthews, R., and Roemer, C., (eds.) *Ancient Perspectives on Egypt* UCL Press. London. pp203-315.

Maenchen-Helfen, O., (1943) 'From China to Palmyra', in *The Art Bulletin*, Vol 25, No 4 (December), pp358-362.

Mankin, D., (1995) *Horace: Epodes.* Cambridge University Press.

Manning, C., (1975) 'Acting and Nero's Conception of the Principate', in *Greece and Rome*, 2nd Series, Vol 22, No 2, pp164-169.

Maranon, G., (1956) *Tiberius: A Study in Resentment*. Hollis and Carter. London.

Mason, S., (2003) 'Flavius Josephus in Flavian Rome: Reading On and Between the Lines', in Boyle, A., Dominik W, (eds.) *Flavian Rome: Culture, Imagery, Text*. Brill. London. pp559-590.

Mathiesen, H., (1992) *Sculpture in the Parthian Empire*. Aarhus University Press. Aarhus.

Matthews, J., (1984) 'The Tax Law of Palmyra: Evidence for Economic History in a City of the Roman East', in *The Journal of Roman Studies*, Vol 74, pp157-180.

Mattingly, D., (2011) *Imperialism, Power and Identity*. Princeton University Press.

Mattingly, H., (1923) *Roman Imperial Coinage*. Spink. London.

Mattingly, H., (1976) *Coins of the Roman Empire in the British Museum*. British Museum Publications. 2nd Ed.

McCrum, M., and Woodhead, A., (1962) *Select Documents of the Principates of the Flavian Emperors*. Cambridge University Press.

McDowell, R., (1935) *Coins From Seleucia on the Tigris*. Ann Arbor. Michigan.

McLynn, F., (2010) *Marcus Aurelius: Warrior, Philosopher, Emperor*. Vintage Books. London.

Millar, F., (1964) *A Study of Cassius Dio*. Oxford.

Millar, F., (1993) *The Roman Near East: 31 BC-AD337*. Harvard University Press. London.

Momigliano, A., (1981) *Claudius: The Emperor and His Achievement*. Greenwood Press. Connecticut.

Morford, M., (1967) *The Poet Lucan: Studies in Rhetorical Epic*. Basil Blackwell. Oxford.

Morwood, J., (1991) 'Aeneas, Augustus, and the Theme of the City', in *Greece and Rome*. 2nd series, Vol 38, No 2, (October) pp212-223.

Morwood, J., (2008) *Virgil: A Poet in Augustan Rome*. Cambridge university Press.

Moscovich, M., (2004) 'Cassius Dio's Palace Sources for the Reign of Septimius Severus', in *Historia: Zeitschrift fur Alte Geschichte*, Vol 53, No 3, pp356-368.

Mounce, W., (1999) *Basics of Biblical Greek: Grammar*. Zondervan. Grand Rapids. Michigan.

Nauta, R., (2008) 'Statius in the Silvae', in Smolenaars, J., Dam, H., Nauta, R., (eds.) *The Poetry of Statius*. Brill. Boston.

Neusner, J., (1999) *The History of the Jews in Babylonia: Part 1, The Parthian Period*. Wipf and Stock. Eugene.

Nisbet, R., and Rudd, N., (2004) *A Commentary on Horace: Odes Book III*. Oxford.

North, J., (1981) 'The Development of Roman Imperialism', in *The Journal of Roman Studies*, Vol 71, pp1-9.

Oates, D., (1956) 'The Roman Frontier in Northern Iraq', in *The Geographical Journal*, Vol 122, No 2 (June), pp190-199.

Oates, D., (1968) 'East Against West: 1. Rome and Parthia', in *Studies in the Ancient History of Northern Iraq*. Oxford University Press. London. pp67-92.

Perowne, S., (1956) *The Life and Times of Herod the Great*. Hodder and Stoughton. London.

Platner, S., (1927) *A Topographical Dictionary of Ancient Rome*. Oxford University Press.

Pollard, N., (2000) *Soldiers, Cities and Civilians in Roman Syria*. Ann Arbor. University of Michigan Press.

Pollard, N., (2007) 'Colonial and Cultural Identities in Parthian and Roman Dura-Europos', in Alston, R., and Lieu, S., (eds.) *Aspects of the Roman East: Papers in Honour of Professor Fergus Millar FBA*. Brepols Publishers. Turnhout. pp81-101.

Pomeroy, S., (1994) *Goddesses, Whores, Wives and Slaves: Women in Classical Antiquity*. Pimlico. London.

Potter, D., (1999) *Literary Texts and the Roman Historian*. Routledge. London.

Powell, A., (1992) 'The Aeneid and the Embarrassments of Augustus', in Powell, A., (ed.) *Roman Poetry and Propaganda in the Age of Augustus*. Bristol Classical Press. London.

Radhakrishnam, M., (2009) 'First Century Spanish Pottery Found in Pattanam', in *India Today*, (7th December) www.indiatoday.into-day.in/site/story/First+century+spanish+pottery+found+in+Patter nam/1/73920.html

Ramaroli, V., Hamilton, J., Ditchfield, P., Fazeli, H., Aali, A., Coningham, R., Pollard, A., (2010) *The chrhr Abad "Salt Men" and the Isotopic Ecology of Humans in Ancient Iran*. Calle Larga Santa Marta. Venice.

Ramsey, W., (1915) *The Bearing of Recent Discovery on the Trustworthiness of the New Testament*. Hodder and Stoughton. London.

Rawlinson, G., (1893) *Parthia*. T. Fisher Unwin.

Regling, K., (1903) 'Romische aurei aus dem Funde von Karnak', in *Festschrift zu Otto Hirschfelds, 60, Geburtstage*. Berlin. p286.

Research Centre for Conservation of Cultural Relics, (1998) *SALTMAN: Scientific Investigations Carried Out on the Saltman Mummified Remains and Its Artefacts*. RCCCR. Tehran.

Rich, J., (1998) 'Augustus' Parthian Honours, The Temple of Mars Ultor and the Arch in the Forum Romanum', in *The Papers of the British School in Rome*, 66,

Rich, J., and Shipley, G., (eds.) (1993) *War and Society in the Roman World*. Routledge. London.

Richardson, P., (1996) *Herod: King of the Jews and Friend of the Romans*. University of South Carolina Press.

Richmond, I., (1963) 'Palmyra Under the Aegis of Rome', in *The Journal of Roman Studies*, Vol 53, pp43-54.

Rose, C., (2005) 'The Parthians in Augustan Rome', in *The American Journal of Archaeology*, Vol 109, pp21-75.

Rostovtzeff, M., (1932) 'The Caravan-Gods of Palmyra', in *Journal of Roman Studies*, Vol 22, Part 1, pp107-116.

Rostovtzeff, M., Bellinger, A., Hopkins, C., Welles, C., (eds.) *The Excavations at Dura Europos: Preliminary Report of the Seventh and Eighth Seasons 1933-1934 and 1934-1935*. Yale University Press. New Haven. (1936).

Roth, J., (2002) 'The Army and the Economy in Judaea and Palestine', in Erdkamp, P., (ed.) *The Roman Army and the Economy*. J C Gieben. Amsterdam. pp375-397.

Rubies, J., (1994) 'Nero in Tacitus and Nero in Tacitism: The Historian's Craft', in Elsner, J., and Masters, J., (eds.) *Reflections of Nero: Culture, History and Representation*. Duckworth. London. pp29-47.

Sailor, D., (2008) *Writing and Empire in Tacitus*. Cambridge University Press.

Sartre, M., (2005) *The Middle East Under Rome*. The Belknap Press of Harvard University Press. London. An abridged edition of Sartre, M., (2001) *D'Alexandre a Zenobie*. Librairie Artheme Fayard.

Schlude, J., (2009) *Rome, Parthia and Empire: The First Century of Roman-Parthian Relations*. PhD Dissertation. University of California. Berkeley.

Schmitzer, U., (2011) 'Roman Values in Velleius', in Cowan, E., (ed.) *Velleius Paterculus: Making History*. The Classical Press of Wales. Swansea. pp177-202.

Schneider, R., (2007) 'Friend and Foe: The Orient in Rome', in *The Age of the Parthians*. I. B. Tauris & Co. Ltd. London. pp50-86.

Scullard, H., (1988) *From the Gracchi to Nero: A History of Rome 133 BC to AD 68*. Routledge. London.

Seager, R., (1979) *Pompey the Great: A Political Biography*. Blackwell. London.

Seager, R., (2005) *Tiberius*. Blackwell Publishing. London.

Sellwood, D., (1967) 'A Die-Engraver Sequence for Later Parthian Drachms', in *The Numismatic Chronicle*, pp18-19.

Sellwood, D., (1980) *An Introduction to the Coinage of Parthia.* Spink and Son Ltd. London.

Sellwood, D., (1983) 'Parthian Coins', in *The Cambridge History of Iran,* Vol 3 No 1, pp279-298.

Seyrig, H., (1950) 'Palmyra and the East', in *The Journal of Roman Studies,* Vol 40, pp1-7.

Sheldon, R. M., (2010) *Rome's Wars in Parthia: Blood in the Sand.* Vallentine Mitchel. London.

Sherwin-White, (1977) 'Ariobarzanes, Mithridates and Sulla', in *The Classical Quarterly,* 5. 27, pp173-183.

Sherwin-White, A., (1992) 'Lucullus, Pompey and the East', in *Cambridge Ancient History,* Vol 9, pp229-273.

Sidebottom, H., (2007) 'International Relations', in Sabin, P., Wees, H., and Whitby, M., (eds.) *The Cambridge History of Greek and Roman Warfare,* Vol 2, Rome From the Late Republic to the Late Empire, pp3-29.

Sidebottom, H., (2007) 'Severan Historiography: Evidence, Patterns and Arguments', in Swain, S., Harrison, S., Elsner, J., (eds.) *Severan Culture.* Cambridge. pp52-82.

Smallwood, E., (1981) *The Jews Under Roman Rule: From Pompey to Diocletian.* Brill. Leiden.

Smith, C., (1972) *Tiberius and the Roman Empire.* Kennikat Press. London.

Smith, R., (1972) 'The Army Reforms of Septimius Severus', in *Historia: Zeitschrift fur Alte Geschtiche,* Vol 21, No 3 (3rd Qtr), pp481-500.

Southern, P., (1997) *Domitian: Tragic Tyrant.* Routledge. London.

Southern, P., (2007) *The Roman Army: A Social and Institutional History*. Oxford University Press. London.

Southern, P., (2010) *Mark Antony: A Life*. Amberley. Stroud.

Speidel, M., (1985) 'Valerius Valerianus in Charge of Septimius Severus' Mesopotamian Campaign', in *Classical Philology*, Vol 80, No 4, (October), pp321-326.

Stadter, A., (2000) 'The Rhetoric of Virtue in Plutarch's Lives', in Stockt, L., (ed.) *Collection D'Etudes Classiques: Rhetorical Theory and Praxis in Plutarch*. Peeters. Louvain. pp493-510.

Stahl, H., (1985) *Propertius: Love and War*. University of California Press. Los Angeles.

Stanton, G., (1975) 'Marcus Aurelius, Lucius Verus, and Commodus: 1962-1972', in *Aufstieg Und Niedergang Der Romischen Welt*. Walter de Gruyter. Berlin. pp478-549.

Stark, F., (1966) *Rome on the Euphrates: The Story of a Frontier*. Harcourt, Brace and World, Inc. New York.

Starr, C., (1993) *The Roman Imperial Navy 31 BC-AD324*. Ares Publishers, Inc. Chicago.

Sullivan, J., (1986) *Petronius: The Satyricon. Seneca: The Apocolocyntosis*. Penguin. London.

Sullivan, J., (1991) 'Introduction', in *Roman Poets of the Early Empire*. Penguin. London.

Syme, R., (1939) *The Roman Revolution*. Oxford University Press.

Syme, R., (1958) *Tacitus*. Oxford. London. Vols. 1 and 2.

Syme, R., (1970) 'Domitius Corbulo', in *The Journal of Roman Studies*, Vol 60, pp27-39.

Syme, R., (1974) 'History or Biography: The Case of Tiberius Caesar', in *Historia: Zeitschrift fur Alte Geschichte*, Vol 23, No 4, (4th Quarter), pp481-496.

Syme, R., (1979) *Roman Papers*. Clarendon Press. Oxford.

Syme, R., (1983) *Historia Augusta Papers*. Clarendon Press. Oxford.

Syndikus, H., (2010) 'The Roman Odes', in Davis, G., (ed.) *A Companion to Horace*. Wiley-Blackwell. London.

Tao, W., (2007) 'Parthia in China: A Re-Examination of the Historical Records', in Curtis, V., and Stewart, S., (eds.) *The Age of the Parthians*. I. B. Tauris. London. pp87-104.

Teixidor, J., (1979) *The Pantheon of Palmyra*. E. J. Brill. Leiden.

Temin, P., (2004) 'Financial Intermediation in the Early Roman Empire', in *The Journal of Economic History*, Vol 64, No 3 (September), pp705-733.

'The Magi's Gifts – Tribute or Treatment?' (2012) *Biblical Archaeology Review*, Jan/Feb, Vol 38, No 1, p16.

Thomas, R., (2011) *Horace: Odes Book IV and Carmen Saeculare*. Cambridge University Press.

Tomber, R., (2008) *Indo-Roman Trade: From Pots to Pepper*. Duckworth. London.

Turner, P., (1989) *Roman Coins From India*. Institute of Archaeology Occasional Publication. London.

Volk, K., (2009) *Manilius and His Intellectual Background*. Oxford University Press.

Wallace-Hadrill, A., (1983) *Suetonius: The Scholar and his Caesars.* Duckworth. London.

Walters, J., (2009) 'Making a Spectacle: Deviant Men, Invective, and Pleasure', in Plaza, M., (ed.) *Persius and Juvenal.* Oxford University Press. pp349-360.

Warmington, B., (1981) *Nero: Reality and Legend.* Chatto and Windus. London.

Watson, L., (2003) *A Commentary on Horace's Epodes.* Oxford University Press.

Watson, W., (1983) 'Iran and China', in *The Cambridge History of Iran,* 3 (1) pp537-558.

Weisehofer, J., (ed.) (1998) *Das Partherreich Und Seine Zeugnisse. The Arsacid Empire: Sources and Documentation.* Franz Steiner. Verlag.

Wells, B., (1923) 'Trade and Travel in the Roman Empire', in *The Classical Journal,* Vol 19, No 1 (October), pp7-16.

Welles, C., Fink, R., Gilliam, J., (eds.) *The Excavations at Dura-Europos, Final Report, Volume V, Part 1: The Parchments and Papyri.* Yale University Press. New Haven. (1959)

Wenke, R., (1981) 'Elymeans, Parthians, and the Evolution of Empires in Southwestern Iran', in *Journal of the American Oriental Society,* Vol 101, No 3 (July-September), pp303-315.

Wheeler, M., (1955) *Rome beyond the Imperial Frontiers.* Philosophical Library. New York.

White, P., (2005) 'Poets in the New Milieu: Realigning', in Galinsky, K., (ed.) *The Cambridge Companion to the Age of Augustus.* Cambridge University Press. pp321-339.

Whittaker, C., (1969) *Herodian: History of the Empire, Books 1-4.* Harvard University Press.

Whittaker, C., (2000) 'Frontiers', *The Cambridge Ancient History*, Vol 11, pp293-319.

Wilkes, J., (1985) 'Review of Lawrence Keppie 'The making of the Roman Army: From Republic to Empire', in *The Journal of Roman Studies*, Vol 75, pp239-243.

Williams, W., (1967) 'Antoninus Pius and the Control of Provincial Embassies', in *Historia: Zeitschrift fur Alte Geschichte*, 16, 4, pp470-483.

Woolf, G., (1992) 'Imperialism, Empire and the Integration of the Roman Economy', in *World Archaeology*, Vol 23, No 3 (February), pp283-293.

Woolf, G., (1993) 'Roman Peace', in Rich, J., and Shipley, G., (eds.) *War and Society in the Roman World.* Routledge. London. pp171-194.

Woolf, G., (1997) 'Beyond Romans and Natives', in *World Archaeology*, Vol 28, No 3 (February), pp339-350.

Wroth, W., (1964) *A Catalogue of Greek Coins in the British Museum: Catalogue of the Coins of Parthia.* Arnaldo Forni. Bologna.

Yarshater, E. (2006) 'Introduction', in *The Cambridge History of Iran.* Cambridge University Press. 3 (1), ppxvii-lxxv.

Zanker, P., (1990) *The Power of Images in the Age of Augustus.* University of Michigan Press. Ann Arbor.

Zeev, M., (2005) *Diaspora Judaism in Turmoil 116/117CE: Ancient Sources and Modern Insights.* Peeters. Leuven.

INDEX

CPSIA information can be obtained at www.ICGtesting.com
Printed in the USA
LVOW11s2035211113

362277LV00024B/1169/P

9 781484 045664